Nils Göde

Clone Evolution

Clone Evolution

Dissertation

Submitted by
Nils Göde

on
12th May 2011

to the
University of Bremen
Faculty of Mathematics and Computer Science

in partial fulfillment of the requirements for the degree of
Doktor der Ingenieurwissenschaften

Supervised by
Prof. Dr. rer. nat. Rainer Koschke
University of Bremen, Germany

and

Prof. James R. Cordy, Ph.D.
Queen's University at Kingston, Canada

Bibliografische Information der Deutschen Nationalbibliothek

Die Deutsche Nationalbibliothek verzeichnet diese Publikation in der
Deutschen Nationalbibliografie; detaillierte bibliografische Daten sind
im Internet über http://dnb.d-nb.de abrufbar.

ISBN 978-3-8325-2920-8

Logos Verlag Berlin GmbH
Comeniushof, Gubener Str. 47,
10243 Berlin
Tel.: +49 (0)30 42 85 10 90
Fax: +49 (0)30 42 85 10 92
INTERNET: http://www.logos-verlag.de

Acknowledgments

I owe my deepest gratitude to my supervisor, Rainer Koschke, who continuously supported me and guided me on my way to becoming a good researcher. I am also heartily thankful to Jim Cordy who co-supervised this thesis.

It is an honor for me to be a member of the Software Engineering Group and I would like to thank all my colleagues for their support. In particular, I thank Jan Harder for countless inspiring discussions and feedback on my work.

I am deeply indebted to Jim Cordy, Mike Godfrey, Elmar Juergens, and Chanchal Roy who welcomed me at their universities and gave me the opportunity to present and discuss my research.

Finally, I would like to apologize to my family and friends, who—once more—did not get the share of my time that they deserved.

Nils Göde, May 2011

"Not all clones are created equal."

Abstract

Duplicated passages of source code—*code clones*—are a common property of software systems. While clones are beneficial in some situations, their presence causes various problems for software maintenance. Most of these problems are strongly related to change and include, for example, the need to propagate changes across duplicated code fragments and the risk of inconsistent changes to clones that are meant to evolve identically. Hence, we need a sophisticated analysis of clone evolution to better understand, assess, and manage duplication in practice.

This thesis introduces Clone Evolution Graphs as a technique to model clone relations and their evolution within the history of a system. We present our incremental algorithm for efficient and automated extraction of Clone Evolution Graphs from a system's history. The approach is shown to scale even for large systems with long histories making it applicable to retroactive analysis of clone evolution as well as live tracking of clones during software maintenance.

We have used Clone Evolution Graphs in several studies to analyze versatile aspects of clone evolution in open-source as well as industrial systems. Our results show that the characteristics of clone evolution are quite different between systems, highlighting the need for a sophisticated technique like Clone Evolution Graphs to track clones and analyze their evolution on a per-system basis. We have also shown that Clone Evolution Graphs are well-suited to analyze the change behavior of individual clones and can be used to identify problematic clones within a system. In general, the results of our studies provide new insights into how clones evolve, how they are changed, and how they are removed.

Table of Contents

Part I

Prelude

Chapter 1

Introduction

Software has become an inevitable part of our daily lives. The importance of software is steadily increasing, and it is hard to imagine domains that do not make use of software in one way or the other. Many areas inescapably depend on software, and unavailability or malfunction of a system has serious consequences. It is, thus, desirable to have high quality software, which is free of defects and can be easily adapted to a changing environment. To ensure the competitiveness and long-term success of a software system, it has to be maintained.

Software maintenance comprises all activities that change a system to correct existing problems, prevent future problems, adapt to an evolving environment, and enhance functionality. The ease and success of software maintenance depends on a multitude of factors, one of which is the presence of duplicated source code passages—*code clones*.

Code clones are similar, or even identical, fragments of source code, which commonly—but not necessarily—originate from copy and paste. An example of similar code fragments, as they appear in real-world software, is shown in Figure 1.1. Such duplicated passages of source code frequently occur in today's software systems as cloning is a prominent strategy for reusing code.

```
1  left.clearHighlight();
2  left.setTitle("unknown");
3  for (Item i : left.items()) {
4      i.setValid(false);
5  }
6  left.deleteItems();
```

(a) First fragment

```
1  right.clearHighlight();
2  right.setTitle("unknown");
3  for (Item i : right.items()) {
4      i.setValid(false);
5  }
6  right.deleteItems();
```

(b) Second fragment

Figure 1.1 – Two similar code fragments—*clones*. The only difference is the first code fragment operating on an object named `left` and the second code fragment operating on an object named `right`.

Cloning has various short-term benefits among which are increased development speed and reduced risk of new defects when reliable code is reused. Nevertheless, clones are a threat to software maintenance in the long run. Copying code multiplies the effort required for subsequent maintenance activities including understanding, changing, and testing the code. In addition, incomplete or incorrect propagation of changes may result in incomplete removal of defects or the introduction of new defects. Given these observations, clones have long been regarded as harmful in general. Fowler and Beck [56] rank clones number one in their stink parade of bad smells and suggest refactoring whenever clones are found.

> *"If you see the same code structure in more than one place, you can be sure that your program will be better if you find a way to unify them."*
>
> — Fowler & Beck [56]

Nevertheless, recent research has shown that clones cannot be considered harmful in general. Apart from the short-term benefits of cloning, clones can be a reasonable design decision to ease future maintenance. For example, cloning can be used to avoid dependencies that might cause problems regarding code ownership or the reliability of existing code. Kapser and Godfrey [101, 103] provide a comprehensive list of situations where cloning can be beneficial.

Despite ongoing and intensive research on software clones, the phenomenon of cloning is not yet sufficiently understood. The conclusion of previous research on software clones is that while some clones certainly threaten the quality of software, others certainly do not. Nevertheless, we cannot yet reliably tell which clones are harmful and which clones are beneficial. Furthermore, individual scenarios and use cases influence this decision. Clones that are regarded as a threat in one situation, may be seen as beneficial in a different scenario.

Consequently, the challenge is to separate the relevant clones—those considered harmful—from the irrelevant clones. This requires being aware and keeping track of duplication in a system in the first place. During the last years, various techniques and tools to detect, inspect, monitor, and remove clones have evolved. These techniques and tools are collectively referred to as *clone management*. The goal of clone management is to mitigate clone-related threats while maintaining the positive effects of clones. Successful clone management, however, requires a sophisticated technique to model and extract clone evolution data, a good understanding of software clones, their life cycle, and their impact on maintainability.

1.1   Problem Statement

Clones threaten the maintainability and, thus, the quality of software in many ways. Most clone-related problems are tightly related to source code changes and the evolution of a system. Hence, analyzing code clones in conjunction with their evolution is essential to better understand the phenomenon of code duplication and associated risks. Until now, however, research has concentrated on detecting and analyzing code clones in a single version of the system only. Based on the state-of-the-art, we identified the following two research problems:

(1) We lack a comprehensive model of clone evolution and a sophisticated technique to extract the model from a system's history.

(2) We lack knowledge about how clones evolve and how they are changed to better understand the nature of clones, assess their risk potential, and chose appropriate counter-measures.

Section 1.1.1 and Section 1.1.2 provide a more detailed description of both research problems. Explicit research questions are given alongside the discussion of related research in Chapter 3.

1.1.1   Modeling Clone Evolution

Analyzing clone evolution requires an adequate model to represent the relevant data. Although some patterns have been presented that describe how individual clones are changed, there is no comprehensive technique for modeling clone evolution in a system. Nevertheless, such a model is needed for analyzing clone evolution from a research perspective, as well as tracking and managing clones in practice.

The next problem is extracting the model from a system's history. Previous studies on clone evolution detected clones in each version of a system separately using a single-version clone detection approach. Tracking clones was done by comparing every clone of a version to every clone of the next version. In summary, existing approaches are computationally expensive and not applicable to large systems with many versions. In particular, they cannot be used for live tracking of clones during development. Hence, we need an efficient algorithm to detect and track clones across multiple versions of a system.

1.1.2   How Clones Evolve

To successfully manage clones in practice, we first need a general understanding of how clones evolve. This includes the number of clones, their lifetime, and information about how they are changed. It is also important to know whether clone evolution is similar between systems and whether findings can be generalized. This general picture of clone evolution is required as a starting point for more in-depth analyses that investigate system-specific peculiarities and identify potentially harmful clones based on deviations in their evolution.

A central problem in clone research is to assess the risks associated with individual clones and to quantify their overall threat potential. Currently, we lack information about how often clones change during their lifetime—that is, how often changes must be propagated—and how often inconsistent changes are unwanted and cause problems. This information is, however, required to identify problematic clones and chose appropriate counter-measures.

One way of mitigating clone-related problems is removing duplication by creating a common abstraction. Still, not all clones are suitable for being removed. Until now, we do not know for which clones removal is an adequate solution. The problem is that we lack information about how developers deal with clones in practice and which clones they consider worth being removed.

1.2   Contributions

This section summarizes the contributions of this thesis categorized according to the two research problems.

1.2.1   Modeling Clone Evolution

In this thesis, we present the *Clone Evolution Graph* as a comprehensive model to analyze clone evolution. The graph allows to quantitatively, as well as qualitatively, investigate how clones evolve and how they are changed. We introduce our visualization tool CYCLONE to inspect Clone Evolution Graphs from different perspectives.

Furthermore, this thesis introduces our incremental algorithm to extract a Clone Evolution Graph from a system's history. The algorithm efficiently detects clones in multiple versions of a system reusing data from the previous version's analysis as much as possible. The algorithm also creates a mapping between clones of consecutive versions. We evaluated the performance of our extraction algorithm to show that it can be used for retroactive analysis of clone evolution as well as providing live clone information during software development.

1.2.2   How Clones Evolve

We conducted three different studies to analyze how clones evolve, how they are changed, and how they are removed. These studies all used the Clone Evolution Graph to represent the relevant data, demonstrating the graph's applicability to analyzing clone evolution.

In our first study, we investigated clone evolution in nine open-source systems and in three industrial systems. Our results show that clone evolution is considerably different between systems making it hard to draw general conclusions. The study shows that clone evolution has its own peculiarities for each system and should be analyzed on a per-system basis.

Next, we have analyzed how individual clones were changed during the evolution of three different systems. We found that the majority of clones was never changed or changed only once during five years of history. Inspecting inconsistent changes in detail, we found that many inconsistencies are intentional and only few changes are carried out unintentionally inconsistent.

Finally, we specifically studied the end of clones' lifetimes by analyzing deliberate removals of duplication. Although not very frequent, we found a number of deliberate clone removals in open-source systems. We have furthermore analyzed which characteristics make clones attractive for removal.

1.3 Project Context

Major parts of this thesis were developed in the context of the project "Empirical Studies on Software Redundancy" funded by the *Deutsche Forschungsgemeinschaft*[1] *(DFG)*. The algorithms described in this thesis were implemented in the context of the *Bauhaus* project.[2] The *Bauhaus* project is a collaboration between the University of Bremen, the University of Stuttgart and the commercial spin-off *Axivion*.[3] It comprises an infrastructure and a variety of tools for program analysis.

The techniques and tools developed in the course of this thesis were applied to and tested with a large number of open-source systems as well as large industrial systems to which—amongst others—access was kindly provided by the *IVU Traffic Technologies AG*[4] and the *Debeka Group*.[5]

1.4 Related Publications

Various parts of this thesis have been previously published. This section lists these publications. For each publication, the chapters indicate where the respective content is located within this document.

- **Incremental Clone Detection [68]**
  European Conference on Software Maintenance and Reengineering, 2009
  Chapter 5

- **Modeling Clone Evolution [73]**
  International Workshop on Software Clones, 2009
  Chapters 4 and 7

- **Mapping Code Clones Using Incremental Clone Detection [62]**
  Softwaretechnik-Trends, 2009
  Chapter 7

- **Evolution of Type-1 Clones [61]**
  Working Conference on Source Code Analysis and Manipulation, 2009
  Chapters 7 and 9

- **Clone Removal: Fact or Fiction? [64]**
  International Workshop on Software Clones, 2010
  Chapter 11

- **Studying clone evolution using incremental clone detection [69]**
  Journal of Software Maintenance and Evolution: Research and Practice, 2010
  Chapters 6 and 7

---

[1] http://www.dfg.de/en/
[2] http://www.bauhaus-stuttgart.de/bauhaus/index-english.html
[3] http://www.axivion.com/
[4] http://www.ivu.com/
[5] http://www.debeka.de

- **Clone Evolution Revisited [63]**
  Softwaretechnik-Trends, 2010
  Chapter 9

- **Not All That Glitters Is Gold [65]**
  Softwaretechnik-Trends, 2011
  Chapter 6

- **Frequency and Risks of Changes to Clones [70]**
  International Conference on Software Engineering, 2011
  Chapter 10

1.5   Thesis Outline

This thesis is organized in four major parts.

Part I provides an introduction to the topic of this thesis. Chapter 2 presents an overview of software clones including reasons for their creation, their detection, the effects they have on a system, and relevant terminology. An elaborate discussion of related work is given in Chapter 3. The chapter points out open questions which are answered in subsequent sections of this thesis. Chapter 4 introduces Clone Evolution Graphs which are used to model clone evolution in a system.

Part II describes our technique to extract a Clone Evolution Graph from the history of a system in detail. Important fundamentals for the incremental extraction of clones from a suffix tree are given in Chapter 5. Chapter 6 is concerned with the efficient detection of clones in consecutive versions of a system. Our approach to map clones between versions and track them throughout the system's evolution is presented in Chapter 7. Performance is an important factor regarding the applicability of our approach. We provide an elaborate evaluation of the algorithm's performance in Chapter 8.

Part III presents our case studies on clone evolution that use the previously described technique to extract Clone Evolution Graphs and analyzes them to gain a better understanding of the phenomenon of software clones. Chapter 9 describes our case study on different aspects of clone evolution in various open-source and industrial systems. Chapter 10 presents our case study on how clones are changed throughout their lifetime. Our detailed analysis of deliberate removal of duplication is given in Chapter 11.

Part IV provides the conclusions of this thesis. Chapter 12 summarizes the findings of this thesis and points out options for improvement and future work.

Chapter 2

Software Clones

What are software clones? Although this question may—at first—seem easy to be answered, it is not. From the very beginning of research on software clones, researchers have struggled to find a precise and universally accepted and applicable definition of software clones. "Clones are segments of code that are similar according to some definition of similarity". This statement by Ira Baxter at the *First International Workshop on Detection of Software Clones* (2002, Montreal) expresses the inherent vagueness of code clones. The "some definition of similarity" is interpreted in many different ways and—in most cases—implicitly dictated by the respective clone detection approach. In absence of a precise and generally accepted definition, an overview of various aspects of software clones helps to characterize them and tell what they are.

This chapter introduces various facets of software clones starting with reasons for their creation and the effects they have on the system. Furthermore, it provides a brief summary of different techniques to detect, track, and manage them. Important concepts and terminology that is used throughout this thesis are introduced at the end of this chapter.

This chapter is intended to be a brief introduction to the field of software clone research. For a more comprehensive overview, please refer to the surveys by Koschke [116] as well as Roy and Cordy [159].

2.1 Reasons

The single most dominant source of clones—similar fragments of source code—is the use of copy and paste. The reasons for using copy and paste are, however, versatile. Roy and Cordy [159] classified these reasons into four categories:

Development Strategy: Reusing existing functionality as a template for new code or without any modification at all. This also includes manual branching of code to implement new functionality without affecting the stable system.

Maintenance Benefits: Reusing reliable code to reduce the risk of introducing new errors, performance benefits, and general design decisions.

Overcoming Underlying Limitations: On the one hand, the programming language might not provide appropriate facilities for abstraction. On the other hand, programmers can be limited by time constraints or lack of expertise.

Cloning by Accident: Unintentional duplication due to missing knowledge of existing functionality or usage of common protocols.

In many situations, it is easier to copy, paste, and modify existing code if it already provides similar functionality to the one that has to be implemented. Kapser and Godfrey [103] refer to this activity as *templating*. By using templates, the implementation of new functionality can be accelerated. In addition, the risk of introducing defects in the new code is reduced if the template code is trusted and known to work reliably [10, 18, 52, 98]. Templating can also be used to experiment with new functionality without risking the stability of the existing system. The relevant code is copied and both the production version and the experimental version can be maintained independently. This allows a developer to try new things without putting the existing code at risk. Reusing existing code may also be induced by the developer's inability to understand the code. Knowing that something provides the desired functionality but not understanding how it is implemented prohibits an extension and facilitates the duplication of the existing solution.

Cloning may also be forced by the structure and the architecture of the system. While it is generally advisable to gather common functionality in a single place, a system's design may not allow creating dependencies between certain subsystems. For example, two packages require the same functionality, but there is no place that both may access. In such cases, cloning is the only option. Code style guidelines may also lead to the creation of clones if similar functionality is required in many places—for example, appropriate exception handling or use of debugging methods. In highly optimized systems, the performance of the system might require the creation of clones. If common functionality is unified in a single place, but required at different locations, the overhead of additional method calls may not be acceptable. When the compiler does not support inlining, cloning may remain as the only option. Nevertheless, this is relevant only for a small subset of systems—for example, real-time or embedded software.

Apart from the intentional duplication of source code, developers may independently implement similar things. This may be due to a lack of knowledge regarding the availability of certain functionality. In addition, the need to implement similar things may emerge from the use of frequent patterns because the programming language lacks appropriate techniques for abstraction. The use of libraries and the need to conform to their protocols (initialization of graphical user interfaces is a good example here) may also result in similarity between independent implementations [18, 98]. Finally, the project context may facilitate duplication that is related to non-technical issues. If developers, for example, are assessed by the amount of code they write in a particular time, this might encourage them to create code clones [10, 52].

Although many reasons have been named, only few studies exist that investigated to which extent these appear in a real system. The in-depth studies that were conducted either observed the reuse strategy of developers [124, 158, 105] or the structure of existing code clones [109, 101, 103] to determine the frequency of individual reasons.

Lange and Moher conducted a study to investigate strategies of code reuse in an object-oriented programming language [124]. The programming activity of a single subject was monitored for the period of one week with special attention on code reuse. More than 85% of new methods have been created by copy and paste using an existing method as template. Concerning the creation of new classes, each of them has been created using an existing class as template. Two major approaches to code reuse have been observed. One is copying the template as a whole and either modifying it afterward or leaving it as a one-to-one copy. The other is gradually copying required blocks of code from the template to the new method.

The code reuse behavior of four experienced programmers has been analyzed by Rosson and Carroll [158]. The subjects were given maintenance tasks that involved enhancing the functionality of an existing program. Examples were provided that illustrated the use of particular program entities related to the given tasks. Rosson and Carroll observed that the subjects made heavy use of the examples provided. In most cases, the usage protocols of existing classes were copied to serve as a template for the new functionality that was to be added. The subjects did not try to get a deep understanding of the classes' functionality from which they copied the usage protocols. This study, as well as the one by Lange and Moher showed that cloning existing code is frequently used to add new functionality to a program.

Kim and colleagues investigated copy and paste practices in an object-oriented programming language [105]. They observed four subjects by directly watching them and five subjects by using an instrumented IDE that was able to replay editing operations. On average, each programmer performed four non-trivial copy and paste operations per hour, each of which covered more than a single line of code. Based on their analysis they identified and categorized different copy-and-paste patterns. Concerning the programmers' intention, cloning was frequently used to create structural templates. Existing code that constitutes how to use a class, implement a module, or express a complex condition was used as template for new but similar functionality. From the design perspective some clones were unavoidable because they had to access their execution context. Other reasons for cloning blocks of code were paired operations, or similar functionality that operates on different data sources.

In another study, Kim and her associates analyzed the evolution of code clones [109]. They presented a clone evolution model that is based on the extraction of clone genealogies from the program's history [106]. Using the genealogies, the lifetime of individual clones was determined. Kim and her colleagues found that the majority of long-lived clones resulted from limitations of the programming language and could not be refactored easily.

Kapser and Godfrey presented several recurring patterns of cloning [101] which they observed in previous studies [99, 100, 102]. They provided a detailed description of each pattern including the advantages and disadvantages of using it. To determine the frequency of these patterns, Kapser and Godfrey performed a case study on two open-source projects [103]. The assignment of a pattern to each clone has been done manually by considering available documentation, code structure, and data as well as control flow dependencies. The most frequent pattern in both subject systems was using existing code as a template for new functionality or cloning it without further modifications. The remaining patterns had roughly the same frequency.

Summarizing the results of the studies, the dominating reason for cloning is using existing code as a template for implementing new functionality. Although evidence of other reasons was found, the reasons categorized as development strategy were predominant. Still, apart from its benefits, cloning activity may seriously threaten the quality of a system as described in the next section.

2.2   Consequences

There is a huge variety of reasons why clones are created—intentionally and unintentionally. While cloning is a reasonable design decision in some situations, the existence of clones threatens the quality of the system. There are different ways in which clones can hinder maintenance and become real problems. Fowler and Beck [56] even argue that all clones are harmful and should be removed where possible. For this reason, code duplication occupies the first place on their stink parade of bad smells.

2.2.1   Size

One of the most apparent drawbacks to code duplication is that the presence of clones increases the size of the system. That is, the system is larger than it needs to be. The size increase affects the source code as well as the final executables. The clone-induced size increase of the source code is the fundamental measure of the analytical cost model presented by Juergens and Deissenboeck [93] to quantify the negative impact of clones. The size increase of executables may not be problematic for most domains given the capabilities of modern hardware. Nevertheless, for some domains—especially embedded systems—the size of the executable is crucial. Having more clones and, consequently, a larger executable may require switching to more powerful hardware with more storage space having a huge financial impact.

2.2.2   Effort

The size of the system does not only affect the resource requirements, but also the maintenance process. During software maintenance, there are a number of activities that are influenced by the size of the system. Among them is the time required to read and understand the source code. Code clones increase the time needed to understand the code, because similar parts have to be read and comprehended multiple times. If clones are similar but not completely identical, identifying the subtle differences can be very time intensive. Subsequent to understanding the code changes might need to be performed. Again, clones increase the effort to change the code. If clones are changed, the changes may need to be propagated to all similar parts. The more clones exist, the more effort is required for change propagation. Attempts have been made to reduce the effort for change propagation using *linked editing* [86, 182]. Nevertheless, available tools can only do the actual propagation. Maintainers still have to decide whether propagation is desired or not. Finally, having clones also increases the effort for testing—which can be a quite resource-intense task.

The relation between the presence of code clones and maintenance effort has been analyzed by Lozano and Wermelinger [136]. To calculate the maintenance effort for a specific method, a combination of the impact a change to that method would have and the likelihood that the method is changed were taken into consideration. They analyzed the history of four subject programs and compared the maintenance effort of methods with clones to methods without clones. It has been found that roughly half of the methods containing clones did not provide evidence of increased maintenance effort. However, in some cases there was a significant increase in maintenance effort. Furthermore, clones of methods that showed the highest increase in maintenance effort were observed in more detail. Although different characteristics of these methods have been examined, no common trend could be observed that would help to identify clones causing high maintenance effort.

2.2.3 Correctness

In addition to the previous consequences, cloning also threatens the correctness of the program. Although cloning can be used to reuse trusted and reliable code, it can also facilitate the propagation of defects. If the original code contains one or more defects, creating copies will inherently cause a duplication of these defects. One of the predominant motivations for creating clones is using existing code as template for implementing new but similar functionality. While the basic structure of the copy is reused, minor modifications are necessary to adopt the copied code section to its new context [18]. Incomplete or wrong adoption of the copy or its new context has been found to be a frequent cause for new defects resulting from cloning activity [90, 130].

Apart from their initial creation, clones threaten the system's correctness throughout their lifetime. Changing a clone always bears the risk of missing to change one or more of its siblings. These situations are referred to as *inconsistent changes* [109]. While inconsistent changes may not immediately cause system failure or data loss, they steadily reduce the similarity between the clones making it harder to keep track of the clone relation. When the change removes a defect from the system, an inconsistent change results in an incomplete removal of the defect, leaving the false assumption that the defect has been removed. Inconsistent changes may also lead to new defects if clones are not modified to conform to a changed environment.

Example 2.1 – Figure 2.1 on the next page provides an example of an inconsistent change. Figure (a) shows two identical clones (lines 1 to 5 and lines 9 to 11). In (b) the missing check for an empty list is added to the first clone. However, the change is not propagated to the second clone although it needs to be. This situation illustrates an incomplete removal of a defect. □

A large-scale case study has been conducted by Juergens and his colleagues to identify defects resulting from copy and paste activity [96]. Developers of each system

```
1   E getFirst(List<E> list) {            1   E getFirst(List<E> list) {
2                                          2     if (list.isEmpty())
3                                          3       return null;
4     return list.get(0);                  4     return list.get(0);
5   }                                      5   }
6                                          6
7   ...                                    7   ...
8                                          8
9   E getFirst(List<E> list) {            9   E getFirst(List<E> list) {
10    return list.get(0);                  10    return list.get(0);
11  }                                      11  }
```

(a) Before change   (b) After change

Figure 2.1 – Inconsistent change to clones. The missing check for an empty list is added to the first clone only making this an incomplete removal of a defect.

were presented clone information and asked to decide whether the clone is related to a fault or not. Depending on the system, 3% to 23% of the clones were found to resemble a defect. The results suggest that clones increase the risk of introducing inconsistencies where similar parts are meant to evolve consistently.

Selim and colleagues [167] have analyzed the relation between code clones and software defects. The relation has been analyzed in two long-lived Java systems using survival models. It has been found that the defect-proneness of cloned methods depends on the respective system. The relation between clones and defects has also been analyzed by Rahman and colleagues [154]. They did not find a significant association between clones and defects and in some cases cloned code was even less error-prone compared to non-cloned code.

Hordijk and associates presented a summary of existing studies related to the effects of clones on software maintenance [80]. It follows that two major effects have been investigated so far: The relation between clones and bugs as well as clones and the system's changeability. Concerning bugs, several studies have shown that defects can be identified which are related to cloning activity. Nevertheless, it could not yet be shown that code clones decrease the changeability of a system.

2.3   Detection

Code clones may be a reasonable design decision on the one hand, but threaten the system's quality on the other hand. Knowledge of where clones reside in a system is the fundamental requirement of clone management which encompasses "all activities of looking after and making decisions about consequences of copying and pasting" [117]. To that end, detecting clones in a system is a central aspect of software clone research. Clone detection refers to the process of locating duplication within a system. An abundance of techniques and tools have been developed to fulfill this task. The different approaches can be categorized according to the representation of the program they operate on. Each approach—more or less implicitly—provides the "some definition of similarity" contained in Baxter's clone definition quoted in the introduction of this chapter.

All approaches have in common that they search for structural similarity in the respective representation of the system. Thus, they cannot detect duplication of domain knowledge that does not result in representational similarity. Furthermore, not every instance of representational similarity originates from duplicated domain knowledge. While some use cases put an emphasis on representational similarity (for example, compression algorithms or plagiarism detection) others are primarily interested in domain knowledge similarity (for example, software maintenance). The latter approaches have to be aware of the possible discrepancy between representational and domain knowledge similarity.

For a detailed comparison of different clone detection approaches and tools, please refer to [19, 161].

2.3.1   Text

The lowest layer of abstraction is the program's source code. Text-based clone detection treats the program's source code as a sequence of characters. Clones are detected by searching similar subsequences within the program's source code. One of the first text-based clone detection algorithms has been introduced by Johnson [91]. The algorithm computes a fingerprint for each line of a source file and detects duplication based on identical fingerprints. A similar approach has been used by Manber [138] fingerprinting text chunks of predefined length.

Ducasse and colleagues [52] compared every source code line to every other source code line to find duplication. To improve performance by reducing the number of comparisons, potentially similar lines were sorted into buckets using hashing. Only lines from the same buckets were considered as candidates of duplication.

Text-based clone detection has several advantages. Operating directly on the source code and using fingerprinting make it very efficient. Many algorithms that are available for string processing can be used for clone detection as well. The detection is also language independent, because the source code is just interpreted as a sequence of characters. Another benefit is that the source code does not need to be syntactically correct and clone detection can be run in any state of development. In addition, the recall—percentage of all existing clones that are detected—is higher compared to other approaches.

The downside of text-based detection is the quality of the reported clones. The lack of syntactic information prevents aligning the borders of clones with those of syntactic units. On the one hand, text-based techniques lack precision—percentage of detected clones that are relevant—because many clones are similar in terms of their textual representation, but less interesting from a developer's point of view. On the other hand, text-based approaches may not detect semantically identical parts if their textual representation is different.

To overcome the disadvantages of text-based detection while maintaining the advantages, Cordy, Synytskyy and Dean [36, 174] used a hybrid approach that

```
1   void do_all_work(int i, int j)      1   void do_all_work (int i,
2   {                                    2                     int j) {
3       /* So much to do... */           3       if (!motivated) // Work?
4       if(!motivated) return;           4           return;
5       ...                              5       ...
6   }                                    6   }
```

(a) First fragment   (b) Second fragment

Figure 2.2 – Two similar code fragments with different comments and layout. Text-based techniques that operate on line level may not detect these fragments as clones.

preprocessed the source code using a parse tree before applying a text-based comparison. The preprocessing ensures that the latter text-based comparison is sensitive to the syntactic structure of the source code. The approach has been applied to web applications and the *TXL* source transformation language [35] has been used for preprocessing. The approach has been constantly improved and applied to programming languages as well [160].

Ducasse and colleagues [51] have evaluated their text-based clone detection approach and shown that it is fast and achieves high recall while maintaining acceptable precision. In addition, adaption to new languages took them less than an hour per language. Nevertheless, overeager normalization can result in too many false positives.

Example 2.2 – Consider the code fragments shown in Figure 2.2. Without appropriate transformation, text-based approaches may not detect these fragments as clones. □

2.3.2   Token

Token-based approaches perform a lexical analysis of the program's source code and join characters into tokens, which are the atomic units of the underlying programming language. The program itself is subsequently represented as a sequence of tokens that can be processed using common algorithms to detect similarity in strings. The additional information that is available to token-based approaches compared to text-based techniques allows them to abstract from whitespace, comments, and the concrete values of identifiers and literals.

Given the sequence of tokens resulting from lexical analysis, a data structure is created that allows detecting duplication efficiently. A frequent choice are suffix trees, which can be created in linear time [9, 95, 98]. To detect parametrized clones, where parameter tokens have been consistently renamed, Baker extended the notion of suffix trees to parametrized suffix trees (*p-suffix trees*) [10, 11]. Other approaches [17, 191] use suffix arrays which offer the advantage of less space consumption. Furthermore, Hofmann [79] has shown that suffix arrays require less time to be computed than suffix trees. However, the downside of suffix arrays is that they cannot efficiently be modified after their initial construction. This makes them less suitable for incremental clone detection. Apart from that, Li and colleagues used frequent subsequence mining techniques to identify duplication in a sequence of tokens [130]. To enable clone detection for very large code bases, Livieri and associates [135] extended an existing approach to enable distributed computation.

Apart from detecting identical sequences of tokens, some approaches also tolerate a certain amount of differences between clones. This can either be directly integrated into the retrieval of clones from the suffix tree [95], or run as a postprocessing step by merging neighboring identical clones [10, 130, 184].

The benefits and shortcoming of token-based clone detection are similar to those of text-based detection. Token-based detection is fast and easy to apply by making use of established string algorithms. The recall is higher compared to tree-based, graph-based, or metric-based approaches. It is not required that the source code is compilable and the techniques are independent of the programming language except for the scanner that performs the lexical analysis. Compared to text-based methods, the additional information allows a more sophisticated preprocessing of the token sequence before the detection itself [98]. This includes, for example, removing irrelevant token sequences and abstracting from the values of identifiers and literals.

Like text-based clone detection, token-based approaches lack precision compared to tree-based and graph-based approaches. Token-based methods are language dependent in the form of a scanner that is able to perform a lexical analysis of the source code for the desired languages. Nevertheless, this is only a minor drawback because scanners are already available or can be created with little effort for most languages.

2.3.3 Abstract Syntax Tree

Tree-based clone detectors do not perform only a lexical analysis of the source code, but also parse it into an abstract syntax tree (AST). Having the AST as a starting point, different techniques are used to detect similar parts of the respective program. The common approach is to identify similar subtrees in the AST that represent similar parts of the program.

Yang [192] used dynamic programming and a generalization of the longest common subsequence algorithm to find similar subtrees. Baxter and colleagues [18] partition subtrees according to a hash function and compare the subtrees within a single bucket for similarity. Different tree similarity algorithms to detect duplication have been compared by Sager and associates [163]. Wahler and her colleagues [186] used a data mining approach on the AST to detect clones. Characterizing a subtree by a numerical vector and searching for similar vectors has been done by Jiang and associates [89]. Another method is to use anti-unification and describe subtrees by patterns which are generalized to identify similar subtrees [27, 53]. Tree-based clone detection has been successfully applied to web documents by using island grammars to parse different languages into a single parse tree [174].

There are a number of hybrid approaches that construct the AST first and serialize it afterward to detect duplication in the token sequence of the serialized tree. Juillerat and colleagues [97] proposed diff-based or data compression algorithms to detect duplication in the serialized AST. Kraft and associates [119] used the Levenshtein distance to compare different node sequences. Analogous to token-based detection, Koschke and his colleagues [118], as well as Tairas and associates [175], used suffix trees to find clones in the serialized node sequence. Kraft and colleagues [119] used a unified tree representation for different programming languages to perform cross-language clone detection. An index-based algorithm that allows detecting clones of a given code fragment efficiently in a large body of source code has been presented by Lee and colleagues [127].

As the syntactic structure of a program is represented inside the AST, tree-based approaches are able to report clones which are usually not detected by the previous methods. These include for example commutative operations where the order of the two operands has been inverted. In general, the precision of AST-based approaches is higher compared to text-based and token-based techniques.

Although the usefulness of reported clones is increased, performance is a critical issue for tree-based detection. The overhead of creating an AST requires more time and space. Tree similarity algorithms generally have a higher complexity than algorithms for detecting duplication in strings. AST-based clone detectors are language depended as they require a grammar to parse the respective language. They also need a syntactically correct program to create an AST.

2.3.4   Program Dependency Graph

Apart from the AST, the program dependence graph (PDG) can be used for clone detection. In addition to the syntactic structure of the program, the PDG also provides the data and control dependencies within the program. Clones can be detected by searching isomorphic subgraphs.

An algorithm that searches for similar subgraphs has been presented by Krinke [120]. Komondoor and Horwitz [113] identified isomorphic subgraphs by using slicing. The problem of detecting software plagiarism was tackled by Liu and colleagues [132]. They used a lossy filter to reduce the search space for isomorphic subgraphs. Gabel and associates [57] proposed an approach to reduce the problem of finding isomorphic subgraphs to tree similarity.

The additional information contained in the PDG can be used to improve the quality of reported clones. Therefore, PDG-based approaches are able to reveal duplications that cannot be detected with any of the other approaches.

The drawback to graph-based detection is the complexity of creating the PDG as well as the algorithms to find isomorphic subgraphs. Like tree-based approaches, graph-based techniques require a syntactically correct program and are language-dependent. The recall is lower compared to text-based and token-based approaches.

2.3.5   Metrics

A rather different approach to detecting clones is based on metrics that are calculated for syntactic units of the program. Most metric-based approaches chose methods, functions, or procedures to be these syntactic units. Others use arbitrary block structures or individual statements. Kontogiannis and colleagues [114, 115] calculated metrics for

AST nodes that represent statements, blocks, and functions. The metrics that are used to identify clones vary between the different approaches. The respective programming paradigm or programming language influence the set of metrics to choose from. For example, Patenaude and associates [152] used Java specific metrics for clone detection.

Metric-based approaches commonly represent the different metrics that characterize a program unit as numerical vector. To detect clones, these vectors are either compared pairwise [141] or clustered using different types of algorithms (e.g. [4, 5, 144, 143]). As pairwise comparison has quadratic complexity, Dagenais and colleagues [37] compared only procedures with similar amounts of statements to reduce running time. Davey and associates [38] used neural networks for clustering metric vectors and identifying clone classes. Metric-based clone detection has also been used to detect clones in web applications [29, 46]. Di Lucca and colleagues [46] used the frequency of HTML elements to characterize web pages.

The advantage of metric-based clone detection is that it performs very well in terms of running time and space consumption. The computation of metric vectors and their comparison has low complexity. The space requirement for storing the metric vectors in memory is also very low.

Nevertheless, metric-based techniques lack recall compared to other approaches. Most approaches are dependent on the programming language because they need to identify the syntactic units which are to be used for comparison and require the syntactic information for calculating the respective metrics. Metrics used for detection have to be carefully chosen, because the choice has major influence on the quality of the results [169]. In addition, metric-based approaches can operate only on program entities of a pre-defined granularity—for example, functions. Consequently, clones that are contained within these entities or span more than one entity cannot be detected.

2.3.6   Assembler

Clone detection based on disassembling binary executables has first been presented by Sæbjørnsen and colleagues [162]. They calculate characteristic vectors for code regions and report regions with similar vectors as clones. Only recently, Davis and Godfrey [39, 40] presented a clone detection approach based on assembler code generated from C, C++, and Java source code. A notable difference is that detected clones are not necessarily contiguous regions in the source code. Assembler-based clone detection is a relatively novel approach and thus, its advantages and disadvantages are still vague.

2.3.7   Beyond Source Code

Clone detection is not limited to the different representations of source code, but can be done using other software artifacts as well. Model-based development of software is gaining increasing significance and so does clone detection in models. A first clone detection technique for models has been presented by Deissenboeck and his colleagues [43, 44] and was applied to industrial models from the automotive domain. Another approach by Liu and colleagues [133] detects clones in serialized UML sequence diagrams using suffix trees. Nguyen, Pham and their colleagues [149, 153] proposed a technique to detect duplication in MATLAB/Simulink models. The approach has been shown to work for small models but has not been tested on larger models. Störrle [173] has analyzed different algorithms and heuristics with respect to their suitability for detecting clones in UML models.

Apart from models, a first approach has been made by Domann and colleagues [47] to detect duplication in requirements specifications. Juergens and colleagues [94] used this approach to detect and analyze duplication in real-world requirements specifications.

2.3.8   Applications for Clone Detection

Applications for clone detection and related techniques are versatile. From a research perspective, clone information can be used to understand a system, its structure, and its evolution. Understandably, clone information is frequently used to understand the phenomenon of cloning—including reasons and effects of clones—itself. Nevertheless, there are other applications for clone detection apart from research.

One application of clone detection is to locate clones within the source code of a system and use that information to support the maintenance of the system. For example, knowledge about clones helps to propagate changes correctly. Clone detection also supports program understanding as structurally similar parts may disclose relations that would otherwise be invisible [155]. Detected clones may also help to detect usage patterns of libraries or objects. Furthermore, clone detection can be also used to identify cross-cutting concerns [24, 25, 26]. Another application for clone detection is the identifaction of library candidates as multiple copies suggest the more general usability of a code fragment [28, 38].

If clones are detected not only for a single system, but a system and another code base, more applications are possible. For example, clone detection can help to find malicious source code inside a system if clones exist between the source code of that system and the source code of software that is known to be harmful [187]. Apart from malicious software, clones between different systems can be used to identify plagiarism and copyright infringement [10, 23, 98, 187]—the latter gaining more and more importance due to the increasing availability of open-source software. Finally, clone information can be used for compression algorithms [32, 42].

2.3.9   Frameworks

There is a huge variety of applications for clone detection each of which has its particular requirements to the respective detection algorithm. While most clone detection approaches are specifically targeted at a single application, more general frameworks have been presented that aim to support a bigger variety of applications. These frameworks define a generic clone detection *pipeline* which allows the user to tailor individual components to his or her needs.

A general framework for clone detection has been presented by Juergens and his colleagues [95] as part of the CONQAT toolkit.[1] The framework offers to configure each of the individual clone detection phases—from reading the relevant source code to

---

[1]http://www.conqat.org

writing the results. Apart from source code, the framework also supports detection of clones in models and natural language documents.

Recently, Biegel and Diehl [21, 22] provided a formal description of a generic pipeline to detect clones in Java source code. Their approach offers an API to easily create an AST-based clone detector that can be configured to be applicable to a variety of applications.

2.4 Management

The mere detection of clones does not suffice to mitigate the problems they cause. To counter their negative effects, clones have to be *managed*. There are different views on which activities are part of clone management. According to Koschke [117], clone management embraces methods to "detect, present, remove, prevent, and compensate clones". The detection of clones has already been discussed in the previous section. In this section, we focus on the further processing of clone information. In particular, removing clones and monitoring changes to clones.

2.4.1 Removing

One possible way of mitigating clone-related problems is removing clones. Fowler [56] already argued that all clones should be removed after being detected. A simple technique to automatically remove clones has been given by Baxter and his colleagues [18]. Duplicated code is extracted into a macro which is invoked in all places where the duplicated code occurred. Parametrization of macros can be used to also remove clones that are not identical but only similar. The downside of this approach is that it is applicable only to programming languages that are preprocessed and extensive use of the mechanism might significantly decrease the comprehensibility of the source code.

A more sophisticated way of removing clones is to apply refactorings. The most prominent example is the *Extract Method* refactoring that has been suggested by many studies [18, 54, 97, 112, 183]. A new method is created that provides the functionality of the cloned fragments. The cloned fragments themselves are replaced with a call to the new method. Such refactorings occur in practice a we have seen when studying the removal of clones. Figure 11.2 on page 178 and Figure 11.5 on page 184 provide examples that we have found in a real system. Apart from the Extract Method refactoring, the Pull Up Method refactoring can be used to move identical functionality from specialized classes to a common base class. Higo and colleagues [77, 78] suggested to filter the output of a clone detector and determine which refactoring is most applicable. Several restructuring scenarios that can be used to remove clones on the function level have been presented by Fanta and Rajlich [54].

While most automated refactorings can be applied to only identical fragments, PDG-based method extraction presented by Komondoor and Horwitz [111, 112] also supports fragments where statements are in different order. The PDG allows the tool to ensure that the refactoring is semantics preserving—a critical requirement for automated refactorings. A technique that is able to refactor not only sequences of statements but also parts of individual statements has been introduced by Juillerat and Hirsbrunner [97]. Clone removal is not limited to source code and was, for example, successfully applied to web documents by Synytskyy and colleagues [174].

The majority of automated refactoring approaches requires that the cloned code is identical. Nevertheless, clones are likely to have subtle differences that must be respected and prohibit the application of a completely automated refactoring. Approaches can, however, analyze clones and their structure to make refactoring suggestions and support semi-automated refactorings [14, 15, 145]. Although clone removal may mitigate clone-related problems and improve the maintainability of a system, it may also introduce new problems when the refactoring is not performed correctly. Consequently, maintainers often refrain from removing clones due to the risk of introducing new problems [34].

2.4.2   Monitoring

Apart from being removed, clones and changes to them can be monitored. Developers are warned whenever changes to existing clones may cause problems. Monitoring helps to reduce the effort for change propagation and to prevent incomplete propagation of changes caused by missing knowledge about clones. To reduce the effort for change propagation, Toomim and colleagues [182] proposed *linked editing*—automated propagation of changes to clones. A similar approach which is specialized to propagate renaming of identifiers has been presented by Jablonski and Hou [86].

To prevent incomplete propagation of changes, Duala-Ekoko and Robillard [48, 49, 50] introduced a first approach to track clones across multiple versions of a system. Whenever changes affect clones, their tool CLONETRACKER informs the developers about potential inconsistencies and supports the propagation of the changes to other cloned fragments. Similar approaches with a slightly different focus have been presented by Chiu and Hirtle [33], de Wit and colleagues [41], and Weckerle [189]. In contrast to the other approaches, de Wit and colleagues [41] performed an extensive evaluation of their tool *CloneBoard*. They found that while the principle of monitoring clones is helpful in general, change propagation often requires more complex strategies than provided by existing tools. Jacob and colleagues [88] proposed and implemented an editor that is aware of copy-and-paste activity, features a differencing algorithm customized to code clones, and visualizes changes to clones.

2.5   Terminology

To complete this chapter on background information about software clones, this section introduces relevant terminology. Unfortunately, the terminology is not consistent across publications. Therefore, we summarize the terms that are used throughout this thesis to describe clone relations and their evolution.

System. When analyzing software clones, we do this in the context of a *system*. A system is seen as a collection of source code files that are relevant to our analysis. In many cases a system corresponds to complete programs. Nevertheless, a system may also denote a subset of a program's files—for example, a selection of certain modules only.

Version. As this thesis is concerned with the evolution of clones, the analyses are not limited to a single state of a system. Let a *version* be the system's source code at a specific point in time. When studying clone evolution, we analyze a sequence of versions of a system that are in a well-defined order. Consequently, there exists a first and a last version that frame the period of the respective analysis.

Token. Our incremental clone detection and tracking tool is a token-based approach, with a *token* being an atomic unit of the respective programming language. Examples of tokens are keywords, operators, and identifiers. Each source code file of the system is regarded as a sequence of tokens.

Fragment. The basic entity of clone evolution analysis is a *fragment*. A fragment refers to a contiguous section of source code. As such, each fragment is a subsequence of tokens that occurs within the respective file's token sequence. A fragment has a well-defined start and end. From the perspective of the algorithms, these are given in terms of token indices whereas for presentation of clone information to humans, start and end are given as line and column information. In general, each fragment is a triple

$$fragment = (file, start, end)$$

with $file$ being the source code file that contains the fragment, $start$ denoting the first token of the fragment, and end referring to the last token of the fragment. All tokens between $start$ and end inclusively are part of the fragment. Nevertheless, fragments do not suffice to analyze software clones without knowing which fragments are similar to each other. Consequently, fragments are grouped into clone pairs or clone classes according to their similarity.

Clone Pair. A *clone pair* combines exactly two similar fragments that are clones of each other. In addition, a clone pair has a *type* that defines the degree of similarity between both fragments. Hence, a clone pair can be described using the following triple:

$$clone\_pair = (fragment_A, fragment_B, type)$$

The type of the clone pair is used to described the degree of similarity between both fragments. We use the categories introduced by Bellon and colleagues [19] that distinguish four different degrees of similarity.

- **Type 1:** For type-1 clone pairs, the token sequences of both fragments are identical disregarding comments and whitespace. The tokens at corresponding locations in both fragments are identical with respect to their type and their textual representation. Figure 2.3 on the next page provides an example of a type-1 clone pair.

- **Type 2:** Type-2 clone pairs are type-1 clone pairs except for the values of identifiers and literals that do not need to match. While all tokens are required to have the same type, the values of identifiers and literals may be different. Type-2 clones are created when code is copied and its structure reused while the identifiers

```
1   int  a  =  0;           1   int  a  =  0;
2   b  =  a  *  a;          2   b  =  a  *  a;  // Comment
3   str  =  "Peter";        3   str  =  "Peter";
```

(a) $fragment_A$ (b) $fragment_B$

Figure 2.3 – A clone pair of type 1.

```
1   int  a  =  0;           1   int  d  =  1;
2   b  =  a  *  a;          2   b  =  d  *  d;  // Comment
3   str  =  "Peter";        3   str  =  "Pan";
```

(a) $fragment_A$ (b) $fragment_B$

Figure 2.4 – A clone pair of type 2.

are changed to conform to the new context. An example of a type-2 clone is shown in Figure 2.4.

Type-2 clones can be further constrained to fragments where identifiers and literals have been consistently renamed—*parametrized duplication*—that is, a one-to-one mapping must exist between the identifiers and literals of the first and of the second fragment. An approach to detect parametrized duplication has been presented by Baker [12].

- **Type 3:** Type-3 clones are defined as type-1 or type-2 clones with gaps—that is, the token sequences of both fragments are mostly identical, but there are tokens that exist in only one of the fragments. As such, type-3 clones can be regarded as a combination of neighboring type-1 and type-2 clones. Type-3 clones are, for example, created when code is copied and new statements are inserted or deleted from the copy. Figure 2.5 illustrates an example of a type-3 clone pair. Some of the tokens are unique to only one of the clone pair's fragments.

- **Type 4:** In contrast to the previous types, clone pairs of type-4 are not defined based on the token sequences of their fragments but on their semantic. A clone

```
1   int  a  =  0;           1   int  a  =  0;
2   b  =  a  *  a;          2   b  =  a  *  a;
3                           3   print(b);
4   str  =  "Peter";        4   str  =  "Peter";
```

(a) $fragment_A$ (b) $fragment_B$

Figure 2.5 – A clone pair of type 3.

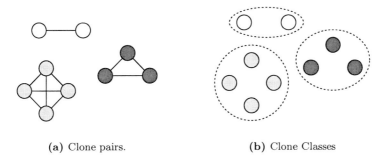

(a) Clone pairs.   **(b)** Clone Classes

Figure 2.6 – Comparison of clone pairs and clone classes.

pair is of type-4 is both fragments are similar in their behavior. These fragments perform similar tasks and are similar in their semantic.

A property of clone pairs is that the similarity relation is symmetric—that is, the existence of a clone pair $(fragment_A, fragment_B, type)$ requires the existence of a clone pair $(fragment_A, fragment_B, type)$. For type-1 and type-2 clone pairs, the relation is also transitive. The existence of a clone pair $(fragment_A, fragment_B, type)$ and a clone pair $(fragment_B, fragment_C, type)$ requires the existence of a clone pair $(fragment_A, fragment_C, type)$.

According to Baker [12], a clone pair is *left-extensible* if the token at position $fragment_A.start - 1$ in $fragment_A.file$ equals the token at position $fragment_B.start - 1$ in $fragment_B.file$. If these tokens are identical, the clone pair could be extended to the left without having an effect on the similarity. Likewise, a clone pair is *right-extensible* if the token at position $fragment_A.end + 1$ in $fragment_A.file$ equals the token at position $fragment_B.end + 1$ in $fragment_B.file$. Furthermore, a clone pair is *maximal* if is neither left-extensible nor right-extensible.

Clone Class. As an alternative to clone pairs, the similarity between fragments can be described in terms of a *clone class*. A clone class combines two or more fragments that are clones of each other. Analogous to clone pairs, the degree of similarity between the clone class' fragments is described in terms of a type. The different types of similarity are adopted from clone pairs. A clone class is a tuple consisting of a set of fragments and the type of similarity:

$$clone\_class = (Fragments, type)$$

We extend left-extensibility and right-extensibility which have been introduced by Baker for clone pairs to clone classes. A clone class is left-extensible if the token to the left of each fragment is identical and right-extensible if the token to the right of each fragment is right-extensible. A clone class is maximal if it is neither left-extensible nor right-extensible. Please note that a subset of the clone class' fragments may be extensible although the clone class itself is maximal.

Clone classes are a more compact representation of the similarity that exists between fragments. While n fragments require $n(n-1)/2$ clone pairs in the worst case, they require only $n - 1$ clone classes in the worst case. This is an important advantage of clone classes over clone pairs since the number of detected fragments can grow huge. The more compact representation and all similar fragments being represented by a single entity make us use clone classes throughout this thesis.

Example 2.3 – This example illustrates the difference between clone pairs and clone classes in Figure 2.6 on the previous page. Each circle represents a fragment and circles of the same shade indicate fragments that are clones of each other. Solid lines indicate the clone-pair relation and dotted ellipses represent the clone-class relation. Figure (a) shows that 10 clone pairs are required to relate the fragments that are clones of each other. In contrast, only 3 clone-class relations are needed as illustrated in Figure (b). □

Chapter 3

Related Research

The importance of software clones is steadily increasing in the research community. Previous studies investigated various facets of the phenomenon of cloning. This chapter introduces existing research related to the topic of this thesis and presents relevant questions emerging from the current state of the art. This chapter is structured as follows. Section 3.1 summarizes related work on clone detection with special focus on incremental detection and the detection of non-identical clones. Related research regarding clone tracking is presented in Section 3.2. Section 3.3 describes previous studies that analyzed the quantitative evolution of clones. Section 3.4 introduces clone evolution patterns that have been used in previous studies to analyze how individual clones evolve. Finally, studies on the occurrence of these patterns in real systems and their relation to clone-related problems is given in Section 3.5. A general overview of the field of software clone research is given by Koschke [116].

3.1 Clone Detection

The detection of clones is—and has been—the central part of research on software clones, because analyzing clones requires to know where they reside in a system. Thus, the goal of clone detection is to locate duplication inside the source code[1]— more specifically, in one of its representations. Clone detection approaches are commonly categorized according to the representation they operate on. The different representations vary in the level of abstraction and, consequently, the amount of information available, the dependency on certain programming languages, and the performance.

The lowest abstraction is used by text-based approaches (for example [52, 91, 92, 128, 138, 140, 190]) that analyze the source code with no or only little preprocessing. These approaches are generally fast and applicable to any form of text at the cost

---

[1]Clone detection is not limited to source code and can, for example, be applied to other software artifacts like models [43, 44, 133, 153, 173] and requirements specifications [47, 94]. Nevertheless, this thesis is concerned only with clone detection in source code.

of not having any language-specific information. Token-based techniques (for example [9, 10, 17, 68, 95, 98, 130, 172, 184, 191]) use a lexer to transform the source code into a sequence of tokens prior to detection. While still being fast, they already require a lexer for the respective programming language, which—on the other hand—is no obstacle for most languages. Tokens provide basic information about the program's structure that is exploited to improve detection. An additional parser is employed by tree-based approaches (for example [18, 27, 53, 89, 97, 118, 119, 150, 163, 175, 186]) that detect clones in the Abstract Syntax Tree (AST) of a program. The AST provides additional information at the cost of performance and the requirement of having a grammar and a syntactically correct program. Graph-based techniques (for example [57, 113, 120, 132]) search for similar subgraphs in the Program Dependency Graph, but are applicable only to small programs due to their performance. Other approaches use metrics (for example, [29, 37, 38, 46, 115, 141, 152]) to find similar program entities based on the similarity of their metrics. Only recently, novel approaches that detect clones based on the assembler code of a program have been presented (for example [39, 40, 162]).

A more elaborate summary of the different approaches is given in Section 2.3. For a general survey of clone detection research, please refer to the technical report by Roy and Cordy [159]. A comparison and evaluation of various clone detection techniques and tools has been presented by Roy, Cordy, and Koschke [161]. A comparative study of different clone detection approaches and tools has been done by Bellon and associates [19]. For this thesis, two aspects of clone detection are particularly relevant: the *incremental* detection of clones and the detection of *non-identical clones*.

3.1.1   Incremental

Clone detection is traditionally targeted at locating duplication within a single version of a system. The need to detect clones in multiple versions is, however, increasing. Clone evolution is a rich source of information, but requires to detect clones in multiple, consecutive versions of a system. A naïve approach is to apply a traditional clone detection technique to every version of the system separately. The problem is that this generates a huge overhead in computation time as code is repeatedly analyzed although it might never change. Assuming the differences between consecutive versions are small, these redundant computations make the naïve approach infeasible for practical applications. Instead, a technique that is designed to be incremental in the first place is required.

We were the first to develop and evaluate such an incremental technique [68, 69] based on the results of my diploma thesis [60]. The underlying idea is to reuse data from the previous version's analysis as much as possible to save unnecessary computations when processing the current version. From a technical perspective, we have extended the suffix tree—the central data structure to most token-based clone detection approaches—to a generalized suffix tree which allows modification of the tree after its initial construction. By modifying the generalized suffix tree instead of creating it from scratch for every version, the incremental algorithm requires on average only 35% of the time compared to the repeated application of a traditional approach when detecting clones in

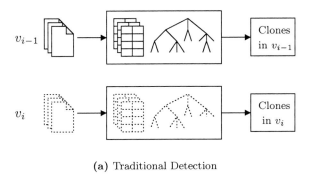

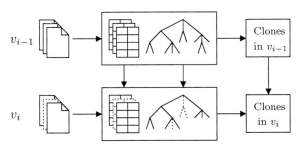

(a) Traditional Detection

(b) Incremental Detection

Figure 3.1 – Comparison of traditional to incremental clone detection. Dotted lines indicate parts that are processed. Incremental detection reuses data from the previous version where possible.

multiple versions. Figure 3.1 illustrates the difference between the repeated application of a traditional approach and our incremental approach.

Although our incremental approach already achieved a great increase in performance, there is still room for improvement. Especially extracting identical clones from the generalized suffix tree is still done in a non-incremental fashion. It requires a notable amount of time that is independent of how much source code has been changed between versions. Particularly regarding small changes between versions, the extraction is the dominating factor accounting for most of the time needed to process a version, making it the bottleneck of the analysis. Thus, it is desirable to extract clones from the suffix tree in an incremental fashion as well—that is, make it depend on the changes between versions.

Kawaguchi and colleagues [104] approached incremental clone detection from the perspective of providing live clone information in an IDE. They introduced a tool named SHINOBI that extracts and presents clone information to the user. The server part of the tool is connected to a source code repository and maintains a suffix array—an alternative to suffix trees—to detect clones. When new versions are commited to the repository, the changed files are parsed and the suffix array is updated. Unfortunately, the authors do not specify how this is done. Most likely, the suffix array is created from scratch, because there is no algorithm to efficiently update a suffix array after its initial construction to the best of my knowledge[2] The client part of SHINOBI is implemented as an IDE plug-in that communicates with the server side. When the developer edits source code, the client sends a clone detection request to the server which, in turn, returns the clones related to the source code that is currently edited. The approach highlights a potential application for incremental clone detection but is not truly incremental itself. First, the suffix array is not updated in an incremental fashion but has to be reconstructed for every version. Second, clone detection is limited to all copies of a given pattern—the source fragment currently edited in the IDE by the developer. This is different from the more general problem of finding all combinations of similar code.

An incremental clone detection algorithm that uses Abstract Syntax Trees (AST) of a program has been introduced by Nguyen and colleagues [150]. Each source file is represented as an AST while the subtrees of the AST are represented as characteristic vectors. Clones are detected by searching for similar vectors. Vectors are hashed using locality-sensitive hashing prior to comparison to improve performance. Only vectors that have the same hash value are compared. This technique is frequently applied by tree-based clone detection algorithms to improve performance despite the worst-case quadratic number of comparisons. Clones correspond to subtrees of the ASTs. When files change, the subtrees of the respective ASTs are added or deleted and the clone information is updated accordingly. The algorithm has been implemented in a tool called CLEMANX. Nguyen and associates show the advantage of their incremental approach by comparing its average running time to that of a traditional approach. Unfortunately, not many details are given about the versions that are analyzed and, in particular, the number of relevant changes occurring between versions. Thus, one might suspect that a lot of versions changed only non-source files irrelevant to the analysis resulting in an unfair advantage for the incremental approach. The major difference to our approach is that their approach is based on ASTs. Consequently, it suffers from all the disadvantages of AST-based clone detection: is requires a parser (which is hard to obtain for certain languages—for example, *COBOL*), the code has to be syntactically correct (which is not always the case during development), and the code must not contain preprocessor directives (which *C* and *C++* code almost always does).

Another incremental approach has been introduced by Hummel and his colleagues [83]. They addressed the scalability of incremental detection in particular. Although being token-based, tokens are aggregated to statements prior to processing. Hence, the basic unit for detection are statements. The central part of the approach is an index that maintains a mapping from sequences of statements to their occurrences. When files are added or deleted between versions, the respective statement sequences are inserted or removed from the index, respectively. The approach is specialized for

---

[2]There is first work on this in the theoretical computer science community—for example [58] and [165]. Nevertheless, the applicability to practical problems is not given yet. Hofmann [79] has evaluated the approach by Salson and colleagues [165] and found that an incremental update of suffix arrays is faster than a complete reconstruction only when the number of modifications is very small.

```
1  account.addMoney(20);              1  widget.setX(30);
2  account.addMoreMoney(1000);        2  widget.setY(10);
3  account.recalculate();             3  widget.updatePosition();
```

(a) First fragment   (b) Second fragment

Figure 3.2 – Two fragments of a type-2 clone class. Although the token sequences are identical with respect to the type of tokens, the fragments are unrelated.

efficiently detecting all clones between a given file and the remainder of the system. An advantage of index-based clone detection is that it can be distributed to many machines, making it very scalable. Hummel and his colleagues show that updating the index and retrieving clones for a given file can be done fast and, thus, the approach is suitable to be used during maintenance of very large systems. Nevertheless, it is questionable whether the approach is beneficial for detection of all cloning relationships in a system and retrospective analysis of clone evolution in a system. Most of the improvement in scalability (compared to our approach [68]) results from aggregating tokens to statements before processing. This significantly reduces the number of atomic units for detection—the factor is the average number of tokens per statement—but also results in loss of detail. If desired, our incremental approach also supports the aggregation of tokens prior to detection.

3.1.2 Non-Identical Clones

We refer to fragments that have similar but not identical token sequences as *non-identical clones*. Hence, non-identical clones are the union of type-2 and type-3 clones. On the one hand, non-identical clones are of great importance, because many relevant clones are non-identical clones due to small differences despite high similarity. Especially these subtle differences between fragments may indicate potential problems. On the other hand, tolerating differences increases the probability that detected clones are in fact unrelated. Tiarks and her colleagues [179, 180] have found that up to 75% of type-3 clones detected by state-of-the-art tools are false positives.

Example 3.1 – Consider the cloned fragments shown in Figure 3.2. The first fragments modifies a bank account while the second fragment is responsible to layout a GUI widget. Although the values of identifiers and literals are different, both fragments have the same sequence of tokens regarding the type of tokens. Still, the fragments are unrelated and, thus, this non-identical clone class can be regarded as irrelevant. □

In general, the challenge of non-identical clone detection is to detect the relevant cases while not detecting irrelevant clones like the one shown in Figure 3.2. Detection of non-identical clones is an inherent feature of clone detection approaches that operate on higher abstractions than tokens. AST-based techniques search for similar subtrees by employing deliberately imperfect hashing—that is, not only identical, but also similar subtrees are assigned the same hash value. Hashing can be done on the subtrees themselves [18], characteristic vectors computed for the subtrees [89], or other patterns derived from the subtrees [53]. Identical as well as similar subtrees that have been detected as clones may differ in their token sequences and, hence, be regarded as non-identical clones. Graph-based approaches search for similar subgraphs of the PDG. This can be done using a variant of slicing [57, 113] or using a search algorithm [120]. Analoguous to subtrees, identical and similar subgraphs are likely to differ in their token representation and are regarded as non-identical clones. Recently, Selim and colleagues [168] introduced another way of detecting type-3 clones using the *Jimple* intermediate representation of Java code. Nevertheless, the AST and the PDG are unavailable to token-based approaches and, thus, subtree and subgraph similarity cannot be exploited.

Assembler-based clone detection searches for similarity in the assembler code that is generated from the source code. This is either done based on the similarity of feature vectors for assembler code regions [162] or using a special search algorithm [39, 40]. Clones detected in the assembler code may not be identical in the source code, because the compiler applies transformations and optimizations to the code. Furthermore, cloned fragments in the assembler code may not even be contiguous regions in the original source code. Hence, the majority of detected clones are non-identical clones. Text-based approaches may detect non-identical clones by applying normalization to the source code prior to clone detection. Furthermore, a similarity threshold can be applied that defines how many differences between cloned fragments are tolerated. This is, for example, implemented in NICAD [160].

Although many different techniques exist to detect non-identical clones, these cannot be easily used in a token-based approach due to the unavailability of the respective program representations. Consequently, token-based clone detection has its own techniques for detecting non-identical clones. The detection of type-2 clones can easily be integrated by redefining the equality of tokens. Type-1 clone detection requires that the types and the values of tokens are identical. To detect type-2 clones, this constraint can be relaxed to only requiring the types to be identical. The same algorithms (for example Baker's DUP [9]) can be used to detect type-2 clones in addition to type-1 clones. Nevertheless, detecting type-2 clones this way yields many irrelevant clones like the one shown in Figure 3.2 on the previous page. To reduce the number of irrelevant type-2 clones, Baker [10] introduced *p-suffix trees* to detect only parametrized clones. While the values of parametrized type-2 clones may still be different, there needs to exist a one-to-one mapping between the token values of the first and the second fragment, respectively. However, many irrelevant clones are not eliminated using this approach. The example shown in Figure 3.2 on the previous page is a parametrized clones and would still be detected.

For type-3 clones, different approaches have been presented. Ueda and colleagues [184] presented an approach to detect type-3 clones in a post-processing step by merging neighboring type-1 and type-2 clones. Whether neighboring clones can be merged is determined by a user-defined fixed threshold that defines the maximum size of a gap between clones. The approach is promising and builds the foundation for the non-identical clone detection presented in this thesis. Another technique has been introduced by Li and colleagues [130]. Their tool CP-MINER uses a frequent subsequence mining algorithm to detect duplication. Identifying similarity despite differences is an inherent feature of the algorithm. The maximum number of different statements that are tolerated is given by the user. This approach is strongly tied to the frequent subsequence mining algorithm and can, thus, not be integrated into a suffix-tree based clone detection approach. An approach that integrates well into suffix-tree based clone detection has been presented by Juergens and his colleagues [96]. Their technique employs an "edit-distance aware" algorithm that retrieves clones from the suffix tree. While traditional approaches consider only identical token sequences, the algorithm by Juergens and his colleagues tolerates differences up to a user-defined maximum. Unfortunately, the approach is not applicable to live clone detection due to its complexity.

3.1.3   Open Questions

A lot of research has been conducted regarding clone detection, with incremental detection gaining increasing importance. Alternatives to our incremental approach either impose strong limitations because of being based on ASTs [150] or do not provide significant advantages [83]. Consequently, we focus on improving the original version of our incremental approach [68]. To increase the performance, the bottleneck of extracting clones from the suffix tree has to be mitigated.

> **Question 1** – *How can clones be extracted from the suffix tree in an incremental fashion?*

The solution to this problem involves a "change-aware" extraction algorithm that processes only those parts of the suffix tree that are affected by change. The technique is described in Section 6.2 and 6.3, while the performance benefit is shown in Chapter 8.

Another problem of our initial incremental approach is its insufficient support for detecting non-identical clones. The naïve detection of type-2 clones is likely to find many irrelevant clones (thus lowering precision) while the missing detection of type-3 clones prevents the detection of potentially relevant clones (thus lowering recall). Accordingly, the algorithm needs sophisticated handling of non-identical clones.

> **Question 2** – *How can non-identical clones be detected incrementally?*

We approach this question with a novel approach for detecting type-2 and type-3 clones which is inspired by previous work by Ueda and colleagues [184]. In contrast to other techniques, we detect type-2 clones not by extracting them from the suffix tree, but in the same manner as type-3 clones by merging neighboring type-1 clones. This eliminates frequent sources of false positives. A detailed description is given in Section 6.4.

The intention of our approach is to reduce the number of irrelevant clones compared to previous approaches. Nevertheless, our technique may—in principle—also miss some of the relevant clones.

> **Question 3** – *How does our detection of non-identical clones compare to previous approaches?*

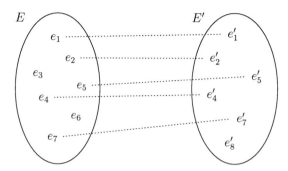

Figure 3.3 – Mapping entities between versions.

To evaluate our technique, we qualitatively compared non-identical clones detected by our approach to non-identical clones detected by previous approaches. The results of this comparison are given in Section 6.4.2.

3.2   Clone Tracking

An essential prerequisite for analyzing clone evolution is being able to track clones across multiple versions of the system, that is, determining a clone's occurrence in different versions of a system. Therefore, the purpose of the tracking is to determine the ancestry of clones. As clones may potentially have an arbitrary structure, the problem can be generalized to that of matching arbitrary source code entities. The situation is illustrated in Figure 3.3. Entities of set E (for example, clones in a particular version) are mapped to their counterparts in E' (for example, the clones' occurrences in the other versions of the source code). The process of determining the ancestry of source code entities is also known as *origin analysis* [71, 195].

Since the problem is not limited to clone evolution and relevant for all kinds of software evolution research, a number of different approaches have evolved both inside and outside the clone research community. Kim and Notkin [107] presented a summary of various techniques used to match software entities for multi version program analysis. The different approaches have been classified according to the program representation upon which they operate. Kim and Notkin identified the following categories:

Entity Name Matching. Entities are matched based on their name. The assumptions are that entities (1) have a distinct name and (2) the name is fixed for different versions of the program [193, 194].

String Matching. If program versions are represented as strings, the best alignment between two versions can be found using common algorithms based on strings [109, 171, 181]. A frequently used approach is the longest common subsequence algorithm (LCS) [7, 85].

Syntax Tree Matching. The availability of a syntax tree allows finding matching entities based on the tree's structure using tree differencing algorithms [192].

Furthermore, the syntactic information can be used in conjunction with other approaches to enhance the quality of matching results [84, 148].

Control Flow Graph Matching. The control flow graphs of two different program versions are matched by computing a one-to-one mapping between the graphs' nodes [6, 125]. Finding matching nodes corresponds to finding matching software entities.

Program Dependence Graph Matching. Another set of algorithms compares the program dependence graphs of two program versions [81, 87]. The applicability of these approaches is very limited due to the non-trivial task of calculating dependence graphs for programs written in modern languages.

Binary Code Matching. Independent of the source code, two program versions can be matched based on their binary representation [188]. The software entities that are matched are blocks of binary data.

Clone Detection. A clone detector can be used to identify similar parts between two program versions, thus creating a many-to-many match. The number of different clone detection approaches and parametrization options allow flexible matching. Although Kim and Notkin [107] list clone detection as a separate category here, each clone detection approach belongs, in fact, to one of the previous categories depending on the program representation.

Origin Analysis Tools. Origin analysis has been introduced by Godfrey and Tu [71] and refers to the process of deciding for a given entity in version v_i whether it has been newly introduced or whether it is the modified version of an entity in v_{i-1}. Origin analysis can be used to reconstruct refactoring events and to calculate the origin of software entities in an earlier version according to a similarity measure based on different criteria [45, 110, 195, 196]. Like clone detection, origin analysis has to compute the similarity between entities based on a specific program representation. As such, it also falls under one of the previous categories depending on the representation actually used.

All approaches perform *state-based* matching by retroactively finding best matches among entities of two program versions. An alternative to state-based matching is *operation-based* matching [131]. Operation-based matching calculates matches between the old and the new version of an entity using the complete set of logical changes between the corresponding program versions [107]. In contrast to state-based matching, there is no need to use a heuristic that matches entities according to a given measure of similarity. Robbes and colleagues [156, 157] proposed to directly capture logical editing operations from an IDE during development to enrich information that is used for analyzing software evolution. Operation-based matching is very promising, but there is hardly any program for which logical changes have been recorded over a reasonable time period to the best of our knowledge. Consequently, existing clone tracking approaches fall back to state-based matching where states are the occurrences of program entities in a particular version.

3.2.1 Matching

Although a number of studies have analyzed how clones are changed, there are only few that suggest techniques to track clones across multiple versions. One of the first techniques to track clones has been presented by Kim and her colleagues [109]. Their study on clone genealogies required them to track clones across multiple versions of their subject systems. Prior to matching clones between versions, they used a conventional clone detection tool, namely CCFINDER [98], to detect clones for each version separately. After that, they employed a hybrid approach to detect best matches between the clones of consecutive versions. The approach consists of a clone-detection component and a string-matching component. The entities that are matched are clone classes.

Matching is done by comparing each clone class of version v_{i-1} to each clone class of version v_i and computing a score for their similarity (the clone-detection component) and the overlapping of their location (the string-matching component). The similarity is based on the duplicated token sequences that both classes represent and defined as the common part's relative proportion to the sum of the lengths of both sequences. The location overlapping calculates how much the locations of fragments from the once class overlap with the location of fragments from the other class. To account for possible movement of fragments due to code modifications between versions, the algorithm exploits the difference information contained in the source code repository. The difference information is used to calibrate the locations before the overlapping score is computed. Matches are detected according to the best scores. If the decision is ambiguous, that is, the clone class in v_{i-1} that has the best similarity score is different from the clone class in v_{i-1} that has the best location overlapping score, both are selected as ancestors of the clone class in v_i.

A different approach has been presented by Bakota and colleagues [13]. In contrast to Kim and her colleagues' approach, they match individual cloned fragments instead of clone classes, resulting in a more detailed mapping. Clones are detected for each version separately using an AST-based approach presented by Koschke and his colleagues [118]. Following clone detection, cloned fragments of different versions are matched. Possible matches are searched not only between consecutive versions, but between every pair of versions, having a significant impact on the complexity. Two fragments of different versions are considered as possible matches only if the respective root of the subtree in the AST has the same type. That is, fragments can be matched only if they represent the same type of structure, for example a method can be matched only to a method, while a class can be matched only to a class. Which of the possible candidates is matched depends on six different measures which are the name of the file that contains the fragment, the position of the fragment inside the clone class, the name of the fragment's root node in the AST (if it has one) or the name of the first named ancestor of the root node, the relative position of the fragment inside its first named ancestor, and the lexical structure of the fragment. Some of these measures depend on the availability of the AST. The individual measures are aggregated into a single similarity score using different weights for the measures. Fragments with the best similarity score are matched. If there are multiple best matches, one of them is chosen randomly to be the ancestor of the respective fragment.

Another technique has been presented by Duala-Ekoko and Robillard [48, 50] and implemented in a tool named CloneTracker [49]. They introduced the notion of a *Clone Region Descriptor* (CRD) that describes the location of a cloned fragment inside a source file. The CRD can be computed for a fragment in a particular version and can be used to locate occurrences of the same fragment in other versions. As such, it can be used to track clones across multiple versions. CRDs are based on the hierarchical structure of a program and contain information about the file, class, method, and block in which the respective fragment is contained. The advantage of the CRD technique is, that clones detected in one version can be located in other versions and, hence, tracked without separate detection of clones in the other version. The disadvantage is that this technique is not capable of detecting clones that are created in later versions. While the approach is robust against certain type of modifications—for example, relocation and renaming—it is susceptible to other types of modifications, for example, altering the hierarchical structure of the source code. In contrast to other approaches, Duala-Ekoko and Robillard have evaluated the precision and accuracy of their approach showing that cloned fragments can be reliably tracked in the majority of situations. Their method has, for example, been used by Bettenburg and his colleagues [20].

Nguyen and colleagues [150, 151] use a hybrid approach based on ASTs to track cloned fragments. In contrast to the other approaches, clone tracking is part of their incremental detection, eliminating the need to detect clones in each version separately before tracking. Clones are detected using characteristic vectors which are computed for subtrees of the AST. If the vectors for subtrees are similar, they are regarded as clones of each other. Similarity is determined using locality-sensitive hashing, that is, similar vectors are assigned the same hash value. Regarding source code changes, the first part of the approach is string-based. The change information from the repository is used to determine which parts of the source code and, hence, the AST have not been changed. The second part is AST-based and consists of calculating an edit script for the remaining parts of the AST that have changed. The edit script is used to determine which subtrees of the AST have changed and, consequently, which vectors have to be removed and added. The removal and addition of vectors allows concluding how clones are affected by the change which, in term, allows tracking them.

3.2.2 Source Code Differencing

An important prerequisite of our clone tracking approach is knowing how the source code has changed between two consecutive versions of a system. Unfortunately, this information is hardly ever recorded while systems are developed and maintained. Consequently, we have to fall back to retroactively analyzing how the source code was modified between different versions of the systems. To achieve this, we have to calculate the differences between two given versions of source code which is analogous to calculating the *Longest Common Subsequence (LCS)* of these two versions.

Probably the best known approach for calculating differences between files is the program DIFF[3] which is based on the algorithm by Myers [147]. Despite the tool DIFF

---

[3]http://www.gnu.org/software/diffutils/

being implemented for sequences of text lines, Myers' algorithm itself can compare two sequences of arbitrary elements. Although the algorithm is widely used, it has some limitations, which include that it can report only additions and deletions of elements. Hence, it is not able to detect changed elements or elements that have been moved to a different location.

To overcome these limitations, Canfora and colleagues [31] have developed a tool named LDIFF that builds upon the line-based DIFF program. LDIFF performs the following three steps to identify changed and moved lines:

(1) Use DIFF to determine which lines are *unchanged.*

(2) Calculate the textual similarity of all blocks that are not classified as unchanged in the previous step.

(3) Calculate the similarity of each pair of lines of the most similar blocks. If the similarity is above a given threshold, the corresponding lines are regarded as changed or moved. Steps 2 and 3 are repeated for a given number of iterations.

LDIFF has two major drawbacks. The first is its recall and precisions. Canfora and colleagues report a recall between 62% and 73% suggesting that a notable number of code changes and movements are not detected. The authors report a precision of 92% indicating that 8% of changes and movements are erroneously detected. The second disadvantage is the running time. The approach is quadratic and the authors report a running time of almost one minute. These disadvantages make the approach not applicable to our clone tracking as we require a much faster difference calculation—especially regarding live clone detection. Furthermore, their approach is line-based whereas we require an approach that operates on sequences of tokens.

Kim and Notkin [108] presented their tool LSDIFF (LOGICAL STRUCTURAL DIFF) that takes the calculation and representation of source code differences to a more abstract level. LSDIFF infers logical rules that describe differences in the structure of two source code versions. However, the approach is not applicable to our clone tracking, as it requires a parser for extracting the information that is needed to perform the difference calculation.

3.2.3   Open Questions

Matching software entities between versions can be done using various program representations. Except for the technique by Kim and her colleagues [109] all approaches require the AST to perform the matching. Unfortunately, information related to the AST is not available to token-based clone detection. Consequently, our tracking is inspired by Kim and her colleagues' approach. The shortcoming of their approach is that using clone classes as basic entities and using line-based locations result in loss of detail. Furthermore, their tracking is non-incremental and has quadratic complexity.

> **Question 4** – *How can a detailed tracking of cloned fragments be integrated into our incremental detection approach?*

```
1   double x = 0.0;          1   double z = 0.0;
2   double y = 0.0;
```

(a) First version   (b) Second version

Figure 3.4 – An ambiguous change to code. There is no way of determining how the code has really been changed between the first and the second version.

We use a tracking that maps individual fragments based on a set of edit operations for the file that contains the respective fragment. Our technique is integrated into the incremental algorithm and exploits information about which files have been changed. Using the edit operations mitigates the need to compare every fragment of one version to every other fragment of the next version, significantly reducing complexity. We present our technique in Chapter 7.

All state-based approaches have in common that they have to deal with ambiguity. Figure 3.4 shows two versions of a code fragment. There is no way of retroactively determining how the code has been changed using state-based matching approaches. Possibilities include the first statement has been removed and y been changed to z, the second statement has been removed and x been changed to z, or both statements have been removed and a new statement has been inserted.

Question 5 – *How can individual fragments be tracked unambiguously?*

We approach this problem by abstracting from the source of the difference information that is used to map fragments. Using a set of edit operations, the new occurrence of a fragment can be precisely calculated allowing the fragment to be tracked unambiguously. When the difference information is obtained by state-based matching, our approach suffers from the same ambiguity as other approaches. Nevertheless, our approach also supports difference information that is obtained by operation-based matching. For example, our approach can—without adoption of the tracking—be integrated into an IDE and make use of edit operations that are captured. Details on how fragments are tracked are given in Section 7.3.

3.3   Quantitative Clone Evolution

The detection of clones and tracking them across multiple versions of a system allow analyzing the evolution of clones. During the last years, clone evolution is gaining more and more importance as it provides rich information to study and understand the phenomenon of cloning.

3.3.1   Clone Ratio

One of the first studies on clone evolution has been conducted by Laguë and colleagues [123] who evaluated the benefits of incorporating clone detection in the development process of a large software system. Clones were detected based on the similarity of metrics that have been computed for functions—a variant of the approach by Mayrand and colleagues [141]. Laguë and colleagues investigated six versions of the system over a three-year period. Despite a noticeable number of clones being removed between versions, the overall clone ratio—that is, the amount of cloning compared to the system's size—remained stable. In addition, they also found that most clones were never changed after their initial creation. Laguë and colleagues conclude that a clone-aware development process may be beneficial and help to reduce the clone ratio and reveal problems before they affect users.

Antoniol and his colleagues [4] introduced a technique to model clone evolution based on time series. Time series were used to predict the future evolution of the average number of clones per function based on the system's history. Again, a metric-based clone detection approach has been employed. Antoniol and his colleagues evaluated their approach and showed that it is able to predict the number of clones per function with relatively low error. They have used the same approach to conduct an extensive study of clone evolution in the LINUX KERNEL [5]. Among their major findings are that the ratio of clones was remarkably low for the whole system as well as for the subsystems. Analogous to Laguë and his colleagues, they observed that the clone ratio remained stable across versions.

Li and colleagues [129, 130] presented a tool named CP-MINER and used it to investigate the evolution of clones in the LINUX KERNEL and FREEBSD over a period of ten years. CP-MINER is a token-based approach that detects clones based on a frequent itemset mining technique. They observed that the clone ratio increased steadily most of the time for both systems. The increase was, however, caused by only a few subsystems. The clone ratio stabilized for the last versions which had been analyzed. Therefore their results do not contradict those of Antoniol and colleagues.

Another study on clone evolution in the LINUX KERNEL has been conducted by Livieri and colleagues [134]. For their analysis, they used the token-based tool D-CCFINDER [135], a distributed version of CCFINDER [98] that allows detecting clones in a large body of source code. They analyzed a total of 136 versions of the kernel and calculated the clone ratio between each pair of versions. The number of clones has been found to be proportional to the size and, therefore, the clone ratio remained stable. In coherence with Li and colleagues, they also found that particular subsystems contributed the majority of clones.

3.3.2   Clones and Maintainability

An attempt to quantify the relation between code clones and reliability as well as maintainability of a system has been made by Monden and colleagues [146]. To detect clones, they used the token-based detection approach presented by Kamiya and colleagues [98]. For their case study they analyzed an industrial system with more than 20 years of history. Reliability of individual files was measured by comparing the number of faults to the size of the respective file. It was found that files containing clones are more reliable on average, that is, they have a lower fault density. Maintainability was measured based on the revision number of files. The higher the revision number, the more changes were required, and, hence, the less maintainable is a file. Monden and colleagues found that files containing clones are less maintainable on average than files without clones.

Geiger and his colleagues [59] analyzed the relation between code clones and change couplings. Clones were detected using CCFINDER [98]. Based on the detected clones, the clone coverage of file pairs was compared to their change coupling that has been extracted from the repository. Although Geiger and colleagues found cases where the relation exists, it could not be verified statistically.

Lonzano and her colleagues [137] analyzed whether functions change more often when having clones. They measured the number and density of changes in methods while these contain clones and while they do not. Clone information was obtained using CCFINDER [98]. Their initial results suggest that functions change more often when they have clones compared to when they do not have clones. To verify this finding, Lozano and Wermelinger [136] conducted another study but found that change effort did not increase for more than half of the methods despite having clones. Again, there seems to be no systematic relation between clones and changes.

A similar study regarding the stability of cloned code compared to non-cloned code has been conducted by Krinke [122]. He analyzed clone evolution in five systems over a period of 200 weeks. Clones have been detected for each version separately using the tool SIMIAN.[4] Stability has been measured by comparing changes that affected cloned code to changes that affected non-cloned code. Krinke concluded that cloned code is more stable than non-cloned code—that is, cloned code is less often changed.

Recently, Hotta and colleagues [82] conducted a similar study. In contrast to Krinke, they analyzed the frequency of changes, not their extent, that is, instead of counting changed source code lines, they counted the number of changed blocks of consecutive source code lines. In total, 15 different subject systems have been analyzed using four different clone detection tools. Their results support Krinke's findings, that cloned code is more stable in general. However, the stability of cloned code is lower in early stages of development. The authors conclude that cloned code does not increase the maintenance costs.

We [66] have partially replicated and extended Krinke's study [122] using a more detailed measurement and considering different parameters for clone detection. In general, we were able to validate his findings. We found that smaller clones are more stable than larger clones. Furthermore, we observed that identical clones are less stable than non-identical clones. We furthermore explored possible reasons to gain a better understanding of why clones are less stable when considering only deletions. Our results show that the instability with respect to deletions is caused by the size of the deletions rather than their frequency. Our manual inspection of the largest deletions showed that cloned code is often deleted in the course of general restructuring and clean-up activity but without clear intent to remove duplication. We extended our study to industrial COBOL systems [76] and, again, found clones to be more stable. However, we did not find clones to be less stable regarding deletions in the COBOL systems.

---

[4]http://www.redhillconsulting.com.au/products/simian/

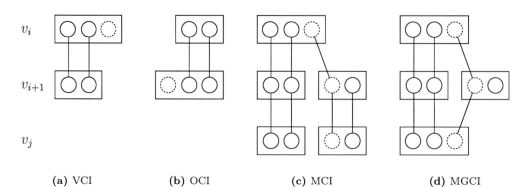

v_i

v_{i+1}

v_j

(a) VCI   (b) OCI   (c) MCI   (d) MGCI

Figure 3.5 – Fragment evolution patterns presented by Bakota and colleagues [13]. Occurrences of fragment f are shown as dotted circles.

3.3.3 Open Questions

The evolution of the ratio between clones and the size of the system is an indicator for whether cloning gets better or worse over time. Laguë and colleagues [123] found that the clone ratio is stable, suggesting that cloning does not necessarily get worse over time. In contrast, Li and colleagues [129] found that the clone ratio steadily increased for the LINUX KERNEL and FREEBSD. Again, Livieri and colleagues [134] report a stable clone ratio.

Question 6 – *How does the clone ratio evolve?*

We analyze the evolution of the clone ratio for nine open-source systems and three industrial system in course of a larger study on clone evolution. The study and its results are given in Chapter 9.

3.4 Evolution Patterns

Apart from analyzing the quantitative evolution of clones, a number of studies have investigated how individual clones evolve using evolution patterns. Clone evolution patterns describe how cloned fragments—or clone classes, respectively—evolve between different versions of a system's source code.

3.4.1 Fragment Evolution Patterns

Bakota and colleagues [13] presented four distinct ways in which individual cloned fragments may evolve. The patterns are based on the ancestry of fragments and the membership of fragments in particular clone classes. Bakota and colleagues refer to a cloned fragment as *clone instance.*

Vanished Clone Instance (VCI) describes the situation where a cloned fragment disappears from one version to the next. Fragment f exists in version v_i, but has no corresponding descendant in a later version. The situation is illustrated in Figure 3.5 (a) on the previous page. This pattern may result from deleting the fragment or changing its structure such that it is no longer similar to its siblings.

An *Occurring Clone Instance* (OCI) is the opposite to a vanished clone instance. A new fragment f appears in version v_{i+1} and has no ancestor in any earlier version. Figure 3.5 (b) on the previous page shows such a situation. The appearing fragment may be created by copy-and-paste activity or reconstituting the similarity between fragments that have diverged previously.

A *Moving Clone Instance* (MCI) describes a fragment that moves to another clone class in-between versions. In version v_i, fragment f and at least one other fragment g belong to the same clone class. In version v_{i+1}, fragment f appears in another clone class. Thus, f and g do not belong to the same clone class anymore. This pattern requires, that fragments f and g never appear in the same clone class for all versions v_j with $j > i + 1$. An example is given in Figure 3.5 (c) on the previous page. In contrast to the previous patterns, this is a long-term pattern since it describes a fragment's evolution across more than two versions. This pattern is caused by a change that is not propagated to all fragments of the clone class. On the one hand, this can be accidentally, on the other hand, this might indicate that the fragments are independent despite of having a similar structure.

The *Migrating Clone Instance* (MGCI) pattern is similar to the MCI pattern. Fragment f and at least one other fragment g belong to the same clone class in version v_i. In the next version v_{i+1}, fragment f has moved to another clone class, such that f and g belong to different clone classes. While the MCI pattern requires that both fragments never appear in the same clone class again, this pattern requires exactly that. Fragment f is said to be a migrating clone instance iff there exists a version v_j with $j > i + 1$ such that f and g belong to the same clone class again. Like the MCI pattern, this is a long-term pattern that affects more than two versions. The situation is illustrated in Figure 3.5 (d) on the previous page. While the MCI provides no information whether the inconsistency was intentional or not, the MGCI pattern shows that the inconsistency was unwanted as the similarity between both fragments is restored.

3.4.2   Clone Class Evolution Patterns

In addition to defining clone evolution patterns for individual fragments, evolution patterns can be defined for clone classes. A clone class evolution pattern describes how a clone class evolves over time. Clone class patterns are based on the ancestry of clone classes, that is, the mapping of clone classes between different versions of source code. The first formal description of these patterns has been given by Kim and colleagues [109] in their study on clone genealogies. Since then, some of these patterns have been used in other studies on clone evolution. These patterns are not exclusive, but combinations of them may appear together. For example, an *Inconsistent Change* always implicates the occurrence of the *Subtract* pattern. Figure 3.7 on the next page shows the relation among the patterns as given by Kim and her colleagues.

The *Same* and *Shift* patterns are the simplest and most frequent of all clone class evolution patterns. The Same pattern refers to a clone class that does not change from

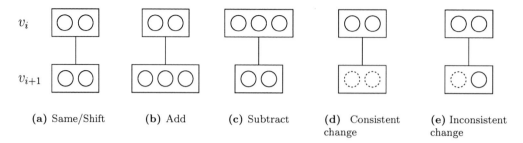

(a) Same/Shift   (b) Add   (c) Subtract   (d) Consistent   (e) Inconsistent
                                                              change   change

Figure 3.6 – Short-term clone class evolution patterns presented by Kim and colleagues [109]. Dotted circles indicate changed fragments.

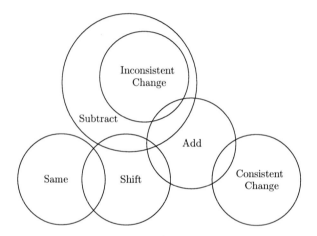

Figure 3.7 – Relation among clone class evolution patterns introduced by Kim and her colleagues (taken from [109]).

version v_i to version v_{i+1}. There are no fragments removed from the clone class and no fragments added to it. The fragments of the clone class are located at exactly the same positions in v_i and v_{i+1} considering potential movement due to the insertion or deletion of code before the fragments. If at least one fragment is found to be slightly out of place—its new location does not exactly match the expected location but overlaps with it—the Shift pattern applies. An example of these patterns is shown in Figure 3.6 (a).

The *Add* pattern applies when at least one fragment is added to a clone class from version v_i to version v_{i+1}. This pattern is strongly connected to the OCI pattern defined by Bakota and colleagues [13], since both patterns refer to the same situation. The pattern is shown in Figure 3.6 (b).

The *Subtract* pattern is the counterpart to the Add pattern and applies when at least one fragment is removed from a clone class between versions v_i and v_{i+1}. This pattern is related to the VCI pattern [13] which applies when a cloned fragment has no

```
 1   if (list.first() == item)          1   if (!list.empty() &&
 2   {                                   2        list.first() == item)
 3     delete list;                      3   {
 4   }                                   4     delete list;
 5                                       5   }
 6                                       6
 7   ...                                 7   ...
 8                                       8
 9   if (list.first() == item)          9   if (list.first() == item)
10   {                                  10   {
11     delete list;                     11     delete list;
12   }                                  12   }
```

          (a) Version v_i **(b)** Version v_{i+1}

Figure 3.8 – Example of an inconsistent change. The check for an empty list is added only to the upper cloned fragment.

descendant. Like the Add pattern, the Subtract pattern has been introduced by Kim and colleagues [109], but was also used by Aversano and associates [8]. It is shown in Figure 3.6 (c) on the previous page.

When cloned code is modified, this can either happen consistently or inconsistently. The *Consistent Change* pattern applies to a clone class whose fragments have been changed identically between versions v_i and v_{i+1}. It is required that some kind of change has occurred, because otherwise the Same or Shift pattern would apply. If code has been deleted, the same amount of code must have been deleted at the same positions from all fragments. If code was added, the same code must have been added at the same locations. When a consistent change happens, the degree of similarity between the fragments of clone class c does not change. The pattern is shown in Figure 3.6 (d) on the previous page. The Consistent Change pattern has been introduced by Kim and colleagues [109] and was used in different studies on clone evolution [8, 61, 63, 121].

The *Inconsistent Change* pattern applies when the fragments of a clone class have been changed differently from version v_i to v_{i+1}. This includes cases where fragments remain unchanged while others are modified. This pattern frequently occurs in conjunction with the Subtract pattern, because the similarity between the fragments of the clone class decreases with every inconsistent change. The Inconsistent Change pattern has been defined by Kim and associates [109]. Since then, it has become a central part of clone evolution research and was analyzed in multiple studies [8, 61, 63, 121, 178]. Figure 3.6 (e) on the previous page illustrates this pattern schematically. A concrete example with soure code is shown in Figure 3.8.

Example 3.2 – This example illustrates an inconsistent change to cloned fragments. The situation is shown in Figure 3.8. In version v_i, the two identical fragments span lines 1–4 and 9–12, respectively. The missing check for an empty list is added to the first fragment only, while the second fragment remains unchanged. Such situations may— but do not always have to—be problematic. The inconsistent change has decreased the similarity between the fragments. □

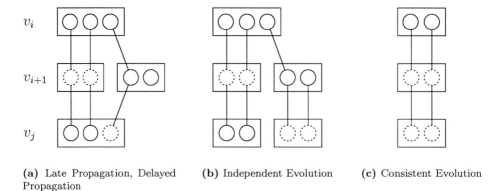

(a) Late Propagation, Delayed Propagation

(b) Independent Evolution

(c) Consistent Evolution

Figure 3.9 – Long-term clone class evolution patterns presented by Thummalapenta and colleagues [178]. Dotted circles indicate changed fragments.

All of the previous clone class evolution patterns were short-term patterns, that is, they described how a clone class changes from one version to the immediately following version. Apart from these, other long-term patterns have been presented that extend these patterns. Long-term clone evolution patterns describe how a clone class evolves over more than two versions. The Late Propagation and Independent Evolution patterns have been introduced by Aversano and colleagues [8] as an extension to the Inconsistent Change pattern defined by Kim and associates [109]. Thummalapenta and colleagues [178] complemented these patterns by introducing the Delayed Propagation pattern—a variant of Late Propagation—and the Consistent Evolution pattern.

The *Late Propagation* pattern applies when the fragments of a clone class are first changed inconsistently, but the change is propagated later to restore the similarity. Therefore, this pattern is one possible follow-up of the Inconsistent Change pattern. The pattern is shown in Figure 3.9 (a). The pattern is related to the MGCI pattern by Bakota and colleagues [13].

The *Delayed Propagation* pattern is a special form of the Late Propagation pattern. Following an inconsistent change, the Delayed Propagation pattern requires that the change is propagated within a certain time span. Thus, it differs from Late Propagation only in the time that passes between an inconsistent change and the reestablishment of consistency. The question is how to select an appropriate time span. Thummalapenta and colleagues [178] chose 24 hours without further explanation.

Independent Evolution is another follow-up of an inconsistent change to a clone class. This pattern applies, when the fragments of the class evolve independently after the initial inconsistent change, that is, the change is not propagated in any of the following versions. The pattern is illustrated in Figure 3.9 (b). This pattern is related to the MCI pattern [13].

The *Consistent Evolution* pattern applies when all fragments of a clone class evolve consistently, that is, they are always changed in the same way during their lifetime. This

Name	Entity	Time	Introduced by	Figure
VCI	Fragment	Short	[13]	3.5 (a), p. 42
OCI	Fragment	Short	[13]	3.5 (b), p. 42
MCI	Fragment	Long	[13]	3.5 (c), p. 42
MGCI	Fragment	Long	[13]	3.5 (d), p. 42
Same/Shift	Clone Class	Short	[109]	3.6 (a), p. 44
Add	Clone Class	Short	[109]	3.6 (b), p. 44
Subtract	Clone Class	Short	[109]	3.6 (c), p. 44
Consistent Change	Clone Class	Short	[109]	3.6 (d), p. 44
Inconsistent Change	Clone Class	Short	[109]	3.6 (e), p. 44
Late Propagation	Clone Class	Long	[8]	3.9 (a), p. 46
Independent Evolution	Clone Class	Long	[8]	3.9 (b), p. 46
Delayed Propagation	Clone Class	Long	[178]	3.9 (a), p. 46
Consistent Evolution	Clone Class	Long	[178]	3.9 (c), p. 46

Table 3.1 – Summary of clone evolution patterns.

pattern is similar to a sequence of Consistent Change patterns. An example is given in Figure 3.9 (c) on the previous page.

3.4.3   Open Questions

This section presented basic clone evolution patterns that have been described in the literature. The patterns are either defined for cloned fragments or for clone classes. They can be categorized into short-term and long-term patterns. Short-term patterns describe how a cloned entity changes from one version to the immediately following version, whereas long-term patterns describe a change that spans more than two versions. The patterns are summarized in Table 3.1.

The clone evolution patterns described in this chapter have been used in various studies and helped to provide valuable insights into the nature of code clones. Nonetheless, there are limitations to these patterns.

- The basic entity for which patterns are defined is important. There are currently two different approaches. Bakota and colleagues [13] defined patterns for cloned fragments whereas others defined patterns for clone classes [8, 109, 178]. Still, these patterns are related. For example, the Late Propagation pattern for a clone class always requires the MCI pattern for at least one of the clone class's fragments. Figure 3.10 shows which patterns always have to occur together. To keep the model simple, it would be beneficial to represent only low-level patterns for fragments, which allow deriving high-level patterns for clone classes.

- Existing patterns are defined based on the ancestry of cloned fragments or clone classes. While this is a reasonable approach, the definitions appear vague as soon as branches occur in the genealogy of clones. If clone classes break apart due to inconsistent changes, the fragments may belong to different clone classes in the later version. They may, or may not be reunited later. These situations are

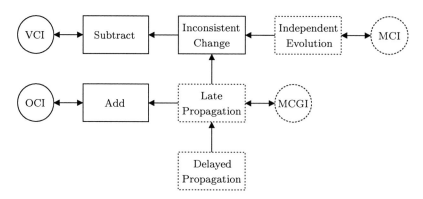

Figure 3.10 – Relation among clone evolution patterns. Circles represent fragment evolution patterns whereas rectangles represent clone class evolution patterns. Solid outlines are short-term patterns and dotted outlines are long-term patterns. Each arrow indicates that an occurrence of a given pattern requires the occurrence of another pattern. Note that this relation is transitive. The patterns *Same/Shift*, *Consistent Change*, and *Consistent Evolution* are not shown as they are not inevitably linked to other patterns.

captured by existing patterns only from the perspective of one class. For example, the MGCI pattern states that a fragment leaves the clone class temporarily and rejoins it later. It might—in the meantime—be part of another clone class. The patterns cannot express the relationship between both classes.

- The definitions of many patterns are to some extent imprecise. An example is the Consistent Evolution pattern defined by Thummalapenta and colleagues [178]. Thummalapenta and associates used a threshold that limited to which extent fragments of a clone class may evolve differently but were still seen as evolving consistently. The fragments were not required to evolve in exactly the same way but may have evolved differently up to the predefined threshold. These definitions may be problematic, since already small inconsistent changes can introduce a new defect or cause an incomplete removal of an existing defect.

These problems express the need for a unified model that captures clone evolution with the highest amount of detail, but also allows aggregating information to obtain more coarse-grained data.

Question 7 – *How can clone evolution be modeled comprehensively?*

Our solution to this problem is the *Clone Evolution Graph* (CEG) that represents the evolution of individual fragments, but also allows deriving the evolution of clone classes. The CEG is based on our observation, that all patterns described in this section can be represented using three essential pieces of information:

- **Membership.** The first is membership of fragments in particular clone classes. This is needed to detect patterns where fragments enter or leave clone classes between versions.

- **Ancestry.** The ancestry of fragments is relevant for long-term evolution patterns that require a fragment to be tracked across multiple versions.

- **Change Consistency.** Knowing whether the fragments of a clone class have been changed consistently or inconsistently from one version to the next is needed for some patterns.

As our model contains all this information, it allows extracting all patterns presented in this section and can, thus, be used as a unified model. The CEG is presented in Chapter 4.

Existing definitions of evolution patterns—especially Consistent Change and Inconsistent Change—do not support or explicitly include non-identical clones. So far, it has not been clarified how the concept of consistent and inconsistent changes can be transferred to clones that are not identical in the first place.

> **Question 8** – *How can the concept of change consisteny be extended to non-identical clones?*

We approach this problem by considering only the common part of non-identical clones for determining the consistency of changes. The details of our solution are given in Section 7.4.

Long-term evolution patterns highlight the need to track fragments although they may temporarily not belong to a clone class—that is, they do not have similar counterparts. To be able to detect these patterns, the CEG needs to be able to handle these situations.

> **Question 9** – *How can temporarily disappearing fragments be tracked?*

To solve this problem, our approach continuously tracks fragments although they may not belong to a clone class. By continuous tracking, we are able to detect these fragments when they reappear and, hence, we are able to detect long-term evolution patterns as outlined in Section 7.1.

3.5   How Clones Evolve

Clone evolution patterns have been used in several studies to investigate the phenomenon of cloning. While some patterns have been used only in a single study, others—for example the Inconsistent Change pattern—have been analyzed frequently. Based on the occurrence of these patterns, different aspects of clone evolution have been investigated.

3.5.1   Lifetime

One of the prominent characteristics of a clone is how long it exists in a system, that is, the time that elapses between its creation and its removal. A first analysis of clones' lifetimes has been carried out by Kim and her colleagues [109]. They investigated clone genealogies in two small Java systems—DNSJAVA and CAROL—measuring the time each genealogy exists. The genealogy information was extracted from the systems using the procedure described in Section 3.2.1. Many genealogies were found to be volatile as clones are removed shortly after their introduction. The results suggest that immediate refactoring of clones may not always be beneficial.

Despite the large number of volatile clones, Kim and her colleagues also detected long-lived clones in the systems. These clones are often *locally unfactorable*, that is, they cannot be removed by applying standard refactorings. In other words, clones exist for a long time because they cannot be removed easily. The study by Kim and her colleagues has been extended to a larger variety of subject systems by Saha and colleagues [164]. They found that for most systems, a large number of clones are long-lived.

The lifetime of clones has also been measured by Bettenburg and his colleagues [20]. They have used an AST-based clone detection approach and tracked clones across versions using Clone Region Descriptors introduced by Duala-Ekoko and Robillard [48]. Clone genealogies were extracted from two different subject systems—APACHE MINA and JEDIT—with 22 and 50 releases, respectively. The average lifetime of a clone genealogy in APACHE MINA is 4.59 releases corresponding to roughly 33 weeks. For JEDIT, clone genealogies exist for 9 releases (approximately 46 weeks) on average. In contrast to Kim and her colleagues' findings, the number of volatile clones is small.

3.5.2   Change Consistency

Clones may cause additional effort when changes must be propagated to similar parts and incomplete propagation of changes may cause problems. To investigate how changes are propagated, several studies analyzed the consistency of changes to cloned code using occurrences of the Consistent Change and Inconsistent Change evolution pattern. Again, one of the first to define and analyze change consistency were Kim and her colleagues [109]. In addition to studying the lifetime of genealogies, they investigated consistent changes to clones. A genealogy is considered as consistently changed if it contains at least one Consistent Change pattern. In DNSJAVA, 36% of all genealogies were found to be consistently changed. For CAROL, 38% of the genealogies have been changed consistently at least once. The numbers show that change propagation is a challenge that maintainers face in practice. Nevertheless, the study does not examine repeated consistent changes and the co-occurrence of consistent and inconsistent changes.

Change consistency is also the focus of a study by Krinke [121]. He investigates the ratio between consistent and inconsistent changes to clones in five open-source systems. For 200 consecutive versions of each system, clones were detected using the SIMIAN clone detection tool. Information about how the source code has been changed was extracted from the repository of each system. Overlaying the clone information with the change information, Krinke was able to tell whether clones have been changed consistently or inconsistently between versions. He found that for every system roughly half of the clones are changed consistently while the other half is changed inconsistently. Thus, both patterns occur with almost the same frequency. Unlike Kim and her colleagues, Krinke did not track clones across versions and, hence, the study does not provide information about repeated changes to the same clone.

Aversano and her colleagues [8] also addressed change consistency and further classified inconsistent changes according to whether the change is propagated later or the clones evolve independently. They conducted a case study using two Java systems— ArgoUML and dnsjava—analyzing 58 and 52 releases, respectively. The procedure to detect consistently and inconsistently changed clones is similar to the one used by Krinke. First, clones are detected for each release separately. Second, change information is extracted from the repository and combined with cloning information to identify changed clones. The distinction between late propagation and independent evolution has been done manually for each inconsistent change. Aversano and her colleagues found that the majority of clones is always maintained consistently. When clones are not changed consistently, they mostly evolve independently, that is, they are deliberately changed differently. Where late propagation of changes was detected, the respective change was mostly non-critical—for example, style changes. An extended version of the study using four different systems has been presented by Thummalapenta and colleagues [178]. Again, most of the clones have been changed consistently or evolved independently. Late propagation has been observed rarely. The relation between certain clone characteristics and the occurrence of specific evolution patterns could not be verified.

3.5.3   Harmfulness of Changes

Incomplete or incorrect changes to cloned code may cause problems. For example, existing defects may not be removed completely or new defects may be introduced. The threat that emerges from update anomalies has been investigated in different studies. In their study on clone maintenance, Aversano and her colleagues [8] analyzed which evolution patterns occur in conjunction with bug fixes. They found that 4 out of 17 bug fixes have been propagated consistently, while another 6 bug fixes have been classified as independent evolution. The remaining 7 bug fixes caused late propagation because the bug fixing change has not been propagated correctly in the first place. The findings show that clones bear the risk of incomplete removal of existing defects and the introduction of new defects.

Bakota and colleagues [13] analyzed *clone smells*—anomalies in the evolution of clones—to identify potential problems. Each clone smell is characterized by one of the patterns presented in Section 3.4.1. The patterns have been searched in 12 consecutive versions of Mozilla Firefox and analyzed manually to evaluate their potential harmfulness. In total, 60 clone smells have been detected of which six were related to defects. Another eight smells resulted from late propagation of incomplete bug fixes that occurred before the period of analysis. The results show that clones—at least in some situations—are harmful as they facilitate incomplete removal of defects or the introduction of new defects. Furthermore, analysis of clone evolution helps to identify problematic situations.

While previous studies concentrated on changes at the revision level, Bettenburg and his colleagues [20] examined changes to clones at the release level. Using AST-based detection and tracking of clones, they identified 458 inconsistent changes in the evolution of APACHE MINA and JEDIT that are potentially harmful. Nevertheless, manually inspecting these changes, only seven of them were found to be related to defects. In addition, many long-lived clones evolve independently and, thus, are less likely to facilitate defects.

3.5.4   Open Questions

Multiple studies have analyzed the evolution of clones moving towards a better understanding of the phenomenon of cloning. Nevertheless, the results of the studies do not allow a general conclusion yet, and are even contradictory regarding some aspects. For example, Kim and colleagues [109] found that many clones are volatile while Bettenburg and colleagues [20] found that the average lifetime of a clone is more than half a year. Krinke [121] reported that consistent and inconsistent changes always appear with roughly the same frequency whereas others [8, 178] found the ratio of consistent changes to vary between systems. These results suggest, that clone evolution is different across systems and may be hard to generalize.

> **Question 10** – *Is clone evolution substantially different across systems?*

We approach this question by conducting an extensive case study on nine open-source systems and three industrial systems. We compare the results of our study with those of previous studies. While previous studies are limited to either small systems, a small number of versions, or single programming languages, our study analyzes a large number of versions of reasonably sized systems written in different programming languages. We use the Clone Evolution Graph (Chapter 4) to collect the relevant data. Our study and its results are presented in Chapter 9.

Changes to clones have been analyzed in multiple studies on clone evolution. Although the ratio between consistent and inconsistent changes has been investigated for the totality of all clones, repeated changes to the same clone have not.

> **Question 11** – *How often are clones changed throughout their lifetime?*

Furthermore, the results of previous studies suggest that many clones deliberately evolve independently and changes to them are intentionally inconsistent.

> **Question 12** – *How many changes to clones are unintentionally inconsistent?*

We conduct a case study to analyze how often clones are changed during their lifetime. Again, the Clone Evolution Graph provides the necessary information and allows us to measure the change frequency of clone genealogies. We further analyze inconsistent changes in detail and evaluate their harmfulness. The study and its results are given in Chapter 10.

Previous studies on clone evolution analyze how clones are changed and how they evolve while they exist in a system. However, the removal of clones from a system has not been analyzed so far. Still, situations where clones are deliberately refactored may provide information about which clones are important and considered harmful by developers.

Question 13 – *Does deliberate clone removal occur in practice?*

To answer this question, we use our Clone Evolution Graph to identify situations where clones disappear from a system and evaluate whether this is due to a deliberate refactoring. We analyze the deliberate removals of duplication and the characteristics of the respective clones. Chapter 11 describes this study and its results.

3.6 Summary

This chapter presented previous research that is related to this thesis. Topics include techniques to detect and extract clone evolution information, represent it, and analyze it to understand the phenomenon of cloning. Previous works provided valuable techniques and insights for analyzing clone evolution. Due to clone evolution being a relatively novel research topic, there are still many open questions, some of which have been mentioned in this chapter. The remaining chapters of this thesis provide answers to these questions, which include technical aspects of extracting clone evolution data as well as the analysis of these data.

Chapter 4

Clone Evolution Graph

Analyzing clone evolution requires a suitable representation of the relevant data that is extracted from a system's history. We have developed the *Clone Evolution Graph (CEG)* as a technique to model how clones evolve in a system. The graph serves as an intermediate representation of the relevant data and thus connects the extraction phase and the analysis phase. A CEG is a general representation of clone evolution that combines ideas and concepts from previous work. As such, a CEG allows us to detect all clone evolution patterns that we have summarized in Section 3.4. The graph is our answer to Question 7 on page 48.

4.1 Definition

As any other graph, a CEG is a tuple consisting of a set of nodes V and a set of edges E:

$$CEG = (V, E)$$

In particular, a CEG is a *hypergraph*, because the set of edges E contains hyperedges. In contrast to a normal edge, which connects only two nodes, a hyperedge connects an arbitrary number of nodes n with $n \geq 2$. The CEG is *undirected* since all edges in E are undirected. The following sections describe a CEG's nodes and edges, respectively.

4.1.1 Nodes

The set of nodes V is the set of cloned fragments detected in the versions of the source code. Each fragment is unique to a single version of the system. If a fragment exists for more than one version, its occurrence in each version is represented as an individual node.

4.1.2 Edges

The nodes of a CEG are connected by the hyperedges in E. A CEG has three different types of edges that represent different relations between cloned fragments. Modeling versions and clone classes using edges of a graph may not be intuitive at first. However, using edges to represent version and clone-class relations between fragments allows us to capture and formalize all relevant concepts in a single graph representation—the clone evolution graph.

- **Version.** Edges of this type connect all nodes that represent fragments contained in the same version of the system. Each node is connected to exactly one edge of this type as every occurrence of a fragment belongs to exactly one version.

- **Clone Class.** Clone class edges connect all occurrences of fragments that belong to the same clone class—that is, they are similar to each other. The fragments, by definition, are contained within the same version of the system. That is, if an edge of this type connects the set of fragments V', there exists a version edge that connects V'' with $V' \subseteq V'' \subseteq V$. Each fragment is connected by exactly one edge of this type.

  Edges of this type have two attributes. The first attribute defines the *type of similarity* among the fragments. This attribute can have one of the values 1, 2, or 3. These types of similarity are described in Section 2.5. The second attribute describes how the fragments connected by this edge have been changed from the version they are contained in to the next. This attribute can have one of three values. The fragments can be *unchanged, changed consistently,* or *changed inconsistently*. By definition, all clone classes in the very last version are *unchanged*.

- **Closest Ancestor.** In contrast to the previous types of edges, ancestry edges are normal edges that connect exactly two nodes—two occurrences of the same fragment—in different versions. If two nodes are connected, both represent occurrences of the same fragment in different versions. To reduce redundant information, these edges connect only *closest ancestors*. Two occurrences of the same fragment in version i and j ($i < j$) are closest ancestors iff there is no occurrence of that fragment in version k with $i < k < j$.

4.2 Visualization

Visualization of CEGs is helpful to analyze and identify irregularities in the evolution of code clones in a system. It also helps to illustrate the concepts and examples described in this thesis. The visualization is inspired by one of the first studies on clone evolution by Kim and her colleagues [109]. In general, visualization of hypergraphs is challenging due to edges connecting more than two nodes. Fortunately, each node of a CEG is connected by exactly one hyperedge of type *Version* and one hyperedge of type *Clone Class*, allowing for a well-arranged visualization.

The visualization is described based on the sample CEG shown in Figure 4.1 on the next page. The nodes of the graph (the occurrences of cloned fragments) are drawn as circles. Edges of type *Version* are indirectly shown as horizontal lines, that is, all fragments in one horizontal line belong to the same version. Hyperedges of type

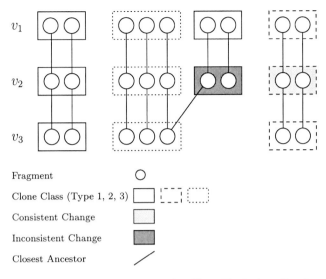

v_1

v_2

v_3

Fragment

Clone Class (Type 1, 2, 3)

Consistent Change

Inconsistent Change

Closest Ancestor

Figure 4.1 – Visualization of a Clone Evolution Graph.

Clone Class are drawn as rectangles surrounding the nodes that are connected by the respective edge. The type of similarity is indicated by the style of the rectangle's border. A solid line represents a clone class of type 1, a dashed line represents a clone class of type 2, and a dotted line represents a clone class of type 3. The information how the clone class' fragments have changed from a version to the next is encoded using the color of the rectangle. White indicates that all fragments remain unchanged, light gray indicates a consistent change, and dark gray indicates an inconsistent change.

The final type of edges—closest ancestors—are shown as solid lines connecting two fragments of different versions. Note that these edges do not necessarily connect fragments of adjacent versions, but may connect fragments of versions further apart if fragments temporarily disappear.

4.3   Tool Support

Clone Evolution Graphs are complex constructs that contain a large amount of diverse information. All of this information can be automatically extracted from the graph without visualizing it. Nevertheless, this requires knowing what to look for. Visualizing the graph and inspecting it allows us to detect and investigate properties and dependencies that are otherwise hidden. To inspect the Clone Evolution Graph and clone evolution data in general, we have developed a tool named CYCLONE [75]. This section briefly summarizes CYCLONE's features. CYCLONE comprises five different views on clone evolution data, each of which has a particular advantage. The views are always kept consistent—that is, selecting entities in one view will also select corresponding entities in the other views. The following sections describe the different views.

4.3.1   Evolution View

The first view CYCLONE offers is the evolution view that visualizes the Clone Evolution Graph according to the description in Section 4.2. The view is shown in Figure 4.2 on the next page. The primary purpose of the view is to explore clone genealogies. One of the major challenges is the amount of data—especially for large systems and many versions. We have implemented several features to manage the complexity:

- **Zoom.** The view offers zooming in and out of the graph allowing for a general overview as well as inspection of details.

- **Exclusion.** Our analysis of how clones are changed throughout their lifetime (presented in Chapter 10) indicates that almost half of all clone genealogies are never changed during their evolution. These can be excluded from the view, because in most situations, only genealogies that change are of interest. Furthermore, genealogies that affect certain source files or that do not affect certain source files can be excluded. Finally, the view can be reduced to only a single genealogy.

- **Highlight.** Given a particular clone class, the complete genealogy of that clone class can be highlighted enabling fast localization of that class in other versions that have been analyzed. This can also be done for individual fragments.

- **Search.** Every occurrence of a clone class and every occurrence of a fragment is identified by a unique ID. CYCLONE provides facilities to search for a given clone class or fragment ID which is, subsequently, highlighted and centered in the view. This can be used to relocate entities between analysis sessions.

The Clone Evolution Graph view also provides hover information for the clone class the mouse is currently pointing at. Apart from the IDs of the clone class and its fragments, the information contains the source code files that contain the fragments and their range in terms of start and end line. Clone classes can also be moved to any other location using drag and drop. This allows the user to create a customized layout and arrange clone classes according to his or her needs.

4.3.2   Comparison View

The purpose of the comparison view is to compare cloned fragments that belong to the currently selected clone class. An example is shown in Figure 4.3 on the next page. The upper part of the view lists the fragments that are part of the clone class along with their properties. Beneath the list, the left and the right part of the panel show one source file each. There a three different modes that the comparison view supports:

- **Single.** Two cloned fragments of the clone class are compared within the same version of the system.

- **Backward.** One of the clone class' fragments is compared to its occurrence in the previous version. This mode can be used to investigate how the fragment has changed from the last version to the current version.

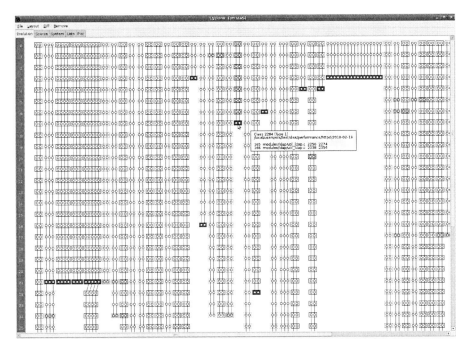

Figure 4.2 – CYCLONE's evolution view.

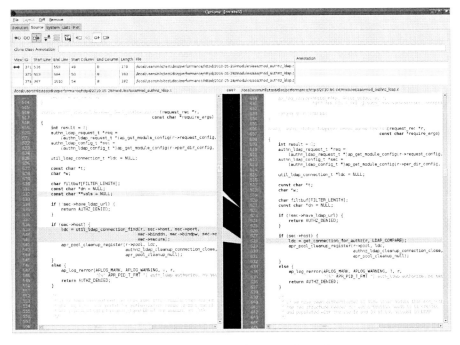

Figure 4.3 – CYCLONE's comparison view.

- **Forward.** One of the clone class' fragments is compared to its occurrence in the next version. This mode can be used to investigate how the fragment has changed from the current version to the next version.

For each of the three modes, the differences between the source code shown in the left and the right panel are highlighted. This can be done either on the token level or on the line level. If done on the line level, the small panel between the source code views links them both helping to identify the locations where changes occurred. The view contains navigation facilities to switch between the fragments of the current clone class or switch to the next or previous clone class.

4.3.3   Treemap View

This view offers a decomposition of a particular version of the system using a treemap [170]. The decomposition is done according to the number of lines of code contained in individual source code files and aggregated lines of code for directories. Each rectangle of the treemap corresponds to one source file of the system. The size of the rectangle is defined by the lines of code of that file while the color intensity of the rectangle is determined by the clone coverage—that is, the percentage of lines that are covered by clones—of the file. White rectangles indicate that there are no clones in the respective file whereas more color-intense rectangles represent higher clone coverages. Figure 4.4 on the next page illustrates an example of the treemap view.

Analogous to the Clone Evolution Graph view, the treemap view provides information about the entity that is currently pointed at. Furthermore, the treemap supports moving up and down the directory tree of the current system version. In other words, every level of the decomposition can be inspected. At the highest level, a single rectangle that fills the whole space represents the root directory of the version. Descending a level decomposes the current rectangles (which represent directories at this point) according to the lines of code contained in the source files and directories it contains. This step can be repeated until every entity corresponds to a source file which cannot be decomposed further. The clone coverage is not calculated only for source files, but also for directories that are shown in intermediate steps.

Another feature of the treemap is setting an arbitrary entity as the root of the treemap. The whole space of the treemap subsequently represents the selected entity. This feature can be used to "zoom" into a particular entity and analyze its decomposition in detail. Finally, the treemap supports selection of individual entities. When an entity is selected, all entities that share clones with the selected entity—that is, there exists a clone class that contains at least one fragment in each entity—are highlighted and visually linked. An additional number indicates the number of clone classes that contain fragments from both entities to quantify the strength of the relation. Future work could be directed at implementing alternative metrics for measuring the strength of the relation—for example, the number of cloned fragments that are contained in each entity. This feature allows the user to analyze whether cloning is a local phenomenon or whether clones are wide-spread throughout the system.

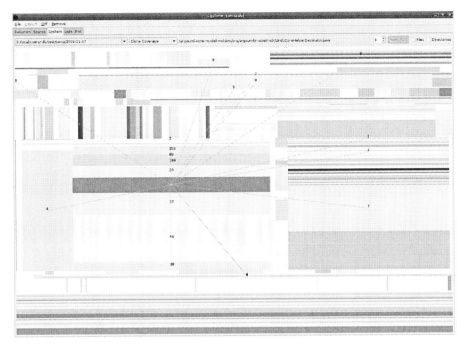

Figure 4.4 – CYCLONE's treemap view.

4.3.4   List View

The list view is a tabular presentation of relevant entities of the Clone Evolution Graph. Three tables include information about the versions that are contained in the Clone Evolution Graph, the clone classes of the selected version and the fragments of the selected clone class. The primary purpose of the list view is to sort entities according to their attributes—for example, sorting clones according to their lengths. The list view is shown in Figure 4.5 on the next page.

4.3.5   Plot View

Finally, the plot view displays data using charts. It currently supports line charts, bar charts, and stacked bar charts. The plot view is of general purpose. It can be used to display the quantitative evolution of data as, for example, the size of the versions, the number of clones, and the clone coverage. Furthermore, it allows the user to investigate how much time was needed to analyze a particular version broken down to individual phases. Nevertheless, the x-axis does not necessarily have to represent the versions of the system. It may, for example, also represent the age of clone genealogies or the change frequency of clone genealogies. An example of the plot view is given in Figure 4.6 on the next page.

The canvas of the plot view is to some degree interactive. The user can select any data point to retrieve its exact coordinates. For convenience, the data that are currently

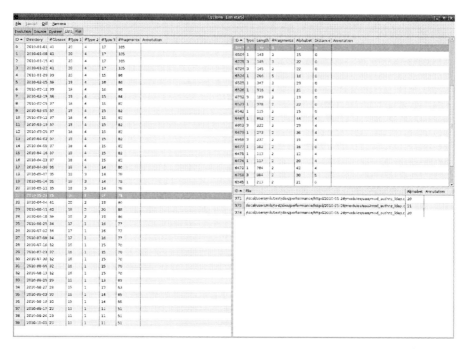

Figure 4.5 – CYCLONE's list view.

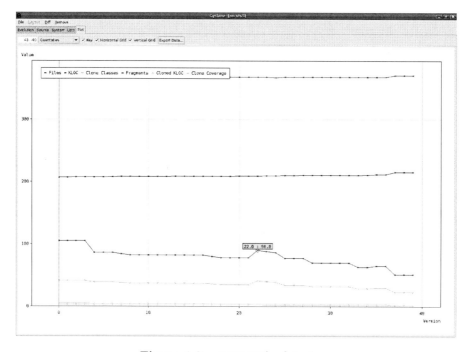

Figure 4.6 – CYCLONE's plot view.

displayed can be exported in plain tab-separated text format. The exported data can than be imported by any other program for further processing.

4.4   Summary

This chapter introduced the Clone Evolution Graph, a technique to model how clones evolve over time. The Clone Evolution Graph is a compact representation of clone evolution serving as interface between data extraction and analysis. The CEG answers Question 7 on page 48 as it supports various aspects of clone evolution. In addition, this chapter presented a short summary of our tool CYCLONE that can be used to visualize and analyze Clone Evolution Graphs. The multitude of different views on clone evolution data allows the user to investigate relevant data from different perspectives. Various features have been added to manage the complexity of large graphs and support the efficient retrieval of relevant information.

The following chapters describe how a Clone Evolution Graph can be efficiently extracted from the history of a system (Chapter 5 to 8) and how it can be used to study and understand software clones and their evolution (Chapter 9 to 11).

Part II

Extraction

Chapter 5

Fundamentals

The Clone Evolution Graph is the interface between the extraction of clone evolution data and its analysis. This chapter concentrates on the extraction and provides an indepth description of the *Incremental Detection Algorithm* (IDA) [60, 68]. IDA analyzes the history of a system by processing its versions in sequence. The two major tasks of the incremental algorithm are to detect clones for every version of the system and to create a mapping between the clones of different versions. The challenge of extracting the CEG is the huge amount of data that needs to be processed. Scalability in both dimensions—number of versions to be analyzed and size of the system—is an important requirement.

This chapter gives a detailed description of the incremental algorithm and its underlying concepts. First, the relevant data structures are introduced in Section 5.1. Second, Section 5.2 shows the overall structure of the incremental algorithm. Section 5.3 outlines how internal data structures are updated according to how the source code has changed—the first of IDA's three major steps. The remaining two steps are described in the following chapters. Chapter 6 explains the detection of clones in the current version while Chapter 7 introduces our approach for mapping clones between versions.

The core of the algorithm originates from my diploma thesis [60] and has been published in its original version in [68]. Although some basic ideas have been kept, major improvements and extensions have been done. The major goal of the algorithm's initial version was to speed up detecting clones in multiple versions of a system. Mapping clones between versions was considered only marginally. In summary, the major improvements compared to the algorithm's original version are:

Clone Classes. The initial version of the algorithm was based on clone pairs. The algorithm has been reworked to use clone classes instead of pairs. This reduces the number of clone relations significantly, because in a sequence of n identical tokens there are $(n-1)^2$ maximal clone pairs while there are only $n-1$ maximal clone classes. Using clone pairs has previously exceeded memory as repetitive structures in the code—which appear frequently—resulted in large numbers of clone pairs.

Change Information. The current algorithm uses detailed information about how the source code has changed to map clones between versions. This allows mapping clones according to how the code has been modified.

Change Consistency. The original version of the algorithm was capable of only detecting whether a clone pair has been changed or not. The improved version analyzes changes in detail to identify whether changes are consistent or inconsistent (considering the similarities and differences between clones).

Disappearing Fragments. Tracking fragments that temporarily disappear because they do not belong to a clone class is also supported. This allows identifying situations where a change to one clone is propagated to the other clones in a later version.

Extracting Clones. In the algorithm's original version, the whole suffix tree had to be searched for clones in every version. The improved algorithm also uses a new modification-aware approach for extracting clones from the suffix tree, by only considering the changes parts.

Non-Identical Clone Classes. The new algorithm is able to merge neighboring identical clones into larger non-identical clones, eliminating frequent sources of irrelevant clones. This is an improved version of previous work by Ueda and colleagues [184].

The improvements that have been done to the original version of the incremental algorithm are numerous. Although the basic idea of efficient extraction of clone evolution data remains unchanged, almost every aspect of the algorithm has been reworked to increase its capabilities and efficiency. The following sections describe the details of the improved algorithm.

5.1   Data Structures

There are two fundamental data structures that are used by the incremental clone detection algorithm: *token tables* and a *generalized suffix tree*.

5.1.1   Tokens and Token Tables

The incremental algorithm performs token-based clone detection, that is, it does a lexical analysis and transforms the source code into a sequence of tokens. A *token* is an indivisible unit of meaning of the respective programming language. Aho and his colleagues describe tokens as follows:

> "[...] tokens, that are sequences of characters having a collective meaning."
> [2]

The set of all tokens is the alphabet of a programming language's syntax. Examples of tokens are keywords, operators, brackets, identifiers, or literals such as a number or string. Each token is characterized by the following attributes:

Index	Type	Value	Line	Column
1	while	while	1	1
2	(	(	1	7
3	Identifier	x	1	8
4	>	>	1	10
5	Literal	0	1	12
6	)	)	1	13
7	{	{	1	15
8	Identifier	x	2	5
9	-=	− =	2	7
10	Identifier	y	2	10
11	;	;	2	11
12	}	}	3	1

Table 5.1 – Token table for the source code fragment shown in Figure 5.1.

```
1   while (x > 0) {
2       x -= y;
3   }
```

Figure 5.1 – Source code for which the token sequence is given in Table 5.1.

- **Type.** The token's type describes the lexical category to which a token belongs. Examples of categories are +-operator, while-keyword, and identifier.

- **Value.** The value of a token is its textual appearance. For most token types, the value is predefined and identical for all tokens of a given type. For example, a specific keyword or operator always has the same textual appearance. However, tokens that are identifiers or literals may have different values and may be differentiated based on these values.

- **Line.** Each token has a clearly defined starting position inside its source code file. This attribute specifies the line in which the token is contained. For tokens that span multiple line, this value equals the line in which the token starts.

- **Column.** This is analogous to the line information and tells in which column the token starts.

The incremental algorithm uses *token tables* to store sequences of tokens. A token table stores tokens along with their relevant attributes. For each file, there exists exactly on token table that holds the token sequence of that particular file. Each token can be accessed inside its token table by an index.

Example 5.1 – The token table shown in Table 5.1 stores the token sequence of the source code fragment shown in Figure 5.1. □

5.1.2   Generalized Suffix Tree

Apart from token tables, the incremental algorithm maintains a generalized suffix tree to identify duplication in the token sequences. Suffix trees have proven to be a versatile data structure which allow efficiently performing different types of searches within a sequence of elements. As such, they also allow for the detection of recurring subsequences of elements—clones—in linear time. Constructing a suffix tree can be done in linear time with respect to the length of the input and the tree requires only linear space to be stored. One of the first algorithms to efficiently create and store a suffix tree has been presented by McCreight [142]. Although suffix trees can be applied to any type of sequence, let us assume that the suffix trees are built for sequences of tokens.

A suffix tree is a compacted trie representation of all suffixes of a token sequence $T = t_1 t_2 \ldots t_n \$$ over an alphabet Σ of tokens including a unique artificial token $\$$ with $t_i \in \Sigma$ and $t_i \neq \$$ for $1 \leq i \leq n$. Every suffix $T_i = t_i t_{i+1} \ldots t_n \$$ is represented by a path from the root of the suffix tree to one of its leaves. Every edge of the tree is labeled by a non-empty subsequence of T. The concatenated labels of the edges on the path equal T_i. To ensure constant space usage of each edge label, the respective subsequence is referred to by a tuple (i, j) indicating the label's start and end position in T.

An important property of suffix trees is that for every node n of the tree and for every token t in Σ, there is at most one edge whose label starts with t from n to its children. In other words, paths representing suffixes share edges as long as the suffixes share a common prefix. Furthermore, suffix trees are augmented with so-called *suffix links*. Suffix links interconnect the inner nodes of the suffix tree. The suffix link of node n points to node p when the path of n shortened by its first token equals the path of p. Traditionally, suffix links are defined only for the inner nodes of the suffix tree. We extend this notion to include the leaves of the tree as well. The suffix link of a leaf representing the suffix T_i will therefore point to the leaf that represents the suffix T_{i+1}—which is the next smaller suffix. The suffix link of the root node is undefined.

Example 5.2 – Consider the suffix tree shown in Figure 5.2 on the next page that represents the suffixes of the sequence $T = abc\$_1 bab\$_2$.[1] The tree has eight leaves each of which represents one of the eight suffixes of T. For instance, the node n, indicated in the figure, represents the suffix $T_6 = ab\$_2$ that can be obtained by concatenating the edge labels on the path from the root to n. $\square$

The concept of suffix trees has been extended by Gusfield and colleagues [72] to *Generalized Suffix Trees (GST)*. While the conventional suffix tree is used to represent the suffixes of a single sequence of elements, a generalized suffix tree represents the suffixes of all sequences inside a set Δ. A GST can be seen as the superimposition of the suffix trees of the individual sequences in Δ. Whenever parts of edge labels are identical, they can be unified into a single edge serving for two or more sequences from Δ. Due to multiple sequences being used, the tuples that label the edges must be expanded. The tuple (i, j) indicating start and end of the label inside a sequence is extended to a triple also providing information to which sequence indices i and j refer.

---

[1]Assume the sequence represents the concatenated token sequences of two separate files each of which is terminated by a unique artificial token ($\$_1$, $\$_2$).

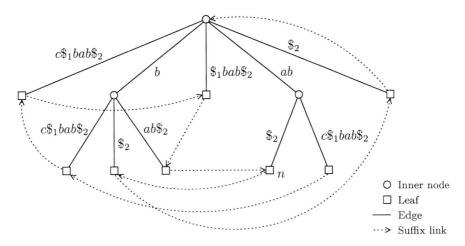

Figure 5.2 – Suffix tree for sequence $T = abc\$_1bab\$_2$.

Consequently, every edge is labeled using a triple (X, i, j), where i and j denote the start and end position inside sequence $X \in \Delta$.

The GST for Δ is isomorphic to the conventional suffix tree of the concatenated sequences in Δ. It differs only in the labels of the edges that connect leaves to their parent nodes. An important property of GSTs is that suffix links always connect leaves representing suffixes of the same sequence in Δ. Note that we have extended the notion of suffix links to also include the leaves of the tree.

Example 5.3 – An example GST for $\Delta = \{abc\$_1, bab\$_2\}$ is given in Figure 5.3 on the next page. The GST is isomorphic to the conventional suffix tree for the concatenated sequences as shown in Figure 5.2. Note that the labels of edges between leaves and their parent nodes are shorter. □

Constructing a suffix tree for large sequences requires fast algorithms. Different algorithms have been presented to efficiently construct a suffix tree in linear time.

McCreight. One of the first algorithms to create a suffix tree in linear time and space has been presented by McCreight [142]. The algorithm adds all suffixes of a sequence of elements from longest to shortest to the suffix tree. The position for adding the next suffix to the tree is efficiently derived from the insertion of the previous suffix using suffix links.

Ukkonen. Ukkonen was the first to introduce a suffix tree construction algorithm that works *on-line* [185]. On-line refers to the algorithm's property of inserting suffixes from shortest to longest. This improvement allows the algorithm to start suffix tree construction before the complete sequence of elements is known. After adding each new suffix to the tree, the suffix tree completely represents the sequence that has been processed so far.

Baker. A different extension to McCreight's algorithm has been presented by Baker [12]. Baker introduced the concept of *parametrized* suffix trees to store

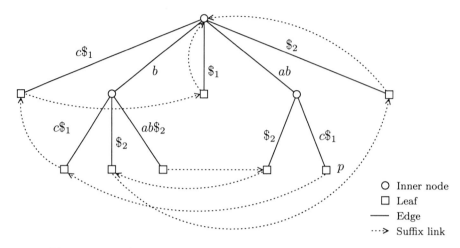

Figure 5.3 – Generalized suffix tree for $\Delta = \{abc\$_1, bab\$_2\}$.

parametrized token sequences. A parametrized token sequence abstracts from the actual values of identifier tokens, but still preserves the order among them.

Unfortunately, Ukkonen's algorithm does not support modifying the suffix tree when the underlying token sequence changes. Baker's suffix tree construction algorithm is unsuitable since it also does not support modification of the suffix tree after its initial construction. Furthermore, it operates on parametrized token sequences whereas our incremental algorithm detects clones using normal token sequences. Consequently, our incremental approach uses a variation of McCreight's algorithm as described by Amir and colleagues [3] to insert suffixes into the generalized suffix tree.

5.2   Algorithm Overview

This section presents the "big picture" of the incremental algorithm. The input to the algorithm is a sequence of versions of a program's source code—more specifically: the changes from the previous version to the current version. The list of versions can be unbounded, because versions are processed in strict order. The analysis of a version is independent from the versions that follow. This makes the algorithm applicable during maintenance where the source code is frequently changed and new versions are created. The output of the algorithm is the Clone Evolution Graph that describes how clones evolved. For research purposes, the complete CEG is returned when all versions have been analyzed. For practical applications and use during maintenance, the algorithm reports only the difference between the current version and the previous version of the CEG. The overall algorithm is sketched in Figure 5.4 on the next page.

The versions of the system's source code are analyzed in strict order. For each version v_i, three successive steps are performed. First, the internal data structures are updated according to how source code files have changed from v_{i-1} to v_i. This includes

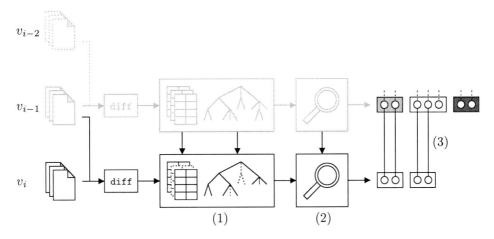

Figure 5.4 – Schematic view of our incremental algorithm.

updating the token tables as well as updating the generalized suffix tree. Second, the clones in version v_i are detected by extracting type-1 clones from the modified parts of the updated suffix tree and inheriting unmodified type-1 clones from version v_{i-1}. Neighboring type-1 clones are merged into larger clones of types 2 and 3. Third, the clones of version v_i are mapped to their closest ancestors in one of the previous versions. Information about the clones in version v_i and the mapping to their ancestors is added to the Clone Evolution Graph. After these steps have been performed, the analysis proceeds with the next version v_{i+1} or terminates if v_i has been the last version.

5.3 Updating Data Structures

The first phase of analyzing a version of a system is processing all changes to source code files. Information about which files and how they have been changed is the input to the incremental algorithm IDA. IDA expects a list of changed files and recognizes four types of changes:

- **Added.** The file has been added. It exists in version v_i, but did not exist in version v_{i-1}.

- **Deleted.** The file has been deleted between both versions. It existed in version v_{i-1}, but does no longer exist in version v_i.

- **Modified.** The file exists in v_{i-1} and v_i but has been changed between both versions.

- **Renamed.** The file has been renamed from version v_{i-1} to v_i. It is now known by a different name.

The change types *Added*, *Deleted*, and *Modified* are exclusive. A change of type *Renamed* may occur in conjunction with a change of type *Modified*. Note that—by definition—all files in the first version v_0 are *Added*. Changed files are processed one after another and independent from each other. Although files may be processed in arbitrary order, deleted files are processed first. This results in a smaller suffix tree reducing the effort for processing other changed files. Depending on the type of change, different actions are required.

5.3.1 Added Files

When a file is added from one version to the next, a new token table is created for that file. IDA performs a lexical analysis of the source code file and stores the resulting token sequence in the newly created token table. Afterward, the token sequence's suffixes are added from longest to shortest to the existing suffix tree. Our incremental algorithm uses the method STI described by Amir and colleagues [3]. Each new suffix requires the insertion of exactly one new leaf to the suffix tree. Depending on the tree's structure, inserting a new suffix into the tree might also require splitting an existing edge and creating a new inner node. Using the position of the last modification, the location for the next modification to the tree can be efficiently retrieved. For details on how to add or delete suffixes, edges and nodes from the suffix tree see [3] and [142].

5.3.2 Deleted Files

A deleted file is processed by removing its suffixes from longest to shortest from the GST. We start by searching the leaf representing the longest suffix of the file's token sequence. This can be done efficiently, because for every edge on the path, we have to check only the first token of its label. Since we know that the leaf exists and due to every edge from a given node having an edge label starting with a different token, we can "jump" over the edge and can advance our search position inside the suffix by the edge's length. The costs of this step could be reduced by storing the suffix tree leaf that corresponds to the longest suffix for each file. Nevertheless, the costs of finding the corresponding leaf are only marginally.

After finding that leaf, we can now follow the suffix links until we reach the root to collect and delete all other leaves that represent a suffix of that file. We exploit the important property of generalized suffix trees that suffix links always point to leaves representing a suffix of the same file. For each suffix of the removed token sequence, one leaf is removed from the tree. This might require merging two edges if the leaf has just a single sibling—nodes with only one child are not allowed in a suffix tree. After all leaves representing suffixes of the deleted file have been removed from the tree, the token table of the file is deleted.

Example 5.4 – Let us revisit the GST shown in Figure 5.3 on page 72. Assume that the token sequence $abc\$_1$ is removed from Δ. We first have to find the leaf corresponding to the longest suffix $abc\$_1$. We start at the root node and select the edge starting with the suffixes first character a. By definition, there has to be exactly one edge from the root node to one of its children starting with a. Having found this edge, we can advance our search position in the suffix by two tokens—the next token to look for is now c. We repeat this process until the leaf (named p in the figure) is found. When p has been found, we can follow the suffix links to collect all leaves representing suffixes of the token sequence $abc\$_1$. Each of this leaves is removed, merging edges where necessary. For instance, when p is deleted, the edges labeled ab and $\$_2$ have to be merged. □

5.3.3   Modified Files

Processing a modified file is broken down to an addition of the file's new version and a deletion of the file's old version. By first adding the file's new version, we are able to reuse some the suffix tree structures that correspond to the file's old version. If we delete the file's old version first, we would not be able to reuse any nodes and edges from the suffix tree. Analogous to addition, a new token table is created for the new version of the modified file and the new suffixes are inserted into the GST. After all suffixes of the new version have been inserted, the suffixes of the file's old version are removed from the tree. Finally, the token table of the file's old version is removed.

To reduce the number of structural modifications to the suffix tree, edges and nodes representing suffixes of the file's old version are reused if they represent the same suffixes of the file's new version. When a new leaf would be inserted into the tree, its potential siblings are checked. If any of the edges leading to a sibling is labeled by the same subsequence as the edge connecting the new leaf, the old edge and leaf can be reused because the corresponding suffix did not change. This prevents any structural modification to the tree. Even better, when a reusable leaf is found, there needs to exist a reusable leaf and edge for any remaining suffix which is to be inserted. We find these by following the suffix links until we reach the root. Leaves that represent suffixes of the old version of the modified file and that have not been reused are removed afterward.

Example 5.5 – Assume the sequence $abcba\$$ is changed to $abdcdba\$$. The last three suffixes $ba\$$, $a\$$, and $\$$ do not change. Since they are represented by exactly the same structures inside the suffix tree, the edges and nodes representing these suffixes can be reused preventing further structural modification of the tree. As soon as a reusable suffix is found—$ba\$$ in this example—all other suffixes are reusable as well since suffixes are processed from longest to shortest. □

The time that can be saved by reusing edges heavily depends on the location of the tokens that changed from the old to the new version of the file. Due to the nature of the suffix tree, the closer a change is to the end of the file, the more suffixes are affected, and consequently, the less there is to gain from reusing edges. A detailed analysis of how much time can be saved by reusing edges is given in Section 8.2.7.

5.3.4   Updating Edge Labels

There is a potential pitfall when the structure of the generalized suffix tree is changed. Recall that edges of a generalized suffix tree are labeled using a triple (X, i, j) with X being the sequence in Δ that contains the edge's label and i and j determining its start and end position. However, when sequence X is removed from Δ, this may result in undefined edge labels. To solve this issue, we apply the approach described by Ferragina and colleagues [55] to update edge labels of a generalized suffix tree. The method describes how edges must be relabeled when the structure of the GST is changed. Updating edges label requires constant time and ensures that edge labels are always valid—that is, they refer to a token sequence contained in Δ.

5.4   Summary

This chapter presented the underlying concepts for our incremental clone detection algorithm. The fundamental data structures include token tables, which store sequences of tokens, and generalized suffix trees, which are used to detect duplication. We described how these data structures are updated when the source code changes. In particular, the addition, deletion, and modification of files has been discussed. The generalized suffix tree is used by our incremental algorithm to extract duplication within the token sequences for which it was built. An elaborate description of how the generalized suffix tree is used to extract clone information is provided in Chapter 6.

Chapter 6

Detection

A major step of `IDA` is detecting the clones that exist in the current version of the source code. The result of this phase is a set of clone classes of types 1, 2, and 3. This phase is broken down into four steps. First, modified and new type-1 clones are extracted from the suffix tree. Compared to other approaches, this is done in an incremental fashion providing an answer to Question 1 on page 33. Second, the new and modified clones are unified with unchanged type-1 clones from the previous version. Third, neighboring type-1 clones are merged to form larger clones of type 2 and 3 answering Question 2 on page 33. Last, clones are filtered to remove irrelevant clones. The overall process is shown in Figure 6.1 on the next page. Before the individual steps are explained in detail, Section 6.1 describes the relation between clones and a suffix tree.

6.1 Clones in Suffix Trees

Suffix trees enable easy detection of duplicated fragments inside a sequence of tokens or multiple sequences of tokens in the case of generalized suffix trees. The important property of suffix trees is that suffixes of token sequences share edges as long as these suffixes have a common prefix.

Example 6.1 – To illustrate this, let us revisit Figure 5.3 on page 72. Consider the suffixes $abc\$_1$ (from the first sequence in Δ) and $ab\$_2$ (from the second sequence in Δ). Both suffixes share the common prefix ab. Consequently, the suffix tree contains a path from the root to an inner node such that the concatenated labels of the edges equal ab.
$\square$

Based on this observation, each inner node of the suffix tree corresponds to exactly one clone class. The token sequence that is duplicated is the concatenation of the edge labels from the root to that inner node. The fragments of the clone class correspond to the leaves that can be reached from the inner node. Each leaf represents exactly one

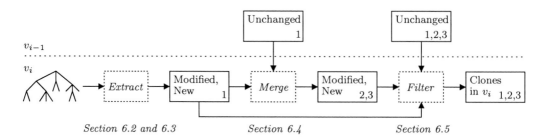

Figure 6.1 – The process of detecting the set of clones that exist in the current version v_i. Individual steps are shown as dotted rectangles. Solid rectangles illustrate intermediate sets of clones with included types given in the bottom right corner. Arrows indicate input and output of individual steps.

fragment of the clone class. The location of the fragment can be calculated from the leaf, because it is known which suffix is represented by the leaf.

Example 6.2 – Consider the generalized suffix tree in Figure 5.3 on page 72. There are two inner nodes and, hence, two clone classes. The first clone class is the duplicated token sequence ab having two fragments (one in each sequence in Δ). The other clone class is the duplicated token sequence b, occurring three times—once in the first sequence and twice in the second sequence. $\square$

6.2   Detecting Type-1 Clones

Using suffix trees for clone detection has been pioneered by Baker [9] and suffix trees have since then proven to be well-suited to identify duplication. Baker's algorithms are, however, based on clone pairs while IDA works with clone classes. Consequently, IDA uses its own algorithm to extract clone classes from a suffix tree, The algorithm is, however, inspired by Baker's algorithm *pdup* [12]. The suffix tree used by IDA compares tokens based on their value. While not making a difference for most token types, identifiers and literals are required to have exactly the same value to be treated as equal. Although this increases the size of the suffix tree as the number of distinct tokens is larger, the extraction of type-1 clones is much easier and faster, because the distinction between identifiers and literals having different values is already encoded in the suffix tree.

IDA's detection mechanism relies on detecting type-1 clones first. The algorithm for extracting type-1 clones is recursive. Starting from a particular node, the search descends into the suffix tree collecting the leaf nodes that can be reached from each inner node. Once the list of reachable leaves has been collected, a clone class can be reported for the respective inner node. For simplicity, we say that two leaves are extensible if the corresponding suffixes are left-extensible. Due to the nature of the suffix tree, it suffices to check for left-extensibility, because all leaves being reached from an internal node are not right-extensible by definition.

The recursive procedure `extract_clones`, which searches clone classes starting from node n in the suffix tree, is given in Figure 6.2. The procedure has two output parameters. The first is the list of leaves being reached from n, the second a Boolean value indicating whether the leaves are left-extensible.

Input: n : Node
Output: *leaves* : Set<Node>; *extensible* : Boolean

```
 1  extensible ← true;
 2  if n is a leaf then
 3  │   leaves ← {n};
 4  else
 5  │   leaves ← ∅;
 6  │   foreach child of n do
 7  │   │   extract_clones (child, child_leaves, child_extensible);
 8  │   │   if extensible then
 9  │   │   │   if not child_extensible then
10  │   │   │   │   extensible ← false;
11  │   │   │   else
12  │   │   │   │   extensible ← is_left_extensible (leaves, child_leaves);
13  │   │   leaves ← leaves ∪ child_leaves;
14  │   if not extensible and n.path_length ≥ threshold then
15  │   │   report clone class for n;
```

Figure 6.2 – Procedure `extract_clones` for extracting clone classes from the suffix tree.

If the node n is a leaf, an empty list of leaves is created into which n is inserted (lines 2 and 3). In that case, the node n is extensible because of being the only node. If, on the other hand, n is an inner node, the procedure is recursively called for each child node of n returning the leaves being reached from that child and whether these are extensible or not (lines 6 and 7). When a child node has been processed, it has to be checked whether all leaves collected so far are still extensible, which is the default assumption. If the leaves from the child are not extensible themselves, the overall list of leaves cannot be extensible (lines 9 and 10). Otherwise, the overall extensibility has to be verified (line 12). The check can be done in constant time by testing the first leaf of the current child list and the first leaf of the leaves collected so far for left-extensibility. It is sufficient to test the first leaf of each list since each list in itself is left-extensible. After checking the overall extensibility, all leaves from the current list of child leaves are added to the overall list of leaves that have already been processed (line 13).

After recursively processing all child nodes, all leaves that can be reached from n have been collected. The Boolean value *extensible* indicates whether the leaves are left-extensible or not. If they are left-extensible, the fragments of the clone class are completely contained within the fragments of another clone class and therefore, no

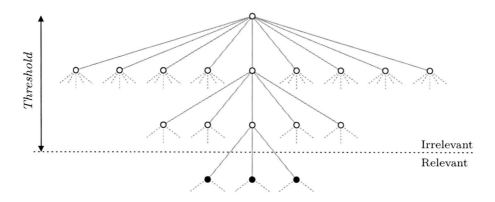

Figure 6.3 – Schematic view of branching in the suffix tree.

class is reported for n. Given that the leaves are not left-extensible and the fragments of the new class are longer than a given threshold, a new clone class is reported for n. This threshold ensures that the type-1 clones have a certain length and meaning. Applying the threshold removes irrelevant clones, for example those that are only one token long. The threshold is defined by the user and depends on the application.

6.3   Start Nodes

An important decision is where to start the search for type-1 clone classes, that is, which node of the suffix tree is passed to the initial call to `extract_clones`. The naïve approach—and the one that has been used in all suffix-tree based algorithms including the original version of the incremental approach—is to call `extract_clones` once passing the root of the suffix tree. There are, however, two options for improvement:

(1) A lot of inner nodes are visited for which no clone class is created, because they are too close to the root, that is, the path from the root to the node is shorter than the predefined threshold. Excluding these nodes would save a lot of unnecessary calculations. Especially when considering that the branching factor (and consequently the number of nodes) is much higher close to the root of the suffix tree. A schematic view of this situation is shown in Figure 6.3.

(2) A lot of inner nodes are processed that are contained in parts of the suffix tree that have not been changed. When nodes and edges of the suffix tree have not been changed, the respective clone classes have not changed as well and can thus be reused from the previous version.

In the first variant of the incremental algorithm, the whole suffix tree was searched for new and modified clones for each version to be analyzed. Although no clones were reported for most of the nodes, each node of the suffix tree had to be processed for each version. Following the idea of processing only modified parts, IDA now uses a new approach to search only the parts of the tree that were modified. The new techniques exploits that nodes contributing clones classes are situated close to the leaves and only in subtrees that were modified when the GST had been updated.

The new technique uses multiple start nodes for the extraction of clone classes instead of running a single search from the root node. This way, most of the inner nodes not relevant for clone classes are omitted. The question remains of how to find the relevant start nodes. Considering the requirements of an inner node to be relevant for a clone class, start nodes must

(1) have a path length greater or equal the predefined threshold,

(2) have a parent node whose path length is less than the predefined threshold, and

(3) have some changes compared to the last version within the subtree of which they are the root.

The black-colored nodes shown in Figure 6.3 indicate potential start node candidates. According to the third property, a node can be a start node only when there is some kind of modification in the suffix tree. Based on this observation, the search for appropriate start nodes is triggered whenever a structural modification is done to the suffix tree. Hence, from the algorithm's perspective, finding start nodes is done when changed files are processed and the data structures are updated. The procedure find_start_node traverses the nodes of the suffix tree to find the correct start node. Each node has an associated Boolean value *visited* that tells whether this node has already been visited by the procedure find_start_node. At the beginning of analyzing a particular version, this value is *false* for all nodes of the suffix tree. Let *PSN* be a set of nodes that contains potential start nodes.

Input: n : Node

```
1  if n ≠ root ∧ not n.visited then
2      p ← n.parent;
3      if p.path_length < threshold then
4          if n.path_length ≥ threshold then
5              n.visited ← true;
6              PSN ← PSN ∪ {n};
7      else
8          n.visited ← true;
9          find_start_node (p);
```

Figure 6.4 – Procedure find_start_node to identify start nodes for searching clone classes.

Figure 6.4 presents the procedure that identifies start nodes in the suffix tree. Starting from a given node n, the procedure recursively makes its way towards the root of the tree until the path length of the parent p of n is below the threshold. Node n

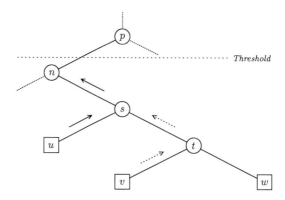

Figure 6.5 – Finding start nodes in the suffix tree.

is added to the set of potential start nodes *PSN*. Because every node has to be processed at most once for each version, all nodes that are traversed are marked as visited. If, in another invocation, the procedure is called for a node n that has already been visited, the procedure can immediately terminate because the corresponding start node has already been identified. Whenever a structural modification is done to the suffix tree, the procedure is called for the respective node that has been added or is going to be deleted. This ensures that all modifications are contained within the subtrees of which the start nodes are the roots. Consequently, all new and modified clone classes are detected by using the start nodes as starting points for the search procedure.

Example 6.3 – An example is given in Figure 6.5. Assume that the procedure find_start_node is first invoked for node u and then for node v due to modification of the suffix tree's structure. When invoked for node u, nodes u, s and n are visited and marked (solid arrows). Node n is added to the set of start nodes because the path length of its parent p is less than the threshold. The next invocation for node v visits and marks nodes v and t (dashed arrows). It terminates at node s because s is already marked and, therefore, the corresponding start node has already been found. □

After all changed files have been processed and the GST has been updated, the set *PSN* contains all potential start nodes. Nevertheless, not every node in *PSN* is a true start node, because a start node might become invalid when further modifications change the tree's structure. According to the example above, n has been identified as start node. If, however, the edge between n and its parent p is split according to a subsequent modification, a new parent p' of n replaces n as start node when p''s path length it still greater or equal the given threshold. Fortunately, this can be solved easily after *PSN* has been constructed by excluding all potential start nodes whose parent's path length is greater or equal the threshold. To finally detect type-1 clones, procedure extract_clones is invoked for every remaining valid start node.

Using multiple start nodes for extracting clones classes yields all new and modified clone classes that exist in the current version. In the end, however, the set of all clone classes is required. Consequently, all unchanged type-1 clone classes are inherited from the previous version and unified with the new and modified clones classes of the current version. A clone class is unchanged if none of its fragments is contained in a changed file. This yields the complete set of type-1 clone classes that exist in the current version. The identification of suitable start nodes and the local search for new and modified clones is our answer to Question 1 on page 33.

6.4   Detecting Non-Identical Clones

In contrast to type-1 clones, the fragments of type-2 and type-3 clone classes—non-identical clones—are not identical but different to a certain degree. For type-2 clones, the values of identifiers may differ, whereas for type-3 clones certain tokens are not part of every fragment (gaps). Although many non-identical clones are relevant, clones of these types are also a frequent source of irrelevant duplication. Tiarks and her colleagues [179, 180] found that up to 75% of type-3 clones detected by different tools are false positives. It is thus a challenge to not report irrelevant type-2 and type-3 clones while still detecting the relevant clones among them. This section provides an answer to Question 2 on page 33 and presents the approach used by our incremental algorithm IDA.

Our technique for detecting non-identical clones is inspired by previous work by Ueda and colleagues [184]. Both approaches merge neighboring clones to form larger clones. In contrast to Ueda and colleagues who used their technique for identifying type-3 clones, we also use our approach for detecting type-2 clones. Furthermore, our algorithm operates on clone classes and allows flexible gaps based on the length of the corresponding neighboring identical clones.

6.4.1   Detection Process

Before describing the algorithm itself, the following example motivates the need for a more sophisticated detection of non-identical clones.

Example 6.4 – Figure 6.6 on the next page shows two clones classes A and B with two fragments each. Both clone classes are of type 2, that is, their fragments differ only in the values of literals and identifiers. Looking at the fragments, however, we can observe that the fragments are unrelated except for having a similar structure. Repetitive structures like the ones shown in Figure 6.6 on the next page are a frequent source of false positives regarding non-identical clones. Even Baker's [11] approach which requires identifiers and literals to be renamed systematically detects many of these false-positive clones. □

Nevertheless, observing these false-positive clones, it appears that they have a common property—there is no larger subsequence of identical tokens within the fragments. Looking at the fragments of clone class B in Figure 6.6 on the next page and comparing the contents of the arrays, we can observe that the first token is different (2 and 1), the second is identical (,), the third is different (3 and 1), the fourth is identical (,), and so forth. Table 6.1 on the next page illustrates this situation. The same applies

```
1   parse("language", language, 0);
2   parse("input", input, 3);
3   parse("length", length, 1);
```

```
1   debug("Nodes:", nodes, 1000);
2   debug("Edges:", edges, 1000);
3   debug("Time:", time, 0);
```

(a) First fragment of A

(b) Second fragment of A

```
1   int[] primes = {
2       2,  3,  5,  7, 11, 13,
3      17, 19, 23, 29, 31, 37,
4      41, 43, 47, 53, 59, 61,
5      67, 71, 73, 79, 83, 89
6   };
```

```
1   int[] picData = {
2       1, 1, 1, 0, 0, 0,
3       1, 1, 0, 0, 1, 1,
4       1, 1, 0, 0, 1, 1,
5       0, 0, 0, 1, 1, 1
6   };
```

(c) First fragment of B

(d) Second fragment of B

Figure 6.6 – Two samples of type-2 clone classes (A and B) with two structurally similar but otherwise unrelated fragments each.

| First fragment | int | [|] | primes | = | { | 2 | , | 3 | , | 5 | ... |
Second fragment	int	[	]	picData	=	{	1	,	1	,	1	...
Identical?	✓	✓	✓	–	✓	✓	–	✓	–	✓	–	...

Table 6.1 – Token equality of clone class B's fragments.

to the fragments of clone class A. In summary, there is no subsequence of tokens within the fragments that is sufficiently large to be somehow characteristic.

Given the observation above, the basic idea of the new approach to detect type-2 and type-3 clones is that there must be a sufficiently large subsequence of identical tokens before we can tolerate any differences. This ensures that both fragments have some characteristic combination of tokens in common apart from their differences. Not surprisingly, these identical subsequences are type-1 clones with a certain length threshold. Given this set of type-1 clones, IDA detects type-2 and type-3 clones by merging neighboring type-1 clones to larger clones. Consequently, each non-identical clone has identical token subsequences of sufficient length. Our detection of non-identical clones is inspired by previous work done by Ueda and colleagues [184].

The input to IDA's non-identical detection are the type-1 clones that have been extracted from the suffix tree or inherited from the previous version, respectively. The output is the set of non-identical clones that exist in the current version of the system. Detection of non-identical clones by merging neighboring clones has to be done based on clone pairs, because a subset of the fragments of two clone classes may form a non-identical clone, while the complete set of fragments does not. Non-identical detection is a three-step process consisting of preprocessing, merging, and reporting.

Preprocessing. At the beginning, the type-1 clone classes have to be expanded to type-1 clone pairs. If a type-1 clone class has only two fragments, the clone class can directly be transformed into a clone pair. If a clone class has more than two fragments, each combination of its fragments is a potential clone pair. For each such pair, IDA checks whether it is maximal—that is, not left-extensible and not right-extensible— because although a clone class is maximal, a subset of its fragments may not. Clone pairs that are not maximal are excluded. Each clone pair has a canonical representation with respect to the location of its fragments. The pairs are sorted into buckets according to the pair of files that contain the pair's first and second fragment respectively. Within a bucket, the clone pairs are sorted according to the location of their first fragments. Each bucket is processed separately, because only pairs whose fragments are contained in the same files can be merged.

Merging. The merging step processes one bucket after another. Merging is done by creating "chains" of subsequent type-1 clone pairs that can be merged into a larger non-identical clone pair. We refer to each such chain as *candidate*. For each bucket— that is, each pair of files—IDA creates a list of candidates. We say a clone pair can *extend* a candidate when it is close enough to a pair of the candidate and both can be merged. Clone pairs are always prepended to candidates when they can extend them. Consequently, the *head* of a candidate is always the last clone pair added to it. Using this strategy, candidates are always inversely sorted according to the location of their head.

The sorted clone pairs of the bucket are processed in sequence. For each clone pair, we have to find the candidate that it can extend or if no such candidate is found, create a new candidate. Consequently, each clone pair belongs to exactly one candidate. This excludes candidates that are completely contained within other candidates, because if a clone pair would extend two or more candidates, one of these candidates has to include all the other candidates. The procedure merge_bucket creates the list of candidates for an individual bucket. The algorithm is sketched in Figure 6.7 on the next page. An accompanying illustration of the procedure is given in Figure 6.8 on the next page.

The first step of the algorithm is to collect all candidates that the current clone pair p can extend (lines 3 to 10). These are added to the list *extendables*. It suffices to check whether p and the head h of the current candidate c can be merged, because the clone pairs of a candidate are sorted according to the location of their first fragments. The head of each candidate is the clone pair that is closest to p. If p and h are twisted, p cannot extend c. Two pairs are twisted if the order of their first and second fragments is different. That is, the first fragment of clone pair A is located before the first fragment of clone pair B, but the second fragment of A is located after the second fragment of B. Twisted pairs cannot be merged because they do not have a well-defined order.

If the pairs are not twisted, the algorithm checks whether both pairs are mergeable according to the first fragment of each pair. Different criteria can be applied to determine whether the fragments of two clone pairs are mergeable. The current implementation of IDA uses the distance between the fragments as criterion. Two fragments are considered mergeable if the distance between them is smaller than the shorter of the two fragments. For example, if the fragments are 47 and 51 tokens long, the gap between them—the

Input: *bucket* : List<Clone Pair>
Output: *candidates* : List<List<Clone Pair>>

1 **foreach** *p in bucket* **do**
2   *extendables* ← empty list;
3   **foreach** *c in candidates* **do**
4   *h* ← head of *c*;
5   **if** *not twisted(p, h)* **then**
6   **if** *mergeable(p.first, h.first)* **then**
7   **if** *mergeable(p.second, h.second)* ∧ *not overlap(p, h)* **then**
8   Prepend *c* to *extendables*;
9   **else if** *no more mergeables* **then**
10   break out of inner loop;

11   **if** *extendables is empty* **then**
12   Prepend new candidate consisting only of *p* to *candidates*;
13   **else**
14   **foreach** *e in extendables* **do**
15   Remove *e* from *candidates*;
16   Prepend *p* to first candidate in *extendables*;
17   Prepend first candidate in *extendables* to *candidates*;

Figure 6.7 – Procedure `merge_bucket` to create non-identical candidates from identical clone pairs.

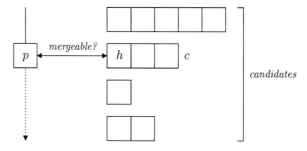

Figure 6.8 – Creation of non-identical candidates by merging clone pairs (shown as boxes).

distance—must be less than 47 tokens for both fragments to be mergeable. The criterion is based on the assumption that the differences between non-identical clones may not exceed their similarities. Although this may potentially lead to non-identical clones with almost 50% of differences, we have observed that the actual difference between non-identical clones is much smaller in practice when clones are merged based on the above criterion.

If the first fragments of p and h are fine to be merged, the algorithm checks whether the second fragments are mergeable as well using the same criterion. In addition, it is checked whether merging would create an overlapping clone pair. This may happen when all fragments are contained within the same file and merging would produce a candidate where the subsequence of tokens covered by the first fragments of the clone pairs overlaps with the subsequence of tokens covered by the second fragments of the clone pairs. If this is not the case, the current candidate c is prepended to the list of candidates *extendables* that can be extended by the current clone pair p. Furthermore, p cannot be a new candidate any longer, because at least one candidate has been found that can be extended by p.

If the first fragments of p and c cannot be merged, we can exploit that candidates are inversely sorted according to the location of the first fragments of their heads for optimization (lines 9 and 10). We can stop checking the remaining candidates at this point if there cannot be any more extendable candidates. As candidates are inversely sorted, the first fragments of the heads of any following candidates will be located closer to the beginning of the file and, consequently, further away from p's first fragment. Nevertheless, whether pairs are mergeable also depends on the length of their fragments. Still, the maximal length of a fragment can easily be determined during preprocessing. Using the maximal length and the current distance, the algorithm checks whether another extendable candidate may exist or not. If not, the algorithm can break out of processing candidates.

Finally, p has to be added to a candidate. If no extendable candidates have been found (lines 11 and 12), p is the first pair of a new candidate. Otherwise, p is added to the first candidate in the list of extendable candidates. Due to the construction, this is the longest candidate—that is, the one that contains all the other extendable candidates. The updated candidate is moved to the front of the list of candidates to preserve the sorting while all other extendable candidates are discarded, as they are now completely contained in the updated candidate. When all pairs in the bucket have been processed, each candidate in *candidates* represents a potential non-identical clone pair.

Example 6.5 – This example illustrates the merging process based on six type-1 clone pairs (a to f), each of which has one fragment in file 1 and one fragment in file 2. Both files and the location of the fragments are shown in Figure 6.9 on the next page. The clone pairs are processed in sequence according to the location of their first fragments.

Clone pair a is the first to be processed. Hence, there are no candidates that could be extended by a. A new candidate is created that consists only of clone pair a: *candidates* $= \{\{a\}\}$. The next clone pair in sequence is b. This pair can extend a, because their fragments are not twisted and mergeable—the distance between a_1 and

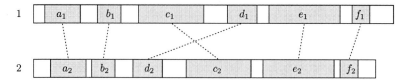

Figure 6.9 – Two files containing fragments of type-1 clone pairs.

b_1 (a_2 and b_2 accordingly) is smaller than the shorter of the two fragments. Therefore, clone pair b extends the candidate containing pair a: $candidates = \{\{b, a\}\}$. Clone pair c cannot extend the candidate consisting of clone pairs a and b. The pairs b and c are not twisted, but the distance between b_2 and c_2 is larger than b_2 (the shorter of both fragments). Hence c cannot extend the existing candidate and is the initial clone pair of a new candidate: $candidates = \{\{c\}, \{b, a\}\}$. Next, clone pair d is processed. This pair cannot extend the candidate containing clone pair c, because the pairs are twisted, that is, their fragments have different order in files 1 and 2 respectively. Furthermore, d cannot extend the other candidate, because the distance between b_1 (the head of that candidate) and d_1 is too large. Consequently, d is the first clone pair of a new candidate: $candidates = \{\{d\}, \{c\}, \{b, a\}\}$. Clone pair e cannot extend the candidate containing d, because d_2 and e_2 are not close enough. It can, however, extend the candidate containing c as the fragments of both pairs are close enough to be merged. The last candidate $\{b, a\}$ cannot be extended by e. Clone pair e is the new head of the candidate $\{c\}$. The candidate is moved to the front of the list of candidates: $candidates = \{\{e, c\}, \{d\}, \{b, a\}\}$. The last clone pair, f, can extend the candidate $\{e, c\}$ as well. The next candidate, $\{d\}$ cannot be extended, because the gap between d_1 and f_1 is too large. At this point we can stop checking the remaining candidates. Due to the sorting of the candidate list, their heads are even further away from f than d. That is, we do not need to check whether f can extend $\{b, a\}$. The final list of non-identical candidates for files 1 and 2 is:

$$candidates = \{\{f, e, c\}, \{d\}, \{b, a\}\}$$

□

Incremental Merging. Merging is expensive in processing time. The complexity is $\mathcal{O}(n^4)$ with respect to the number of cloned fragments (see Section 8.1 for details). To prevent redundant calculations and decrease the actual time needed for this phase to an acceptable level, merging is performed in an incremental fashion. Before merging, clones are represented as pairs and sorted into buckets according to the files that contain the respective clone pair's fragments. Identical clone pairs within a bucket are subsequently merged to non-identical clone pairs. To avoid redundant processing, the intermediate results—that is, the non-identical clone pairs—are kept for every combination of files. When the next version is processed, these results are reused for all pairs of files where the files have not changed since the last version. This prevents the creation of a bucket for the respective file pair and the costly merging procedure. The non-identical clone pairs within the respective files that have been detected in the previous version are reused and directly passed to the next step. The amount of processing time that can be saved obviously depends on the number of files that change between versions and the number of identical clones that are contained within these files. A detailed analysis of the worst-case complexity and time consumption is given in Chapter 8.

Reporting. The final step of detecting non-identical clones is creating clone classes from the candidates resulting from the merging phase. The candidate extracted from each bucket are processed in the following way. First, IDA checks whether the candidate contains more than one clone pair. If the candidate contains only a single clone pair, it is discarded as potential non-identical clone as nothing has been merged. If the candidate contains two or more clone pairs, these are merged into a single non-identical clone pair. The clone pairs of the candidate are sorted inversely with respect to their fragment's locations in the files. Hence, the start of the non-identical clone pair is defined by the last pair of the candidate, whereas the end of the non-identical clone pair is defined by the first clone pair of the candidate.

As mentioned previously, IDA works with clone classes, while merging is based on clone pairs. Consequently, the non-identical pairs need to be combined to non-identical classes. This is done based on the concatenated token sequence of the type-1 clone pairs that were merged to a non-identical clone pair. If the concatenated token sequence of the identical part of two non-identical clone pairs is the same, the fragments of both pairs are combined in a single non-identical clone class. This approach is based on the assumption that clones represent duplication in token sequences and, hence, clone classes are created according to the identical parts of non-identical clone pairs.

Finally, the type of the non-identical clone class is determined. Each non-identical clone class can be either of type 2 or type 3. To find the correct type, IDA examines the gaps between the identical parts of the non-identical clone class. If the gaps contain only identifiers and literals, the non-identical clone class is of type 2. If there are any other tokens apart from identifiers and literals contained in the gaps, the clone class is of type 3. The resulting set of non-identical clone classes is—together with the initial set of type-1 clone classes—passed to the filtering stage.

6.4.2 Comparison to Other Approaches

The non-identical clone detection approach has been designed to avoid false positive clones that are frequently reported by traditional non-identical clone detection techniques. To test this assumption, we compare clones detected by a traditional technique to clones detected by the approach described in this thesis. More specifically, we identify and present categories of clones that are commonly detected by traditional approaches but no longer detected using the technique presented in this thesis. Consequently, this section answers Question 3 on page 34. In this thesis, we restrict the comparison to type-2 clones. A similar comparison for type-3 clones is left for future work.

One way to evaluate our approach for detecting non-identical clones would be a human oracle that assesses the detected clones. The precision that is computed from the assessment results could be compared to that of previous approaches. However, different judges may classify clones differently since the relevance of clones is to some degree dependent on specific use cases. Consequently, we believe it is more appropriate to evaluate our approach based on categories of non-identical clones that are no longer detected. This allows everyone to decide on his or her own whether these categories of clones are relevant. We categorize the clone according to their structure.

Procedure

Our evaluation is based on a comparison of type-2 clones detected by our new approach (described in Section 6.4.1) and by a simple technique that just ignores the textual representation of identifiers and literals—that is, all identifiers and literals are considered to be equal. For our comparison, we use the source code of JABREF[1] from January 1, 2009. JABREF is a bibliography manager written in Java and the version we analyzed comprises almost 63 KSLOC. We performed different preprocessing steps prior to clone detection to eliminate frequent sources of irrelevant, but unavoidable duplication. First, we excluded all generated source files, namely ANTLR-generated parsers. Second, we removed files that contained test code. We also excluded all `import` statements form the remaining source files. Finally, we removed all array initializations (repetitive sequence of literals and commas).

After preprocessing, we ran the simple type-2 detection algorithm resulting in the set F_2 that contains all cloned fragments that belong to clone classes of type 2. Similarly, we executed our new approach resulting in the set $F' = F'_1 \cup F'_2 \cup F'_3$ where F'_1, F'_2, and F'_3 contain the fragments of type-1, type-2, and type-3 clone classes, respectively. For both approaches, we used 50 tokens as minimum clone length. For our new technique, we set the minimum length of identical subsequences that are subsequently merged to non-identical clones to 5 tokens. Since our new approach is more restrictive in detecting type-2 clones, every type-2 clone detected by our new approach is also detected by the simple approach—that is, $F'_2 \subset F_2$. Hence, our focus is on categorizing the type-2 clones that are no longer detected: $F_2 \setminus F'_2$.

Unfortunately, the detection of type-2 clones cannot be separated from the detection of type-3 clones in our new approach. This is due to our algorithm, which does not differentiate between different types of non-identical clones. This leads to type-2 clones that are only parts of—and consequently reported as—type-3 clones. In other words, fragments from F_2 may not necessarily be found in F'_2 and may have a slightly different location and extent. To mitigate this problem, we analyze the set $F_2 \setminus F'$. To account for slight variations in the fragments' locations, we consider fragments to be equal as soon as their source code locations overlap. Since the objective of our new type-2 detection approach is to exclude as many irrelevant clones as possible, using this tolerant definition of equality is an underestimation of our technique's potential.

---

[1]http://jabref.sourceforge.net

Category	Fragments	%
Sequences of **method calls**	92	34.2
Sequences of **new-instantiations**	60	22.3
Sequences of variable **declarations**	21	7.8
Sequences of **assignments**	21	7.8
Sequences of statements used to configure **GUI** elements (for example, a layout manager); an example is given in Figure 6.10 on the next page	17	6.3
Iteration loops and associated statements; Figure 6.11 on the next page shows an example	15	5.6
Definitions of **anonymous classes**	9	3.3
Sequences of **if-statements**	6	2.2
Declarations of **arrays**	2	0.7
Concatenation of **string literals**	2	0.7
Other *clones without any predominant characteristic*	24	8.9
All	**269**	**100.0**

Table 6.2 – Categories of type-2 clones that are not detected using our new approach.

Results

The first thing to be noted is the significant difference between the size of set F_2 with 404409 fragments and the size of set F' with 3719 fragments. However, F_2 contains a large number of overlapping and subsumed fragments. We removed all subsumed fragments before our manual inspection. In terms of clone classes, the simple approach detected 2854 clone classes, whereas our new technique reported only 1471 clone classes. That is a decrease of almost 50%.

In total, the set $F_2 \setminus F'$ contained 269 cloned fragments that were left for manual inspection. We manually categorized each such cloned fragment according to its structure. Note that a clone may have characteristics of more than one category. Therefore, we have categorized each clone according to its predominant characteristic. Hence, our judgment is a potential threat to the validity. In summary, we identified 11 different categories of type-2 clones that are no longer detected using our new approach. Table 6.2 summarizes the categories and the fragments that fall into each category.

Discussion

Summarizing our results, we consider all clones not categorized as *others* as irrelevant. Although being structurally similar, these cloned fragments are conceptually unrelated.

```
1    inputPanel.add( fieldScroller ) ;
2    con.fill = GridBagConstraints.HORIZONTAL ;
3    con.weighty = 0;
4    con.gridwidth = 2 ;
5    gbl.setConstraints( radioPanel, con ) ;
6    inputPanel.add( radioPanel ) ;
```

(a) First fragment

```
1    wordPan.add(removeWord);
2    con.anchor = GridBagConstraints.WEST;
3    con.gridx = 0;
4    con.gridy = 0;
5    gbl.setConstraints(fieldNameField, con);
6    fieldNamePan.add(fieldNameField);
```

(b) Second fragment

Figure 6.10 – Type-2 clone in GUI setup.

```
1    int piv = 0;                         1    int i = 0;
2    for (Iterator<BibtexEntry> i =       2    for (Iterator<File> iterator =
3        set.iterator();                  3        files.iterator();
4        i.hasNext();) {                  4        iterator.hasNext();) {
5    BibtexEntry entry = i.next();        5    File file = iterator.next();
6    idArray[piv] = entry.getId();        6    fileNames[i] = file.getPt();
```

(a) First fragment   (b) Second fragment

Figure 6.11 – Type-2 clone in iterations.

In total, we consider 90% of the clones that are no longer detected by our new approach as irrelevant. However, our subjective judgment is a potential threat to the validity.

We have compared our new approach to a technique that simply ignores the textual representation of identifiers and literals. One might argue that a more sophisticated type-2 detection approach, as for example the one by Baker [10], might be less susceptible to structurally similar but otherwise unrelated clones. However, we have found that for most of the type-2 clones we have analyzed, identifiers have been renamed consistently—the clone shown in Figure 6.11 is an example. Consequently, Baker's approach for detecting parametrized duplication is not significantly better than the simple technique to which we have compared our new approach.

Nevertheless, there are clones that we considered relevant, but which are no longer detected by our new approach—namely those found in the category *others*. Most of these clones were close to the minimum length of 50 tokens and had parameters at the front and back. Our new approach would detect only the identical middle sequence, which is in itself shorter than the minimum clone length. Decreasing the minimum clone length, however, would again increase the number of clones that are detected but are irrelevant. Further research could be directed at finding parameters that provide the best trade-off.

A hypothetical alternative to our approach would be applying simple type-2 detection first and then excluding type-2 clones based on the frequency of parameters. However, we have experimented with different measures and found that they cannot reliably be used to identify irrelevant clones. This is due to a number of relevant type-2 clones containing even more parameters than irrelevant type-2 clones.

In summary, the results of our comparison suggest that our new approach avoids many categories of clones that are commonly considered irrelevant. Our conclusion is that our new approach of detecting non-identical clones is a reasonable alternative to the simple technique. It increases precision, as it avoids many clones that are irrelevant and for which there is no common abstraction.

6.5   Filtering

The final step of detecting clones is to remove irrelevant clones from the set of all clones. The input to this phase are the type-1 clones extracted from the generalized suffix tree and the non-identical clones (type 2 and type 3) that result from the merging step. Filtering excludes clone classes from the input according to different criteria.

The most important criterion is a user-defined minimum length that clones are required to have. This minimum length is measured in number of tokens. The filter removes all clone classes where at least one of the fragments (fragments of non-identical clone classes may have different length) is shorter than the given minimum length. Note that the minimum length is different from the threshold used to extract type-1 clone classes from the suffix tree. Usually, the threshold for type-1 clone extraction is much smaller than the minimum length that the final clones are required to have.

Apart from excluding clone classes whose fragments fall below the minimum length, filtering also removes subclasses. A clone class a is a subclass of another clone class b if all of a's fragments are contained within the fragments of b. In other words, for each fragment f of clone class a, there exists a fragment g in clone class b such that f and g are contained in the same file, the start of f is greater or equal the start of g and the end of f is less or equal the end of g. This situation occurs when clones are merged to non-identical clones. Filtering removes all subclasses from the results.

The filtering algorithm proceeds in the following way. Our extraction of identical clones from the suffix tree already ensures that no type-1 clone class is a subclass of an other type-1 clone class. Merging non-identical clones ensures that no non-identical clone class is a subclass of an other non-identical clone class. Furthermore, a non-identical clone class cannot be a subclass of a type-1 clone class, since the former are created by merging the latter. Consequently, it suffices to check whether any type-1 clone class is a subclass of a clone class of type 2 or 3.

In general, filtering has quadratic complexity with respect to the number of clone classes. In practice, we improve the runtime by different optimizations. For example, we reduce the number of comparisons by sorting clone classes according to their number of fragments as a subclass can never have more fragments than the clone class that contains it. Since fragments within a clone class are sorted according to the file that contains them and their location within that file, testing a subclass relationship is straightforward. This holds in particular for clone classes with the same number of fragments.

Example 6.6 – Let us revisit Figure 6.9 on page 88. When clone pairs a and b are merged to a larger non-identical clone pair, both pairs are subpairs (or subclasses respectively) of the newly created non-identical clone pair. For each of their fragments, there is a fragment of the non-identical clone pair that completely contains the fragment. □

At the end of the detection phase, the set of type-1, type-2, and type-3 clone classes that have been found in current version has been constructed. If only the location of clones is of interest, the incremental algorithm could proceed with the next version. To model clone evolution, however, the mapping between clones of different versions is required. Creating the mapping is IDA's next step in processing a version of the system, which is described in Chapter 7.

6.6   Summary

This chapter presented our technique to extract clones from the generalized suffix tree. The extraction is necessary to determine the set of clone classes for each version that is analyzed. A major contribution compared to the original version of our incremental algorithm [68] and other suffix-tree-based approaches is a local search for new and modified clones. Reusing the clones that have definitely not changed from the previous version and combining these with the new and modified clones is faster than a full retrieval of all clones from the suffix tree. This incremental extraction of clones answers Question 1 on page 33. Furthermore, this chapter presented our approach to detect non-identical clones based on small identical chunks of tokens. By requiring non-identical clones to have identical parts of a certain length, our method avoids detecting irrelevant duplication that is frequently reported by other approaches. The algorithm is our answer to Question 2 on page 33.

Although detection of clones is one of the most important aspects, it does not suffice to analyze the evolution of clones. Using the techniques described in this chapter still yields independent sets of clones—one for each version. To be able to analyze clone evolution, clones have to be mapped between these sets—in other words, individual clones have to be tracked. The next chapter gives an elaborate description of the tracking employed by our incremental algorithm.

Chapter 7

Mapping

The third and final step of the incremental algorithm IDA creates a mapping between the clones detected in the current version and their ancestors. This mapping is required to track clones throughout their lifetime and analyze how they evolve. Previous studies [13, 109] created a mapping between clones of consecutive versions according to the best matches found by comparing all clones of one version to all clones of the other version. Although providing a potential solution, there are several drawbacks to this technique.

First, the approach is computationally expensive due to its quadratic nature. Every clone from one version has to be compared to every clone from the other version. Although a number of comparisons can usually be avoided by presorting the clones, the quadratic nature remains. Second, the approach is based on similarity measures. Since large parts of a clone may be changed between versions, old and new versions of a clone may not be mapped to one another, because the similarity between the two versions is too low. Third, clones are traditionally mapped only between successive versions. This prevents mapping clones that temporarily disappear and are not visible in each version.

The mapping approach used by IDA mitigates these problems as much as possible. This chapter describes our approach in detail and answers Question 4 on page 39. In summary, the improvements to mitigate the previously mentioned problems are as follows. Exploiting information about how files have changed, IDA can map them much more efficiently. Using this difference information, clones can be mapped unambiguously and independently of the extent to which clones are changed between versions. IDA expects the difference information as input, making the algorithm itself independent from how this information is obtained. It can, for example, be retroactively calculated using standard tools like DIFF or be directly recorded by an IDE. Finally, IDA is able to track fragments that temporarily disappear between versions.

7.1   Ancestry of Fragments

This section describes our method for inferring the ancestry of multiple occurrences of a fragment in different versions of the system. The goal of the mapping approach is

```
1   while (line != null) {              1   while (line != null) {
2       while (line.length() > w) {      2       while (line.length() > w) {
3           result += "\n"               3           result += "\n"
4           line = line.substring(w);    4           line = line.substring(w);
5       }                                5       }
6       result += (line + "\n");         6
7       line = reader.readLine();        7       line = reader.readLine();
8   }                                    8   }
```

(a) Version v_i (b) Version v_{i+1}

Figure 7.1 – Both fragments in (a) are closest ancestors of the fragment in (b) when the content of line 6 is deleted between versions v_i and v_{i+1}.

to retroactively establish these relations. An important decision that must be made is which granularity is to be used for the mapping. Previous studies mapped either clone classes or individual fragments between versions. Analogously to the approach used by Bakota and colleagues [13], IDA maps individual cloned fragments between versions. The advantage is that mapping individual fragments provides the highest amount of detail while other mappings (for example between clone classes) can be created using the mapping between fragments.

Each fragment has an arbitrary number of ancestors in the previous versions of the system. When analyzing a version, it is, however, sufficient to determine only the *closest ancestors* of a fragment as the ancestor relation is transitive. The closest ancestors of a fragment are its immediately preceding occurrences. That is, fragment g is a closest ancestor of f if there is no fragment h contained in a version between g's version and f's version such that h is an ancestor of f and g is an ancestor of h. It may, at first, seem unlikely that a fragment has more than one closest ancestor. However, overlapping fragments may result in multiple closest ancestors as shown in the following example. These overlapping fragments occur when a subset of the fragments of a clone class with more than two fragments are left-extensible or right-extensible. These fragments form another clone class with less, but longer fragments that overlap with the other clone class' fragments.

Example 7.1 – Consider the situation illustrated in Figure 7.1. Assume that in (a) there are two overlapping fragments. One starting in line 2 and ending in line 5 (dashed), the other starting in line 2 and ending in line 6 (solid). In (b), the content of line 6 has been deleted. This does not affect the first fragment, which still spans lines 2 to 5. However, the second fragment is changed because its last line is removed. Like the first fragment, the updated fragment now spans lines 2 to 5. Both fragments now match exactly and, hence, are the same fragment (dotted). Consequently, the single fragment in (b) has both fragments from (a) as closest ancestors. □

Analogously to its ancestors, each fragment may have an arbitrary number of descendants which are its occurrences in the following versions of the system. Nevertheless, each fragment has at most one *closest descendant* which is its subsequent occurrence.

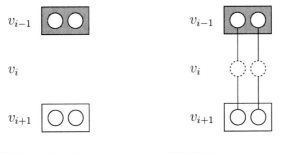

(a) Without ghost fragments   (b) With ghost fragments

Figure 7.2 – Tracking clones without and with using ghost fragments (dotted circles).

Cloned fragments are defined based on the similarity between them. Consequently, a fragment cannot exist without a similar counterpart. When a fragment "drops out" of a clone class due to inconsistent changes to the clone class' fragments, the fragment at first disappears and can no longer be tracked. However, changes that are inconsistent first, may be propagated later—that is, the similarity between fragments may be restored in a later version. To detect these situations, fragments must continue to be tracked although they temporarily disappear and do not belong to a clone class. We refer to any such fragment that does not belong to a clone class as *ghost fragment*. Ghost fragments are treated by IDA in the same way as normal fragments. They are, however, used only internally and are not part of the Clone Evolution Graph. The use of ghost fragments answers Question 9 on page 49.

Example 7.2 – Let us look at Figure 7.2. The figure shows two situations in which the fragments of a clone class are changed inconsistently from version v_{i-1} to v_i. The similarity between the fragments is not given any longer and, hence, they do not form a clone class in version v_i. Nevertheless, the change is propagated from version v_i to v_{i+1} restoring the similarity and the clone class. If ghost fragments would not be used—shown in (a)—the fragments cannot be tracked and their lifetime breaks apart. Tracking these fragments as ghost fragments when they are not part of a clone class, allows detecting propagation of the change and continuously track the fragments as shown in (b). □

Example 7.3 – Figure 7.3 on the next page provides an example to illustrate the ancestry of fragments. The figure shows the ancestors and descendants of a fragment f in version v_i. The fragment has two closest ancestors (dark, dotted) inside the version v_{i-1}. In addition, the fragment has two ancestors in version v_{i-2} (dark, solid). In total, f has two closest ancestors and four ancestors. Fragment f has one closest descendant (light, dotted) in version v_{i+1}. and another descendant in version v_{i+2} (light, solid). The respective clone class has disappeared between versions v_{i+1} and v_{i+2}. Nevertheless, IDA continues to track the fragments as long as they are not completely removed. The

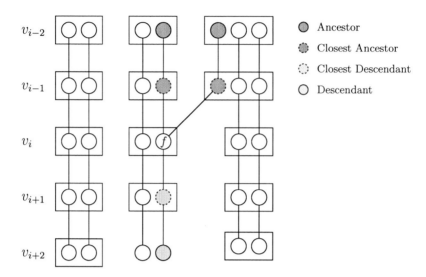

Figure 7.3 – Ancestry of fragments.

ancestry of fragments is independent from whether fragments belong to clone classes or not. $\square$

From a technical perspective it suffices to determine the closest ancestors for each fragment that exist in the version that is currently being analyzed. Further ancestors and descendants can be derived from the information about closest ancestors. The result of IDA's previous step—detecting the clones that exist in the current version—is then used and for every fragment, IDA determines its closest ancestors in the mapping phase. The mapping is heavily based on information about how the source code has changed between versions.

7.2   Source Code Changes

The central characteristic of a system is that it changes over time. Assuming that a system does not change, clones would just exist but not evolve. Changes to the system's source code from one version to the next are the driving force of clone evolution. Hence, changes also play an important role in the extraction of clone evolution data.

The information about which files of the system have been modified and how they have been changed is available to IDA and has already been used for updating the internal data structures. This information is also used in the mapping stage which, again, is independent from the source of the difference information. IDA supports detailed input of external difference information but is also capable of internally calculating the differences between token sequences using Myers' [147] algorithm adopted to operate on token sequences. Another possible scenario is, that the change information could be recorded and provided by the IDE when the system is maintained. Whatever method is used, in the end, IDA has access to a list of the deltas between a modified file's old and new versions.

Each delta δ represents a contiguous modification of the file's token sequence. IDA differentiates between two different types of changes: *addition* and *deletion*. Traditional differencing algorithms also support modifications of tokens. However, these are broken down to a deletion of the old tokens and an addition of the new tokens. This allows easier representation and processing of changes. Each delta is—inspired by the UNIX DIFF utility—characterized in the following way:

$$\delta = (type, s_1, e_1, s_2, e_2)$$

type The type of the delta indicates whether tokens have been added to the file's token sequence or removed from the file's token sequence. Therefore, *type* can take the values *ADD* and *DEL*.

s_1 This is the start index of the location that is affected by the change in the file's old version. For additions, s_1 equals the index of the token directly after which the new tokens are inserted. For deletions of tokens, s_1 equals the index of the first token that is removed from the old token sequence.

e_1 This represents the last index of the location in the file's old version that is affected by the change. For additions, this value equals s_1 and equals the token directly after which the addition takes place. If tokens are deleted, this index defines the last token that is removed from the file.

s_2 This represents the start of the change's location in the file's new version. For additions, this value equals the index of the first token that has been added to the file's token sequence. For deletions, this is the index of the token directly after which the removed tokens were before they have been removed.

e_2 This is the end index of the location that is affected by the change in the file's new version. For additions, this is the index of the last token that has been newly added to the file. For deletions, this value equals s_2.

Example 7.4 – Figure 7.4 on the next page shows an example of two deltas—an addition and a deletion of tokens. In Figure (a), tokens 3 and 4 in version v_i have been added after token 2 in version v_{i-1}. Figure (b) shows a deletion of tokens 4 and 5 in version v_{i-1}. The token directly before the removed tokens is token 3 in version v_i. $\square$

The list of deltas is used to update the fragments known from the previous version and check whether an occurrence exists in the current version.

7.3   Creating the Mapping

Creating the mapping consists of updating all—normal and ghost—fragments from the previous version v_{i-1} and checking whether they are a closest ancestor of a fragment contained in the current version. The approach discussed in this section answers

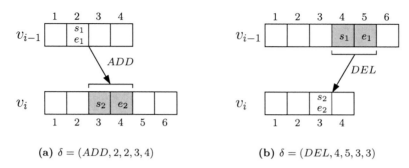

(a) $\delta = (ADD, 2, 2, 3, 4)$ (b) $\delta = (DEL, 4, 5, 3, 3)$

Figure 7.4 – Changes of a file's token sequence from version v_{i-1} to v_i.

Question 5 on page 39. Mapping clones contained in unchanged files is straight-forward. The fragments contained in the previous version of an unchanged file do not need to be updated as they are found at the very same location in the current version. For modified files, the procedure **update** updates a given fragment f according to the list of deltas Δ that contains information about how the file containing f has changed. The procedure is shown in Figure 7.5 on the next page.

The deltas in Δ are sorted according to their location and processed in sequence. Fragment f' represents the updated version of f. At the beginning f is assigned to f'. After that, the deltas are processed as long as they affect the fragment. Once a delta is located behind the fragment, the procedure can terminate due to the deltas being sorted and all other deltas being located behind the fragment as well.

If the current delta δ is of type ADD, the algorithm distinguishes two situations. When the addition is located before the fragment, the fragment's start position is adjusted. That is, the fragment is moved by the number of tokens that have been inserted. When the addition is located within the fragment's bounds, the start position of the fragment remains the same but its length is increased by the number of tokens that have been inserted.

For a delta of type DEL, three different situations may occur. First, the deletion may affect all tokens of the fragments (lines 9 and 10). In such a case, the fragment does not exist any longer (indicated by ε) and the procedure can terminate. Second, the deletion affects tokens before the fragment (lines 11 to 13). The start of the fragment is decreased by the number of tokens that have been deleted and were not part of the fragment. The length of the fragment is reduced by the number of tokens that have been deleted and were part of the fragment. Third, the deletion does not affect any tokens located before the fragment. In this case, the start of the fragment remains the same, but its length is reduced by the number of tokens that have been deleted and were part of the fragment.

When all relevant deltas have been processed, f' is the updated version of f and thus resembles the fragment's occurrence in the current version that is analyzed. For each fragment f from the previous version IDA checks whether it is the closest ancestor of a fragment contained in the current version. This is the case when the updated version of

Input: f: Fragment, Δ: List<Delta>
Output: f': Fragment

1 $f' \leftarrow f$
2 **foreach** $\delta \in \Delta$ **do**
3   **if** $\delta.type = ADD$ **then**
4   **if** $\delta.e_1 < f.start$ **then**
5             $f'.start \leftarrow f'.start + (\delta.e_2 - \delta.s_2 + 1)$
6   **else if** $\delta.e_1 < f.end$ **then**
7             $f'.length \leftarrow f'.length + (\delta.e_2 - \delta.s_2 + 1)$
8   **else**
9   **if** $\delta.s_1 <= f.start \wedge \delta.e_1 >= f.end$ **then**
10            $f' \leftarrow \varepsilon$
11   **else if** $\delta.s_1 < f.start$ **then**
12            $f'.start \leftarrow f'.start - (min(f.start, \delta.e_1) - \delta.s_1)$
13            $f'.length \leftarrow f'.length - max(0, (\delta.e_1 - f.start + 1))$
14   **else if** $\delta.s_1 <= f.end$ **then**
15            $f'.length \leftarrow f'.length - (min(f.end, \delta.e_1) - \delta.s_1 + 1)$

Figure 7.5 – Procedure `update` that takes a fragment f and a list of deltas Δ and updates f's location accordingly.

f (f') exactly matches one of the fragments detected in the current version. As every fragment is unique with respect to its location, IDA can check in constant time (using hashing) whether the updated version f' matches any fragment g in the current version. If such a fragment g is found, f is a closest ancestor of g and registered as such. If no such g is found, f' is subsequently tracked as ghost fragment. The procedure is sketched in Figure 7.6 on the next page.

Example 7.5 – Several examples are provided to illustrate the use of the `update` procedure. Let a fragment be a tuple $(start, length)$, where $start$ denotes the index of the fragment's first token and $length$ is the number of tokens being part of the fragment.

Figure 7.7 on the next page shows the addition of tokens to a file between versions v_{i-1} and v_i. In (a), the tokens (dark gray) are added before the cloned fragment (light gray). This affects the start index of the fragment but not its length. If we call the procedure `update` with fragment $f = (4, 3)$ and $\Delta = \{(ADD, 2, 2, 3, 4)\}$, it returns fragment f' which equals f regarding length but has a different start. The start of f' is adjusted according to line 5 in Figure 7.5. Assuming that this is the first change, the previous value of $f'.start$ equals $f.start$ according to line 1 of the procedure `update`.

$$f'.start = f'.start + (\delta.e_2 - \delta.s_2 + 1) = 4 + (4 - 3 + 1) = 6$$

The updated version of fragment f is $f' = (6, 3)$.

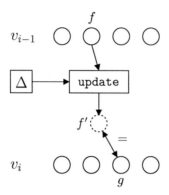

Figure 7.6 – Finding closest ancestors. Clone classes are not shown as they are irrelevant for the mapping.

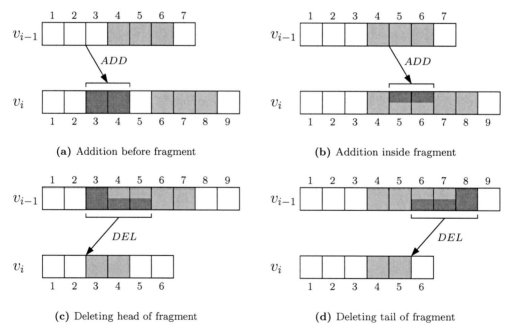

(a) Addition before fragment

(b) Addition inside fragment

(c) Deleting head of fragment

(d) Deleting tail of fragment

Figure 7.7 – Impact of a change (dark gray) to the token sequence on a fragment (light gray).

The second example in (b) shows an addition of tokens within the bounds of the fragments. Procedure update is called with $f = (4,3)$ and $\Delta = \{(ADD, 4, 4, 5, 6)\}$. In contrast to the previous example, this does not change the fragment's start index, but its length. The length of the fragment increases by the number of tokens that are inserted (line 7 in procedure update). Again, assuming this is the first change to f', the previous length of f' equals the length of f.

$$f'.length = f'.length + (\delta.e_2 - \delta.s_2 + 1) = 3 + (4 - 3 + 1) = 5$$

In this case, the updated version of fragment f is $f' = (4,5)$.

Deletions are more complicated than additions of tokens. For the example given in (c), the change deletes tokens before the fragment as well as from the beginning of the fragment. This affects both the start of the updated fragment and the length of the updated fragment. Passing the fragment $f = (4,4)$ and changes $\Delta = \{(DEL, 3, 5, 2, 2)\}$ to the procedure update results in fragment f' as follows:

$$f'.start = f'.start - (min(f.start, \delta.e_1) - \delta.s_1) = 4 - (min(4,5) - 3) = 3$$
$$f'.length = f'.length - max(0, (\delta.e_1 - f.start + 1)) = 4 - max(0, (5 - 4 + 1)) = 2$$

The procedure update returns fragment $f' = (3,2)$.

The final situation given in (d) illustrates the deletion of tokens from the end of a fragment as well as subsequent tokens. The fragment's location does not change. The length of the fragment is shortened by the size of the overlap between the fragment and the deletion. Thus, calling update with $f = (4,4)$ and changes $\Delta = \{(DEL, 6, 8, 5, 5)\}$ yields:

$$f'.length = f'.length - (min(f.start + f.length - 1, \delta.e_1) - \delta.s_1 + 1)$$
$$= 4 - (min(4 + 4 - 1, 8) - 6 + 1) = 2$$

The fragment returned by procedure update is $f' = (4,2)$. Although all examples illustrated only a single change, update is capable of processing multiple changes that influence the start and the length of the given fragment. $\square$

7.4 Consistency of Changes

Changes to clones play an important role when analyzing their evolution and assessing their harmfulness. Consequently, the Clone Evolution Graph includes information about the consistency of changes. Every clone class in the CEG has an attribute having one of three possible values:

- **Unchanged.** None of the clone class' fragments has been changed between this version and the next.

- **Consistent.** All of the clone class' fragments have been changed and the same changes have been applied to all fragments between this version and the next.

- **Inconsistent.** At least one of the clone class' fragments has been changed, but not all fragments have been changed in the same way. This includes fragments that have not been changed at all or were changed differently.

This information is also encoded in the visualization of the Clone Evolution Graph. The color of the rectangles representing clone classes tells which value the attribute has. White indicates that the fragments were unchanged, light gray tells us that the fragments have been changed consistently, and dark gray indicates that the fragments have been changed inconsistently.

To determine how the fragments of a clone class have changed, the changes to the respective source code have to be analyzed. Thus, it is reasonable to combine analyzing the consistency of changes with the mapping of fragments, because the procedure update already processes all changes to fragments. Every fragment contained in a modified file is passed once to the procedure update. The basic idea of our approach is to record the changes that affected each fragment and—after the changes to all fragments are known—compare the change sets of the fragments of each clone class. If all change sets are empty, the fragments have not changed and the clone class is classified as *unchanged*. If the change sets are not empty and all of them are identical, the clone class is classified as *consistent*. If at least one change set is non-empty but not all change sets are identical, the clone class is classified as *inconsistent*.

The first step is determining the change set for each fragment. To avoid confusing changes to fragments with the deltas used to describe changes to files, we refer to fragment changes as *edits*. An edit is a triple

$$\epsilon = (type, offset, length)$$

where *type* has one of the values ADD or DEL, *offset* denotes the location of the edit with respect to the start of the fragment, and *length* determines how man tokens have been added or deleted. Thus, an edit can be regarded as a *localized* delta. While the indices of deltas refer to the complete token sequence of a file, the offset of an edit refers to the token sequence of the fragment. This eases the comparison of edits for different fragments. The change set of a fragment is a list of edits. Not surprisingly, the change set for all fragments contained in unchanged files is empty. For fragments contained in modified files, the changes set is determined while changes are processed in procedure update.

The changes relevant for a fragment f are those that affect (and change) the token sequence of the fragment. Any change that happens before or after f is irrelevant, because it does not affect the fragment's token sequence. For additions, all deltas δ with $\delta.type = ADD$, $\delta.s_1 \geq f.start$, and $\delta.s_1 < f.start + f.length - 1$ are considered relevant. In other words, the addition has to take place after the first token and before the last token of f. The localized addition is:

$$\epsilon = (\delta.type, \delta.s_1 - f.start + 1, \delta.e_2 - \delta.s_2 + 1)$$

For deletions, any delta that affects at least one token of the fragment is considered relevant, that is, all deltas δ with $\delta.type = DEL$, $\delta.e_1 \geq f.start$, and $\delta.s_1 <$

$f.start + f.length$. A deletion may affect tokens beyond the fragment's bounds. Hence, deletions need to be cropped so that the corresponding edit refers to only tokens of the fragment. The localized and cropped deletion is:

$$\epsilon \;=\; (\delta.type, max(0, \delta.s_1 - f.start), (\delta.e_1 - \delta.s_1 + 1) - \\ (max(0, f.start - \delta.s_1)) - (max(0, \delta.e_1 - (f.start + f.length - 1))))$$

The length of ϵ is constructed from three different terms. First, $(\delta.e_1 - \delta.s_1 + 1)$ is the total number of tokens that are deleted. Second, the number of tokens deleted before the fragment, $(max(0, f.start - \delta.s_1))$, is subtracted from the total number. Third, the number of tokens deleted after the fragment, $(max(0, f.start - \delta.s_1))$, is subtracted. The remaining value is the number of tokens deleted from the fragment itself—the length of the edit ϵ.

Example 7.6 – Let us revisit Figure 7.7 (b) on page 102. The fragment $f = (4, 3)$ is affected by the addition $\delta = (ADD, 4, 4, 5, 6)$, because $4 \leq 4$ and $4 < 4 + 3 - 1$. The localized edit ϵ that is recorded for f is:

$$\epsilon = (ADD, 4 - 4 + 1, 6 - 5 + 1) = (ADD, 1, 2)$$

This means, after token 1 of the fragment, 2 tokens have been added. This is independent from the fragment's location inside the file. The fragment $f = (4, 4)$ in Figure 7.7 (c) on page 102 is affect by the deletion $\delta = (DEL, 3, 5, 2, 2)$, because $5 \geq 4$, and $3 < 4 + 4$. The localized edit ϵ that is recorded for f is:

$$\epsilon \;=\; (DEL, max(0, 3 - 4), (5 - 3 + 1) - (max(0, 4 - 3)) - \\ (max(0, 5 - (4 + 4 - 1)))) \\ =\; (DEL, 0, 2)$$

In other words, after token 0—that is, at the very beginning of the fragment—2 tokens have been deleted from the fragment. $\square$

When all changes to fragments have been processed, the change set containing localized edits is known for each fragment. The second step in determining change consistency is to compare the change sets of the fragments of each clone class that is known from the previous version. Note that when version v_i is analyzed, change consistency is calculated based on the clone classes in version v_{i-1} as the changes happen between the two versions, Understandably, analyzing change consistency between version v_i and v_{i+1} is not possible since version v_{i+1} is not known yet.

The clone classes of the previous version are each processed separately. If each fragment of a clone class has an empty change set, the clone class is *unchanged*. If at least one change set is non-empty, all sets are compared for equality. If any two sets are found to be different, the clone class is classified as *inconsistent*, otherwise—if all sets are identical—classified as *consistent*. The equality of two change sets is compared using the following steps:

```
1  if (condition) {                       1  if (condition) {
2      return list.first();              2      return list.first();
3  }                                       3  }
```

(a) Fragment f in version v_{i-1} (b) Fragment g in version v_{i-1}

```
1  if (condition &&                       1  if (condition &&
2      list.isEmpty() == false) {         2      list.size() > 0) {
3      return list.first();              3      return list.first();
4  }                                       4  }
```

(c) Fragment f in version v_i (d) Fragment g in version v_i

Figure 7.8 – Inconsistent addition of tokens.

(1) Compare the length of both sets. If the sets have different length, they cannot be equal.

(2) Compare the edits contained in both sets. The edits are sorted, hence, comparing them takes linear time with respect to the number of edits. Two edits are equal if their *type*, *offset*, and *length* are identical. If any discrepancy is found, the change sets are not equal.

(3) Compare the tokens that have been added. When tokens are deleted from identical fragments and the edit is the same, the tokens have to be the same as well. In contrast, when tokens are added, different tokens may be added. For a change to be consistent, IDA requires that the same tokens are added in all fragments. Consequently, for each edit that resembles an addition, the corresponding tokens that are added are checked for equality. If different tokens have been inserted, the change sets are not equal.

Example 7.7 – Figure 7.8 shows two fragments, f and g, of a clone class. Figures (a) and (b) show the identical fragments in version v_{i-1}. Both fragments are changed between versions v_{i-1} and v_i. The respective edit $\epsilon = (ADD, 3, 8)$ is the same for both fragments. However, different tokens have been inserted making the clone class containing fragments f and g be changed inconsistently. □

Consistency of changes to non-identical clones. So far, we have assumed that the fragments of a clone class are identical before being changed. Therefore, a direct comparison of the edits was possible. This technique is, however, not directly transferable to non-identical clones that contain gaps—non-identical parts—in their token sequence. If the gap of a clone is changed, this change can never be consistent, because the other fragments do not contain the respective token sequence. Nevertheless, the consistency of change is relevant only for the identical parts of fragments—the duplicated part—disregarding any gaps. In summary, the previous approach requires some refinement to be applicable to non-identical clones as well.

The basic idea of the refinement is to disregard any gaps in the clones when comparing their change sets. This requires two steps. First, we have to determine which tokens of the fragment belong to the identical part and which do not. Second, we have to use that information to *normalize* the edits and make them comparable—even for non-identical clones.

To identify the identical and non-identical parts of the fragments of a given clone class, IDA computes a longest common subsequence (LCS) of the fragments' token sequences. In fact, large parts of the LCS are already known from the creation of non-identical clones. When identical type-1 clones are merged to larger non-identical clones, the concatenated token sequences of the type-1 clones are already a subsequence of the LCS. What is missing are the gaps between neighboring type-1 clones. Parts of these gaps may belong to the LCS, although they have not been detected as type-1 clones due to the length threshold.

Consequently, IDA uses a traditional algorithm to compute the LCS only for the gaps between the type-1 clones from which the respective non-identical clone has been merged. The additional information is incorporated into the LCS obtained from the concatenated token sequences of the type-1 clones. Although computing an LCS is computationally expensive, this approach is feasible, because the gaps have shown to be very small in practice (often below ten tokens). When all gaps in the LCS have been "filled", a complete LCS is known for the non-identical clone class and, hence, we can tell for every token of a fragment whether it belongs to the identical part or not.

Based on the LCS, the edits in a fragment's change set can be *normalized*. Any addition of tokens that is located in the non-identical parts of a fragment is discarded. The offset of the remaining additions is decreased by the number of non-identical tokens before the addition's original offset. In other words, the normalized edit represents a change as if there were no gaps. For deletions, the corresponding edits are moved and cropped. Like additions, the edit's offset is decreased by the length of the gaps before the edit. The edit's length is reduced by the number of non-identical tokens that are affected. When all edits have been normalized, the change sets of all fragments (including those of non-identical clone classes) can be compared to analyze whether changes are consistent or inconsistent. In summary, the analysis of change consistency has been reduced to the identical parts among fragments of a clone class.

Example 7.8 – Consider the non-identical clone class shown in Figure 7.9 on the next page. The original fragments f and g are shown in (a) and (b), respectively. The fragments differ in line 3, because f has an additional call to a debugging method. From version v_{i-1} to v_i, another line is added in both fragments. The change is consistent, because exactly the same tokens have been inserted at exactly the same location with respect to the identical parts of both fragments. □

7.5 Summary

This chapter presented our technique for mapping clones between consecutive versions, allowing us to track individual clones as the software evolves. The mapping is created using a two-step process. First, the expected location of all known clones from previous

```
1   set.add('a');
2   set.add('b');
3   debug("Size:␣" + set.size());
4   for (char c : set) {
5       print(c);
6   }
```

(a) Fragment f in version v_{i−1}

```
1   set.add('a');
2   set.add('b');
3   // This is a gap, no debug call
4   for (char c : set) {
5       print(c);
6   }
```

(b) Fragment g in version v_{i−1}

```
1   set.add('a');
2   set.add('b');
3   debug("Size:␣" + set.size());
4   for (char c : set) {
5       update(c);
6       print(c);
7   }
```

(c) Fragment f in version v_i

```
1   set.add('a');
2   set.add('b');
3   // This is a gap, no debug call
4   for (char c : set) {
5       update(c);
6       print(c);
7   }
```

(d) Fragment g in version v_i

Figure 7.9 – Consistent change to fragments of a non-identical clone class.

versions is calculated using information about how the relevant source code has changed between versions. Second, the algorithm checks whether any clone detected in the current version matches an updated clone from a previous version. If so, the clone from the previous version is the ancestor of the clone in the current version. The mapping integrates well with our incremental detection of clones and, thus, the technique described in this chapter is our answer to Question 4 on page 39. The mapping abstracts from the source of the difference information which may be calculated retroactively or directly recorded by an IDE. With an appropriate source of precise difference information our approach allows a precise tracking answering Question 5 on page 39.

The approach presented in this chapter also supports tracking clones that temporarily disappear and, hence, answers Question 9 on page 49. This chapter also extends the concept of change consistency to non-identical clones. The answer to Question 8 on page 49 is considering only the subsequence of identical tokens when determining change consistency for non-identical clones. In summary, the incremental tracking of clones is an important extension of clone detection providing the foundation for an in-depth analysis of clone evolution.

The following chapter evaluates the performance of our incremental approach and shows that it is suitable for retroactive analysis of clone evolution as well as live tracking during development. We have used our technique of tracking clones across versions in various case studies of clone evolution which are presented in Chapters 9 to 11.

Chapter 8

Performance

An important property of the incremental detection algorithm IDA is its performance. The envisioned usage scenarios are not limited to research, but also include integration into the daily maintenance practice. The requirement to provide live clone evolution data while a system is maintained imposes restrictions on the time and memory available to process the evolving source code. This chapter provides an in-depth analysis of the algorithm's time and memory consumption to show that IDA is applicable to both research and practice. The analysis includes theoretical considerations as well as practical evaluations using real systems.

8.1 Complexity

This section provides an analysis of the theoretical complexity of IDA's individual phases. The analysis is done with respect to a single version that IDA processes. To obtain the overall complexity, the results would need to be multiplied by the total number of versions that are analyzed. However, this value may differ greatly between different scenarios or may not even be known in advance.

8.1.1 Time

Updating Data Structures. The first thing IDA does is update its token tables and the generalized suffix tree according to the files that have changed from the last version. When a file is added, it is first scanned to extract its token sequence. This requires time linear in the number of characters—which correlates with the number of tokens—in the file. Next, the file's suffixes have to be added to the suffix tree. The number of suffixes equals the number of tokens in the file. IDA uses the algorithm described by Amir and colleagues [3] to insert each suffix into the GST. Amir and colleagues show that in the case of all suffixes of a file being added, the insertion of each suffix requires constant time amortized over all suffixes. Thus, inserting all suffixes of a file is linear in the number of tokens in the file. Consequently, processing an added file requires linear time with respect to its length.

When a file is deleted, its suffixes have to be removed from the GST. IDA does this by first searching for the leaf that corresponds to the file's longest suffix, which is bounded by the length of the file. Each leaf corresponding to the next shorter suffix can be identified in constant time by following the suffix links. Removing a leaf and consequent modification of the suffix tree can be done in constant time according to Ferragina and colleagues [55]. Thus, updating the GST when a file is removed requires linear time with respect to the file's suffixes which equals the file's length measured in tokens.

Processing a modified file is treated as deletion of the file's old version followed by the insertion of the file's new version and can be done in linear time, accordingly. Reusing edges and nodes of the suffix tree may further reduce the runtime, but has no effect on the worst-case complexity. If the file's last token changed, all suffixes are affected and nothing can be reused.

In conclusion, independent from the type of change, processing each changed file requires time linear with respect to the number of tokens contained in the file. Consequently, updating the data structures has linear complexity $\mathcal{O}(n)$ with respect to the total number of tokens contained in all changed files.

Detecting Type-1 Clones.   Following the data structure update, type-1 clones are extracted from the GST. This phase depends on the number of nodes in the suffix tree and, hence, the accumulated lengths of all files that exist in the current version, because the number of suffix tree nodes correlates with the length of the underlying token sequence. Nodes are processed recursively using the procedure extract_clones shown in Figure 6.2 on page 79. Processing a single node takes constant time. Consequently, detecting type-1 clones has linear complexity $\mathcal{O}(n)$ with respect to the aggregated number of tokens in all files. The identification of start nodes using the procedure find_start_node given in Figure 6.4 on page 81 does not change this, as every node of the tree is processed at most once.

The actual runtime of this phase is strongly influenced by the threshold that defines the minimum length of identical clones and the start nodes that are used for the initial calls to extract_clones. Nevertheless, both do not affect the worst-case complexity as a theoretical threshold of 0 and a GST that changed completely still require all nodes to be processed.

Detecting Near-Miss Clones.   Based on the type-1 clones that are detected in the current version, type-2 and type-3 clone classes are merged. For merging, the type-1 clones have to be represented as clone pairs. If there are p cloned fragments contained in type-1 clone classes, the number of clone pairs is bounded by p^2. Assuming the worst case, each clone pair has to be compared to every other clone pair to check whether both of them can be merged into a non-identical clone pair. This results in $p^2 \cdot p^2$ comparisons. Consequently, the complexity of this phase is $\mathcal{O}(p^4)$ with respect to the number of fragments detected as type-1 clones. Nevertheless, this worst-case bound applies only when all fragments are contained in a single clone class and are located within the same file.

In practice, there are a number of optimizations to reduce the actual time needed for this phase. First, most clone classes have only two fragments in the first place. Consequently, the number of clone pairs is only marginally higher than the number of clone classes which, in term, is only marginally higher than twice the number of fragments. Second, only pairs whose fragments are located in corresponding files are compared. Third, the clone pairs are sorted and their order is exploited to avoid unnecessary calculations. Another optimization is using an incremental approach by reusing intermediate results from the previous version. All clone pairs for which the files that contain the fragments have not changed are reused from the previous version. This prevents repeated merging for clone pairs in files that did not change.

Filtering. During the filtering step, clone classes whose fragments are completely contained within the fragments of another clone class are removed from the results. As outlined in Section 6.5, every type-1 clone class has to be compared to every type-3 clone class for a subclass relationship in the worst case. The test itself is bounded by the maximum number of fragments of a clone class. Given there are p clone classes of type 1 and q clone classes of type 2 and 3, filtering requires $p \cdot q$ comparisons and therefore has quadratic worst case complexity with respect to the number of clone classes.

Mapping. After the clones existing in the current version have been detected, they have to be mapped to their closest ancestors. To identify ancestry relationships, all fragments known from the previous version are updated using the procedure `update` shown in Figure 7.5 on page 101. The procedure applies the deltas—bounded by the number of tokens of the respective file—to each fragment. Assuming the worst-case that all fragments are contained in the same modified file and each fragment is affected by every delta, the complexity of this phase is $\mathcal{O}(n^2)$ with respect to the number of cloned fragments. Again, most fragments are contained in unchanged files or are not affected by change in practice.

Change Consistency. Calculating change consistency is the final step of the incremental algorithm. The changes that affect fragments are recorded when clones are mapped. Change consistency has to be determined for every clone class of which at least one fragment is located in a changed file. Transforming a delta into an edit (a localized delta for the respective fragment) is done in constant time. Comparing the change sets of a clone class' fragments for consistency requires $q^2 \cdot r$ steps with q being the number of fragments contained in the clone class and r the number of edits in a fragment's change set. This results in a total of $p \cdot q^2 \cdot r$ steps with p being the number of clone classes that have at least one fragment in a changed file. Consequently, the overall complexity is $\mathcal{O}(n^4)$. In practice, p is very small—two in most cases. In addition, the number of edits that affect a fragment, q, is also very small. Consequently, the calculation is feasible despite its high worst-case complexity.

Summary. Large parts of the incremental algorithm are of linear complexity. Updating data structures is linear with respect to the number of tokens contained in changed files and detection of type-1 clones is linear regarding the number of tokens in all files. In contrast, detection of type-2 and type-3 clones has complexity $\mathcal{O}(n^4)$ with respect to the number of cloned fragments. The number of fragments may—depending on the parameters—be large and is a major contributor to the overall complexity. Mapping fragments and checking change consistency both have to process changes that affect individual fragments. Although both phases are above linear complexity, the relevant variables are very small in practice. Regarding the theoretical complexity, we conclude that detecting non-identical clones is the bottleneck of processing a version. Nevertheless, the complexity of all phases strongly depends on the parameters used. Consequently, the next section presents our detailed analysis of the actual performance and how it is influenced by certain choices of parameters.

8.1.2 Memory

The main memory consumers are the internal data structures—the token tables and the generalized suffix tree. The token tables store sequences of tokens and require memory linear to the number of tokens contained in the program.

The generalized suffix tree contains one leaf for each suffix of the program. The number of suffixes, in term, equals the number of tokens in the program. Since every inner node has at least two children, the number of inner nodes is bounded by the number of leaves. For every node of the tree, there is exactly one edge connecting the node with its parent (except for the root node). Therefore, the number of edges equals the number of nodes minus one. Each node and each edge requires constant memory to be stored. Hence, the generalized suffix tree requires memory linear to the number of tokens which are analyzed.

Apart from the token tables and the generalized suffix tree, memory is required for storing cloned fragments, clone classes, and other data structures that are needed to process a version. However, we neglect these, since the token tables and the generalized suffix tree dominate the memory consumption. In summary, the memory requirement is linear to the number of tokens in the program to be analyzed.

8.2 Time

Although the theoretical complexity provides first hints to the performance of the incremental algorithm, concrete time measurement is needed to show that it is suited for practical applications. Following from the theoretical analysis, most phases of the incremental algorithm depend on the changes between two versions. Hence, we need a measurement to express how much of the system has changed between two versions. Since the incremental approach is a token-based technique, we define the *Degree of Change (DC)* of a version i based on token quantities:

$$DC_i = \frac{\#\text{Tokens in files that changed between versions } i-1 \text{ and } i}{\#\text{Tokens in all files of version } i-1}$$

For files that are modified between versions $i-1$ and i, both the tokens contained in the file's old version and the tokens contained in the file's new version are counted. For the very first version, we define DC_0 to be 1. If nothing has changed between versions $i-1$ and i, DC_i is 0. A DC_i of 1 indicates that as many tokens as contained in the files of version $i-1$ are contained in changed files. The DC can, however, grow beyond a value of 1. Imagine a hypothetical case where all files from version $i-1$ are removed. This results in a DC_i of 1. If, in addition, some new files are added, this further increases the DC, which—in theory—is unlimited.

The DC is subsequently given as percentage. According to our observation of the theoretical complexity, higher DC values increase the processing time.

For time measurement, we distinguish between two scenarios which differ strongly in their DC values. As the DC has a major impact on the results, both scenarios are analyzed separately. The first scenario is targeted at the retrospective analysis of clone evolution while the second scenario resembles live analysis of clone evolution integrated into an IDE.

Evolution. Researchers or practitioners analyze a series of versions retroactively to investigate how clones evolved. This scenario is characterized by varying intervals between versions, resulting in different degrees of change. Depending on how the interval between versions is defined, the degree of change between versions may strongly differ from one version to the next. The duration between consecutive versions depends on the specific task or research interest. An example are released versions with an accumulation of many changed files. In general, the degree of change is much higher than in the IDE scenario.

IDE. The incremental algorithm is part of an integrated development environment (IDE) and therefore actively contributes to the maintenance process. When modifications are made to the source code of the program, the modifications are tracked by the IDE and reported to the incremental tool. The incremental approach treats the modifications as a new version of the program and updates the Clone Evolution Graph accordingly. Based on these updates, changes to clones contained in the source code are reported to the programmer, which allow her to immediately learn how her changes affect the system's redundancy. The characteristic of this scenario is that changes between consecutive versions are very limited. Assuming that saving a file triggers the update of the clone information, every two consecutive versions differ only in a single file. Thus, the DC is always very low.

Not only do both scenarios differ in the degree of change, they also have different requirements regarding performance. The evolution scenario is less restrictive. Updating the Clone Evolution Graph is done using predefined intervals and the results are less critical for the current development activity. In contrast, the IDE scenario requires fast processing due to the interaction with the maintainer. Clearly, live analysis of clone evolution is feasible only if response times are low.

Time measurement has been done using different subject systems. As we are interested only in performance, the type of systems, their purpose, and the programming

System	Short	Lang.	KLOC	KTokens
JabRef	JABREF	Java	117–119	495–505
Apache HTTP Server	HTTPD	C	207–215	778–813
GNU Compiler Collection	GCC	C	2049–2088	8332–8490

Table 8.1 – Subject systems used for performance study.

language they are written in are of minor interest. Consequently, three prominent systems have been chosen—two of medium size and one large system. The subject systems that have been selected are listed in Table 8.1.

8.2.1 Phases

Time is not measured only in total for a version, but for the individual phases of the incremental algorithm. This allows us to spot bottlenecks and possibilities for improvement. The phases that are measured align well with the technical descriptions in the previous sections. The time required to process each version is broken down into the following steps:

Token. This phase includes scanning all added and modified source files to extract their token sequences and create a corresponding token table. Furthermore, token sequences are filtered to discard irrelevant parts.

Tree. All modifications to the suffix tree are recorded in this phase. This includes removing the suffixes of deleted and the old version of modified files as well as adding the suffixes of added files and the new versions of modified files. The identification of start nodes for clone extraction is also part of this phase.

Extract. New and modified type-1 clones are extracted from the suffix tree and merged with unmodified type-1 clones from the previous version.

Merge. Based on the type-1 clones from the previous step, non-identical clones are detected by merging neighboring identical clones. Everything related to the detection of type-2 and type-3 clones is part of this phase.

Filter. Filtering transforms the clone data from the previous steps into clone classes that are used for mapping and output. The filter also removes overlapping clones.

Map. Within this phase, the clones are mapped between versions. The expected location of existing clones is calculated and compared to the clone information of the current version to determine the ancestry of clones.

Other. This phase collects everything not belonging to one of the previous steps. For example, this phase includes initialization and clean up actions.

The sum of the phases listed above equals the total time required to process the respective version.

8.2.2 Parameters

There are two different parameters that significantly influence the time needed to process a version. These are the minimum length of clones and the minimum length of identical subsequences for non-identical clones:

min_{cl} The minimum clone length which is given in tokens. The minimum length applies to all clones independent of whether they are identical type-1 clones or non-identical clones that have been merged. Choosing a high value limits the number of clones that are detected. Selecting a low value increases the number of clones that are found.

min_{sl} The minimum length of identical subsequences that are used to merge non-identical clones. Analogous to min_{cl} the value influences the number of clones that are considered for merging non-identical clones. As the merging procedure is computationally expensive, the parameter has a notable effect on the performance. This parameter resembles the threshold indicated in Figure 6.3 on page 80 and Figure 6.5 on page 82.

We first analyze the evolution scenario and the IDE scenario using a standard setting for both parameters. The impact of both parameters is analyzed separately in Section 8.2.5. All time measurement was done on a single machine with a 64-bit architecture using one of its eight processors with a speed of 3GHz. The machine has 32GB of main memory.

8.2.3 Evolution Scenario

For the evolution scenario, we have analyzed consecutive versions of the subject systems with a fixed interval of one week. We have chosen a fixed interval between versions which significantly eases further interpretation of the results. One week was chosen to capture different degrees of change—assuming that there are very busy weeks on the one hand and weeks where nothing has been changed on the other hand. For each system, we have analyzed its versions from the beginning of year 2010 up to the start of our analysis in October. The very first version of each system is from 1 January 2010 while the last version is from 1 October 2010. Using the fixed interval of one week, we obtained 40 consecutive versions for each system. The minimum, maximum, and average values of the degree of change (DC) for our subject systems are listed in the first part of Table 8.2 on the next page.

To analyze the performance of our incremental algorithm, we executed it for each subject system. We first parametrized our clone detector with standard settings. In particular, we searched for clones of type 1, 2, and 3 using a minimum clone length (min_{cl}) of 100 tokens which corresponds to roughly 15 lines of code excluding comments and blank lines. We required non-identical clones to contain identical subsequences of tokens (min_{sl}) that are at least 20 tokens long.

JabRef. The degree of change (DC)—the number of tokens contained in changed files compared to the number of tokens in all files of a particular version—is important

	Evolution			IDE		
System	Minimum	Average	Maximum	Minimum	Average	Maximum
JABREF	0.0	4.5	39.2	<0.1	1.6	5.3
HTTPD	0.0	19.4	162.3	<0.1	1.7	5.6
GCC	17.3	49.1	105.6	<0.1	0.3	1.5

Table 8.2 – Degree of change (DC) for the subject systems. The DC is the percentage of tokens contained in changed files compared to the total number of tokens. The maximum DC does not include the first version. The minimum DC for the IDE scenario is always above 0, because we have deliberately selected versions that changed files. In contrast, the minimum DC for the evolution scenario may be 0, because versions were selected according to a fixed interval irregardless of whether files have been changed.

when analyzing the time that is needed to process a version of a system. Figure 8.1 (a) on the next page shows the DC of each individual version of JABREF. According to the definition of the DC, the first version of each system always has a DC of 100%. Apart from that, many versions of JABREF have a DC of 0% indicating that no changes have been performed between that version and the previous one. The time that is required to process each version of JABREF is shown in Figure 8.1 (b) on the next page.

The bar at index 0 shows that the incremental algorithm required roughly 2.4 seconds to process the very first version. All internal data structures had to be created from scratch as there is no previous version from which anything could be reused. The time is dominated by two phases, namely *Token* and *Tree*. Reading the relevant source code files and transforming them into token sequences required almost one second. Another 1.3 seconds were required to create the generalized suffix tree. All remaining phases have only a minor impact.

All versions that have a DC of 0 require a constant amount of time to be processed. The time that is required is primarily contributed by general housekeeping functions and updating the Clone Evolution Graph. All remaining versions with $DC > 0$ are dominated by phase *Token* and *Tree*. Interestingly, the ratio between both phases changes slightly. For the very first version, *Tree* required only slightly more time than *Token*. For the other versions, *Tree* requires significantly more time than *Token*. This is caused by the degeneration of internal data structures—for example, hash tables. Comparing Figure (a) and (b) of Figure 8.1 on the next page emphasizes the dependency between the time needed to process a version and the DC. The version with the highest DC requires the most time, the version with the second highest DC requires the second most time, and so forth. Although this does not hold for all versions, a general tendency can be observed.

httpd. Figure 8.2 (a) on page 119 illustrates that almost all versions of HTTPD have, in contrast to JABREF, a DC greater than 0%. In addition, the average DC for HTTPD is more than four times larger compared to the average DC of JABREF. Interestingly, version 23 has a significantly higher DC of 162.3% compared to the other versions.

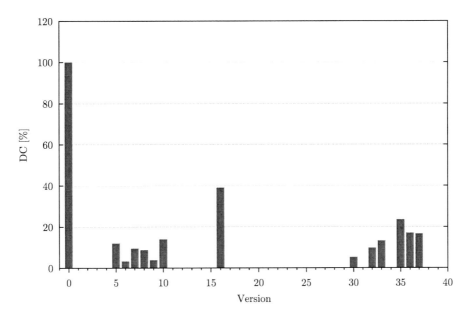

(a) Degree of Change (DC)

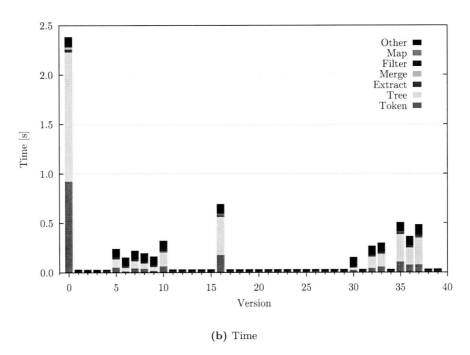

(b) Time

Figure 8.1 – DC and performance measured for JABREF using the parameter settings $min_{cl} = 100$ and $min_{sl} = 20$.

Analyzing the relevant messages from the version control system, we found that the high value was caused by changing central macros that resemble a cross-cutting concern and affect almost all files. The time that is required to process each version of HTTPD is shown in Figure 8.2 (b) on the next page.

Analyzing the first version of HTTPD requires almost 4 seconds. Again, the time is dominated by transforming the relevant files into token sequences and constructing the generalized suffix tree. The following versions all require notably less time than the first version with versions 23 being the only exception. In version 23, the outstanding DC of 162.3% increases the processing time for that version to almost 4.4 seconds. Most of the remaining versions confirm the relation between the DC and the processing time.

GCC.   In comparison to the other two systems, GCC has the highest average DC of 49.1%. Figure 8.3 (a) on page 120 shows that only one version has a DC below 20%. There is one version that has a DC above 100%. The high value is caused by cleaning up deprecated include directives. The processing time for GCC's versions is shown in Figure 8.3 (b) on page 120.

The first version of GCC required almost 90 seconds to be processed. In contrast to the other systems, the time is not dominated only by *Token* and *Tree*. Instead, merging identical snippets to non-identical clones is the most expensive phase. The theoretical complexity of this phase is $\mathcal{O}(n^4)$ where n is the number of identical fragments that are used for merging. Due to its size, GCC contains significantly more identical fragments— that is, n is much larger—compared to the other systems. Other phases that have hardly been visible for the other systems can now be clearly identified. Nevertheless, they still have only a minor impact.

The time needed to process the following versions of GCC are all lower than the time to process the first version. While the phases *Token* and *Tree* vary between versions depending on the DC, the phases *Filter*, *Map*, and *Other* require approximately constant time. The latter phases are dominated by non-incremental calculations that have to be done for each version independent from how much code has been changed. Interestingly, the phases *Extract* and *Merge* also require roughly constant time although both depend on the DC.

Despite its dominance in the very first version, the phase *Merge* has a lower impact on the processing time of the other versions—although, for example, version 21 has a DC of more than 100%. We conclude that reusing the results of our non-identical clone detection is a worthwhile optimization. Analogous to the previous systems, the results suggest a strong relation between the DC and the processing time. We provide a more detailed analysis of this relation in Section 8.2.6.

8.2.4   IDE Scenario

Apart from the perspective of an retrospective clone evolution analysis, using the incremental algorithm during software development to provide live clone evolution data is one of the envisioned usage scenarios. The performance of the algorithm is even more important compared to the evolution scenario because clone data have to be kept up-to-date without a notable delay for the developer. The IDE scenario is characterized by a

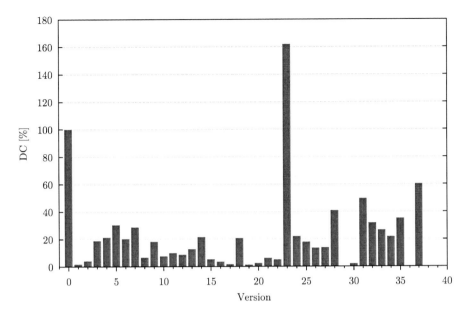

(a) Degree of Change (DC)

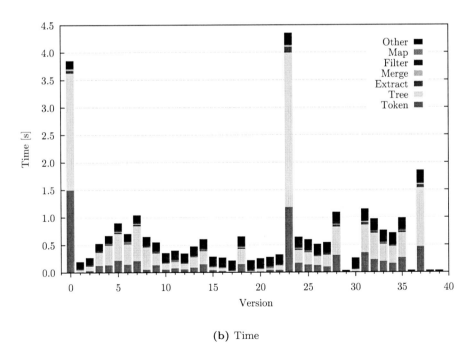

(b) Time

Figure 8.2 – DC and performance measured for HTTPD using the parameter settings $min_{cl} = 100$ and $min_{sl} = 20$.

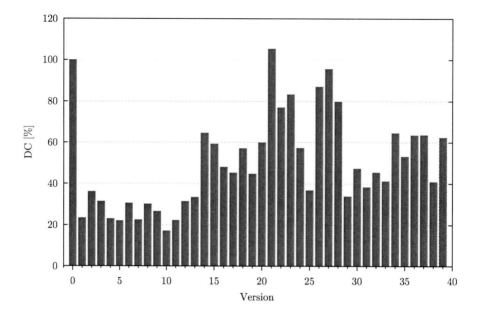

(a) Degree of Change (DC)

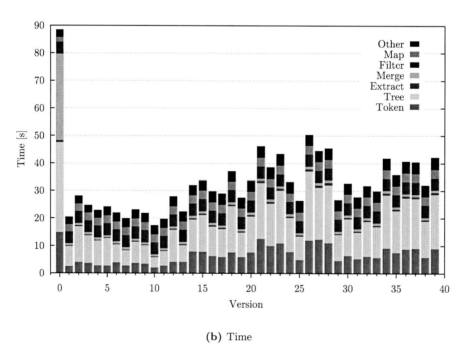

(b) Time

Figure 8.3 – DC and performance measured for GCC using the parameter settings $min_{cl} = 100$ and $min_{sl} = 20$.

significant lower DC compared to the evolution scenario. Whenever a single file is saved, the incremental algorithm treats this as a new version which is processed accordingly.

For the IDE scenario, our setup intends to simulate a continuous clone detection whenever a file is ready to be committed in the absence of the real order of file saving during development for our subject systems. We analyzed the first version from 1 January 2010 of every subject system as we have done for the evolution scenario. Then we retrieved the list of all file modifications from the remaining versions. The list was sorted according to the version the modifications appeared in. The closer a version is to the very first version, the closer are its respective file modifications to the head of the list. The ordering among the file modifications that occurred in the same version was random. It may happen that a file occurs more than once in this ordering because the same file can be modified in several versions. Then we extracted the first 39 file modifications and constructed an artificial version for each of them. The total number of 40 versions has been processed by our incremental algorithm. For comparability, we used the same parameters ($min_{cl} = 100$, $min_{sl} = 20$) as for the evolution scenario. The minimum, maximum, and average values of the DC for the IDE scenario are listed in the second part of Table 8.2 on page 116.

JabRef. The results for JabRef are shown in Figure 8.4 on the next page. The average DC excluding the first version has dropped to 1.6%. The highest DC apart from the very first version is 5.3%. As we have expected, the time needed to process the first version is similar for the evolution scenario and the IDE scenario. The remaining versions are dominated by the phase *Other*. That is, the core parts of the incremental algorithm have only a minor impact while most time is required for general operations that have to be done for every version.

httpd. The average DC for HTTPD decreased to 1.7% for the IDE scenario with its maximum being 5.6%. Figure 8.5 on page 123 presents the results for HTTPD. The picture is similar to JabRef. All versions but the first are dominated by phase *Other*. All versions were processed in less than one fourth of a second.

GCC. For GCC, the average DC is even lower compared to the other two systems. GCC has an average DC of 0.3% while the maximum DC is 1.5%. The results for GCC are given in Figure 8.6 on page 124. All versions but the first require roughly 10 seconds each to be processed. In contrast to the other systems, phases *Filter* and *Map* are now recognizable. They require almost constant time for every version due to their non-incremental nature. The time for every version could, in principle, be reduced when only identical clones are to be detected. Non-identical clone detection requires significantly more effort and organization than the detection of identical clones. Consequently, the processing time could be decreased to an acceptable level for live clone detection when only identical clones are of interest.

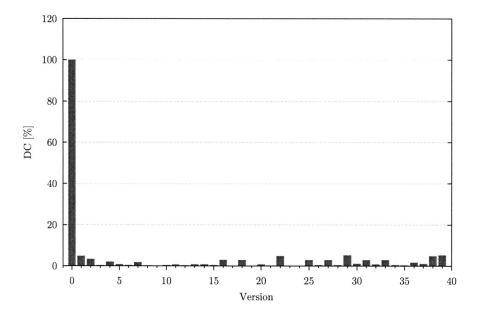

(a) Degree of Change (DC)

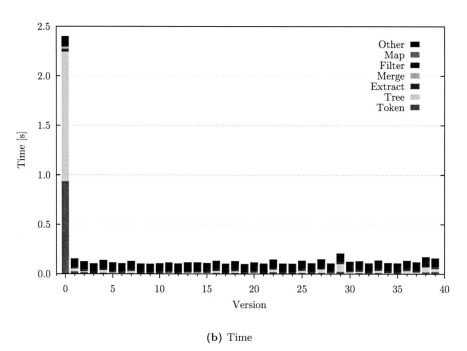

(b) Time

Figure 8.4 – DC and performance measured for JABREF using the parameter settings $min_{cl} = 100$ and $min_{sl} = 20$.

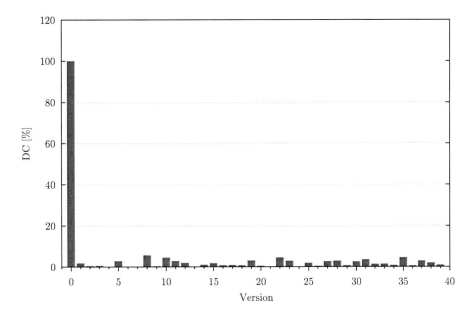

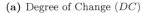

(a) Degree of Change (DC)

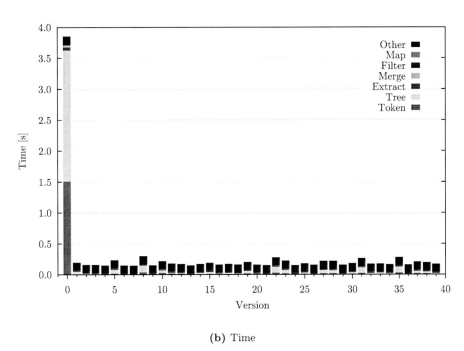

(b) Time

Figure 8.5 – DC and performance measured for HTTPD using the parameter settings $min_{cl} = 100$ and $min_{sl} = 20$.

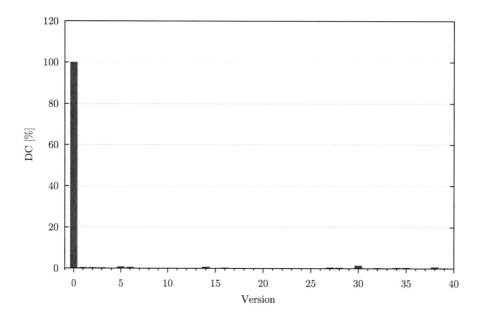

(a) Degree of Change (DC)

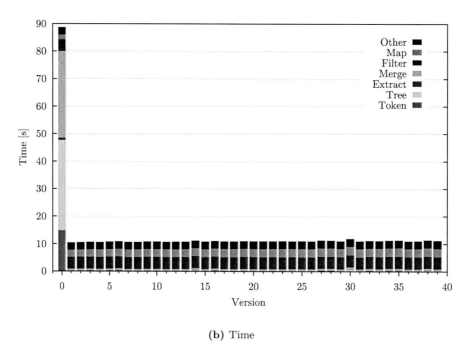

(b) Time

Figure 8.6 – DC and performance measured for GCC using the parameter settings $min_{cl} = 100$ and $min_{sl} = 20$.

System	min_{cl}	Extract	Merge	Filter	Map	Total
JABREF	50	99	59	902	326	5881
	100	96	43	391	118	4920
	150	97	31	229	66	4690
HTTPD	50	670	347	1055	417	26105
	100	682	304	490	147	24735
	150	670	286	308	88	24307
GCC	50	19353	34103	223483	180241	1377813
	100	18698	32217	172048	118435	1227592
	150	18408	31461	133179	81058	1113377

Table 8.3 – Influence of the minimum clone length min_{cl} on the performance. Values are given in ms.

8.2.5 Parameter Impact

The parameters min_{cl} and min_{sl} have a notable impact on the performance of the incremental algorithm. To better understand their influence, we measured the performance for our subject systems using different values for these parameters.

Minimum Length (min_{cl}). For our analysis of the overall performance, we used 100 tokens as minimum length for clones. To evaluate the impact of the minimum clone length, we choose two additional values of 50 and 150 tokens—one being smaller and the other being larger than our standard setting. Consequently, we measure and compare the algorithm's performance using these three distinct values. To ensure comparability of the different measurements, we used a fixed value of 20 tokens for the second parameter min_{sl}. To measure the impact of the parameter, we compare the time aggregated for all versions of each subject systems. The measurement is done for the total time as well as individual relevant phases. The phases *Token* and *Tree* are not shown as they are not influenced by the parameters. However, the total time refers to the sum of all phases including the aforementioned. The results are shown in Table 8.3.

When the minimum clone length is lowered to 50 tokens, the overall processing time increases due to the higher number of cloned fragments. Compared to $min_{cl} = 100$, the processing time increased by 20% in JABREF, 6% in HTTPD, and 12% in GCC. The strength of the increase depends on the ratio between duplication and the system's size. For example, JABREF has the highest ratio of duplication and also shows the strongest increase in processing time when min_{cl} is lowered to 50 tokens. The increase in processing time does not hold only for the total time, but also for individual phases. While the time increases only slightly for phase *Extract* (regarding HTTPD it even decreases) and *Merge*, it more than doubles for *Filter* and *Map*. Increasing min_{cl} from 100 tokens to 150 tokens decreases the time needed for processing. The overall time decreased by 5% in JABREF, 2% in HTTPD, and 9% in GCC.

System	min_{sl}	Extract	Merge	Filter	Map	Total
JABREF	10	383	1108	693	249	7101
	20	96	43	391	118	4920
	30	58	16	263	78	4647
HTTPD	10	1867	6220	839	284	34730
	20	682	304	490	147	24735
	30	480	140	434	142	24092
GCC	10	46559	611915	261770	208749	2077764
	20	18698	32217	172048	118435	1227592
	30	13863	15242	123288	80138	1093540

Table 8.4 – Influence of the minimum subsequence length min_{sl} on the performance. Values are given in ms.

Minimum Identical Subsequences (min_{sl}). We have analyzed the overall performance of our incremental algorithm using a minimum length of 20 tokens for identical subsequences that are subsequently merged to non-identical clones. To evaluate the influence of this parameter, we perform another measurement using a smaller value of 10 tokens and a larger value of 30 tokens respectively. For the minimum clone length we used a fixed value of 100 tokens. The results of our analysis are shown in Table 8.4.

When using 10 tokens for the parameter min_{sl}, a significant increase in the processing time can be observed. The total time increases by 44% for JABREF, 40% for HTTPD, and 69% for GCC. The strong increase is caused by much more nodes of the suffix tree becoming relevant and, consequently, a much larger set of identical fragments that is used as the basis for merging non-identical clones. This can also be seen in the large increase of processing time for phase *Merge*. The time for this phase increases by 2476% in JABREF, 1946% in HTTPD, and 1799% in GCC. These numbers fit our theoretical observation where we found the theoretical complexity of phase *Merge* to be n^4 with n being the number of identical fragments. Although there is a notable increase in the time for the other phases, the increase is much weaker compared to *Merge*.

Setting min_{sl} to 30 tokens reduced the overall processing time for all systems. Fewer nodes of the suffix tree become relevant and the input to phase *Merge* is much smaller. For all three systems, phase *Merge* requires less than half the processing time compared to using 20 tokens. The total time decreased by 6% in JABREF, 3% in HTTPD, and 11% in GCC. In summary, the parameter min_{sl} has a stronger influence on the processing time than min_{cl}. Especially small values for min_{sl} significantly increase the processing time and should, hence, be chosen carefully.

8.2.6 Break-Even Analysis

The previous sections consistently indicate the relation between the degree of change (DC)—the percentage of tokens contained in changed files—and the processing time. A higher DC increases the processing time while a lower DC decreases the processing time. In this section, we analyze this relation in more detail by correlating the DC of a version with the time needed to process that version. Instead of the total time for a version, we measure the analysis speed as time per token, because the versions of our subject systems are of different size. We used the default setting of $min_{cl} = 100$ and $min_{sl} = 20$ for our investigation.

Figure 8.7 on the next page illustrates the results of our analysis for each subject system separately. For each system, we processed 40 versions which provide us with 40 distinct samples. The x-value of each sample is given by the DC of the respective version. The corresponding y-value is determined by dividing the total time needed to process that version by the size of the version measured in tokens. To ease comparability, we have chosen identical x-ranges and y-ranges for all three subject systems. In addition to the samples, we have included a horizontal line that approximates the speed required by a non-incremental analysis. The y-value of the line was calculated by dividing the processing time of the very first version by the number of tokens of the very first version. Since the first version cannot reuse any data from the previous version, it resembles a good estimate of the time needed by a non-incremental analysis. According to this calculation, the y-value of the sample of the very first version with a DC value of 100% equals the y-value of the non-incremental line. Finally, we included a fitting line obtained by linear regression of the samples that approximates the processing speed of the incremental analysis.

Not surprisingly, the speed of the incremental analysis decreases with increasing DC values. Furthermore, higher DC values increase the variation in the processing speed indicating that not only the number but also the nature of changes has an impact. The intersection of the non-incremental line and the incremental line is an estimation of the break-even point between a non-incremental analysis and an incremental analysis. As long as the DC is lower than the x-value of the intersection point, the incremental analysis is beneficial. In contrast, a non-incremental approach is preferable when the DC is higher than the x-value of the intersection point. The DC of the break-even point is 105% for JABREF, 134% for HTTPD, and 172% for GCC.

8.2.7 Reusing Suffix Tree Structures

We have described our technique of reusing nodes and edges of the generalized suffix tree in Section 5.3.3. As tree modifications are expensive, the goal of reusing these structures is to prevent unnecessary modifications to the tree and, consequently, reduce the processing time. In this section, we measure how much processing time is saved by reusing edges and nodes of the suffix tree. We used our default setting of $min_{cl} = 100$ and $min_{sl} = 20$ because updating the generalized suffix tree is independent from both values. For each of the three subject systems, we measure the time needed for the phase *Tree* as well as the total time aggregated over all versions but the first. We deliberately excluded the first version, because reusing suffix tree structures is applicable only when files are modified—which can happen only in versions that have a predecessor. We compare the values for the two different settings: tree structures not being reused and tree structures being reused. The results are given in Table 8.5 on page 129.

For all three subject systems, the overall processing time as well as the time needed for phase *Tree* is lower when suffix tree structures are reused. The highest drop can be

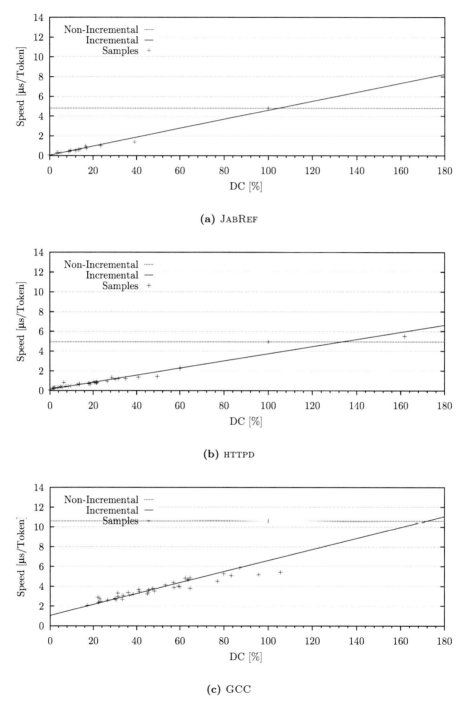

(a) JABREF

(b) HTTPD

(c) GCC

Figure 8.7 – Processing time per token for different *DC*s.

System	Tree			Total		
	No [ms]	Yes [ms]	Δ [%]	No [ms]	Yes [ms]	Δ [%]
JABREF	2560	1789	−30.1	5866	4920	−16.1
HTTPD	15102	11479	−24.0	29209	24735	−15.3
GCC	620340	488296	−21.3	1608631	1227592	−23.7
∅	–	–	−25.1	–	–	−18.4

Table 8.5 – Time saved by reusing nodes and edges of the generalized suffix tree.

System	All	$min_{sl} = 10$	%	$min_{sl} = 20$	%	$min_{sl} = 30$	%
JABREF	27816728	580351	2.1	209052	0.8	124549	0.4
HTTPD	44410075	2507508	5.6	1014121	2.3	659018	1.5
GCC	480015029	46748452	9.7	15546879	3.2	8630915	1.8

Table 8.6 – Number of suffix tree nodes processed.

observed for JABREF where the processing time for phase *Tree* decreases by 30.1% when suffix tree structures are reused. On average, reusing nodes and edges saves 25.1% of processing time when the suffix tree is updated. The saving achieved by reusing nodes and edges is also notable when looking at the total processing time. In JABREF, the total time is reduced by 16.1%. On average, reusing tree structures causes the overall processing time to decrease by 18.4%. We conclude that reusing suffix tree nodes and edges is a reasonable strategy that can save up to almost one fourth of the time needed to update the generalized suffix tree.

8.2.8 Start Nodes

Another optimization of the incremental algorithm is to extract clones only from the modified parts of the suffix tree and reuse all clones from the previous version that are not changed. Section 6.3 describes the procedure in detail. In this section, we investigate how much processing time is actually saved using this technique. Before measuring the time itself, we evaluate the improvement in terms of the number of suffix tree nodes that are processed. For our analysis, we set $min_{cl} = 100$ as the parameter is used only for subsequent filtering of clones and, therefore, does not influence the extraction of clones from the suffix tree. In contrast, min_{sl} is relevant, since it determines the minimum length of identical sequences that are extracted from the suffix tree. For min_{sl}, we use the three values of 10 tokens, 20 tokens, and 30 tokens. The three distinct values allow us to analyze the impact of the parameter on the results.

The results with respect to the number of suffix tree nodes are summarized in Table 8.6. The second column indicates the number of all suffix tree nodes that have been encountered during the analysis. That is, the number can be seen as the aggregated size of the suffix trees of all versions. The remaining columns contain the number and

System	Extract			Total		
	No [ms]	Yes [ms]	Δ [%]	No [ms]	Yes [ms]	Δ [%]
JABREF	11449	96	−99.2	23145	7306	−68.4
HTTPD	19901	682	−96.6	54113	28585	−47.2
GCC	248214	18698	−92.5	3535131	1316057	−62.8
∅	−	−	−96.1	−	−	−59.5

Table 8.7 – Time saved by searching only for new and modified clones.

percentage of suffix tree nodes that have been processed during the analysis for each of the three different values of min_{sl}.

The results show that only a small subset of all suffix tree nodes is processed. This subset does, however, contain all nodes that are relevant to detect new and modified clones—that is, there is no loss of information. Using $min_{sl} = 20$, only 0.8% of all suffix tree nodes are processed in JABREF, 2.3% in HTTPD, and 3.2% in GCC. When min_{sl} is decreased, the percentage of processed nodes increases, because more nodes become relevant. If, on the other hand, min_{sl} increases, fewer nodes are relevant, reducing the number of nodes that are processed even more. These findings already suggest that much processing time can be saved by searching only for new and modified clones in contrast to a complete retrieval of all clones from the suffix tree.

Apart from the number of suffix tree nodes that are processed, we investigated how much processing time can be saved by the incremental extraction of new and modified clones. We present our results only for $min_{sl} = 20$. The effect of decreasing or increasing min_{sl} on the processing time corresponds to the impact on the number of suffix tree nodes that are processed. Analogous to our evaluation of reusing suffix tree structures, we compare the time for a complete retrieval of all clones to the optimized retrieval of only new and modified clones. We measure the time for phase *Extract* as well as the total time aggregated over all versions. This time we include the first version, because it also uses and benefits from the incremental extraction. The results are given in Table 8.7.

The results show that searching only new and modified clones has a strong impact on the processing time. For the phase *Extract*, the time required is reduced by 99.2% in JABREF, 96.6% in HTTPD, and 92.5% in GCC. The decrease in processing time once more depends on the *DC*. A high *DC* leads to less reduction whereas a low *DC* contributes to a higher reduction. The decrease in processing time can also be seen in the total time needed to process all versions. While phase *Extract* is reduced by 96.1% on average, the total time to process all versions is reduced by 59.5% on average. Although phase *Extract* resembles the core of extracting duplication from the suffix tree, other phases (for example *Merge*) benefit from the incremental extraction as well. Consequently, we conclude that incremental extraction of only new and modified clones from the tree is an essential strategy that significantly reduces processing time.

Parameter	#1	#2	#3	#4	#5
min_{cl}	100	100	100	150	50
min_{sl}	10	20	30	20	20

Table 8.8 – Parameter settings for measuring the memory consumption.

8.3   Memory

The applicability of our incremental approach does not depend only on the time it requires but also on the memory that is consumed. This section presents our analysis of the memory consumption of our incremental approach. To measure the memory consumed by our algorithm, we use two different approaches.

(1) **procfs.** The Linux proc file system provides information about running process. In particular, it can tell how much memory is dedicated to a given process. The advantage of this type of measurement is that the memory consumption can be measured at any point in time—for example, after a version has been processed. The disadvantage is the imprecision of the measurement. Being dedicated to a process does not mean the process really uses all the memory. Furthermore, only the total memory usage is reported.

(2) **Valgrind™.**[1] To gain better insight into how much memory our process really uses and which parts are dominating, we use the Valgrind tool set to investigate the memory consumption. The disadvantage of Valgrind is that the measurement cannot be triggered from within our algorithm.

8.3.1   procfs

We have first analyzed the memory consumption of our incremental algorithm using the data from the proc file system. At the end of processing each version, we have measured the amount of memory that was dedicated to the respective process. For each subject system we have measured the memory consumption using five distinct settings. The first is our default setting with $min_{cl} = 100$ and $min_{sl} = 20$. The other four are derived from the default setting by varying min_{cl} or min_{sl} respectively. Table 8.8 lists the five settings used.

The results of our analysis are shown in Figure 8.8 on the next page. Figure (a) illustrates how much memory was dedicated to the incremental algorithm after processing JABREF's versions. For all but one setting, the algorithm required roughly 180MB of memory. Only when using 10 tokens for min_{sl}, the memory consumption is slightly higher due to the notably larger number of clones that are detected, processed, and stored. At the end of the analysis, there is a sudden increase in the amount of memory dedicated to the process. This is a common phenomenon that has several reasons. First, the subject systems grow in size during our analysis—that is,

---

[1]http://valgrind.org

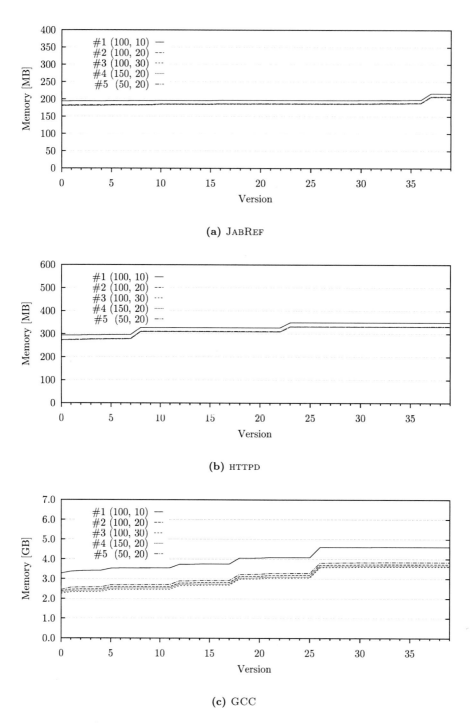

(a) JABREF

(b) HTTPD

(c) GCC

Figure 8.8 – Maximum memory usage for each version.

later versions are larger than earlier versions. Second, internal data structures of the incremental algorithm degenerate over time. Third, various data including the Clone Evolution Graph is kept in memory and written to disk only at the end of the analysis. This behavior is imposed by the format that is used to store the data but could be changed for other scenarios. The increase of the memory consumption is not continuous but happens in intervals due to the operating system dedicating memory in larger chunks to individual processes.

The memory consumption when analyzing HTTPD's versions is given in Figure (b). Memory consumption starts at 270MB and increases to 340MB at the end of the analysis. Analogous to JABREF, using 10 tokens for min_{sl} increases the overall memory consumption slightly. Two situations can be observed where additional chunks of memory are dedicated to the process.

In contrast to the other systems, analyzing GCC requires significantly more memory as shown in Figure (c). GCC's first version requires around 2.3GB of memory whereas the last version requires 3.8GB of memory. Small differences between individual settings can be observed. The memory consumption for $min_{sl} = 10$ is once more higher compared to the other settings. Several allocations of additional memory can be observed throughout the analysis period. The more frequent and stronger increase of the memory consumption compared to the other systems is caused by the higher number of clones—and, consequently, higher amount of data that needs to be stored—in GCC.

8.3.2   Valgrind

Measuring memory consumption using the proc file system is an overestimation of the real amount of memory required by a process. Furthermore, the data does not provide information about which parts of our algorithm are responsible for the memory consumption. To get a more detailed picture of the memory used, we used the MASSIF tool which is part of the *Valgrind* profiling tool set. In particular, the following information is of interest to us:

(1) The peak memory consumption

(2) The parts of the algorithm responsible for the memory consumption

We have analyzed the version of each subject system once more using VALGRIND. However, this time we used only one setting with the highest memory consumption ($min_{cl} = 100$ and $min_{sl} = 10$) for JABREF and HTTPD. For GCC we have used $min_{cl} = 100$ and $min_{sl} = 30$, because using $min_{sl} = 10$ made the analysis tool VALGRIND itself fail due to memory limitations. Table 8.9 on the next page lists the peak memory usage for each subject system and which parts of the algorithm are responsible for the memory consumption.

VALGRIND reported a peak memory usage of 158 megabytes for JABREF, whereas the proc file system has previously reported 217 megabytes. Hence, the incremental algorithm required only 73% of the memory dedicated to it. For HTTPD, VALGRIND reported a peak memory consumption of 310 megabytes. That is roughly 87% of the 358 megabytes that have been reported using the procfs measurement. For GCC, however,

System	Peak [MB]	Token Tables	GST	Other
JABREF	158	5%	79%	16%
HTTPD	310	6%	82%	12%
GCC	4202	6%	75%	19%

Table 8.9 – Detailed memory consumption.

the situation is different. VALGRIND reported a peak memory requirement of 4,202 megabytes. The consumption measured by VALGRIND is larger (111%) compared to the consumption of 3,788 megabytes that was measured using procfs. This suggests a malfunction of either procfs or VALGRIND, because the memory consumption measured using procfs should always be larger compared to the value measured using VALGRIND.

Looking at the different parts responsible for the memory consumption, we were able to clearly separate two main contributors. First, 6% of the total memory—5% for JABREF—are required for the token tables that store the token sequences of the files relevant to the analysis. Second, the generalized suffix tree data structure showed to be the main memory consumer. Storing the nodes and edges of the generalized suffix tree requires 75% to 82% of the total memory. Although they require linear space with respect to the size of the token sequences, generalized suffix trees have an even higher memory consumption than traditional suffix trees caused by additional references that are required for modifying the tree after its initial construction. The remaining 12% to 19% are required by various other parts of the algorithm among which is storing information about clones.

8.4 Summary

This chapter presented our in-depth analysis of our incremental algorithm's performance regarding time and memory consumption. We analyzed multiple versions of three distinct subject system of different size and showed that the time required to process each version depends on the number of changes that happened since the previous version. The more changes were applied, the more processing time was required. In general, the incremental analysis is significantly faster than a repeated single-version analysis. Processing versions is dominated by tokenizing new and modified files as well as updating the generalized suffix tree.

The choice of parameters has a strong influence on the processing time. We have analyzed the impact of two prominent parameters and shown that more tolerant settings—that is, more clones are detected—notably increase the processing time. In particular, the detection of non-identical clones can be quite costly. Our empirical results match our theoretical considerations at the beginning of this chapter. We have further shown that our optimization of reusing suffix tree structures saves almost 20% of processing time and an incremental extraction of only new and modified clones saves more than 50% of total processing time.

In addition, we have analyzed the memory consumption of our algorithm. As a rule of thumb, analyzing one million lines of code requires roughly 2GB of memory. A more detailed analysis revealed that around 80% are required for the generalized suffix tree data structure. Another 5% are required for storing the token tables and the remaining 15% are needed to store other data among which is the information about clones.

With our implementation we have tried to find a reasonable trade-off between time and memory consumption. Currently, the algorithm operates on individual tokens. To further increase the algorithm's speed and decrease its memory consumption, one could unify multiple tokens (for example a statement) into a single token. Although this decreases the algorithm's precision slightly, time and memory consumption can be significantly reduced.

In summary, this chapter has shown that our incremental algorithm has a reasonable performance that makes it suitable for retroactive analysis of clone evolution as well as live analysis during development. Extracting relevant clone evolution data is done in considerably less time compared to previous approaches that often required hours or days for comparable amounts of source code.

Part III

Studies

Chapter 9

Diversity of Clone Evolution

Analyzing clone evolution is an important step towards understanding the phenomenon of cloning. Previous studies have investigated different aspects of clone evolution, including the clone ratio, the lifetime of clones, and the consistency of changes to clones. Although previous studies provide important results, the amount of data that has been considered is fairly small. The limitations include small subject systems [109], a small number of versions that have been analyzed [13, 20], and consideration of a single programming language only [8, 109]. Furthermore, the results of earlier studies are contradictory to a certain degree.

- **Clone Ratio.** A stable clone ratio is reported by Laguë and colleagues [123] as well as Livieri and colleagues [134]. In contrast, Li and colleagues [130] observed a steadily increasing clone ratio.

- **Lifetime.** Kim and colleagues [109] conclude that many clones are volatile whereas Bettenburg and colleagues [20] found that clones live for more than half a year on average.

- **Change Consistency.** Krinke [121] found that consistent and inconsistent changes to clones appear with roughly the same frequency. Others [8, 178] report that consistent changes to clones are more frequent.

The disagreement may—at least partially—result from the use of different techniques to collect data and the analysis of different subject systems. The goal of this case study is to clarify the contradictions by using an improved technique for data collection and running an extensive analysis using multiple subject systems written in different languages. Specifically, the case study answers Question 6 on page 42 and Question 10 on page 52. The original version [61] of the study analyzed clone evolution in nine different open-source systems. Later, the study has been extended to three industrial systems [63] to investigate potential differences between open-source and industrial projects.

System	Language	KSLOC	First	Last	#Versions
GIMP	C	339–411	06/05	04/09	200
HTTPD	C	138–130	06/05	04/09	200
NAUTILUS	C	84–135	06/05	04/09	200
FILEZILLA	C++	22–105	06/05	04/09	200
KMAIL	C++	90–116	06/05	04/09	200
UMBRELLO	C++	74–93	06/05	04/09	200
ANT	Java	125–129	11/05	04/09	175
ARGOUML	Java	92–126	06/05	04/09	200
JABREF	Java	37–72	06/05	04/09	200
KV-KL	COBOL	530–623	11/07	03/10	125
ZY-ZG	COBOL	148–153	11/07	03/10	125
ZY-ZP	COBOL	422–448	11/07	03/10	125

Table 9.1 – Subject systems used for studying clone evolution.

9.1 Setup

This section describes the subject systems that have been used in this case study and the procedure that has been used to collect relevant data.

9.1.1 Subject Systems

The case study was conducted using nine different open-source systems and three industrial systems. An important criterion for choosing the systems was that they are of reasonable size, because—understandably—cloning can be controlled much easier in small projects making clone evolution look significantly different. For this study, the average size of a system's version had to exceed 50K SLOC. Systems have been selected to make different programming languages be represented in the study. The open-source systems used are ANT, ARGOUML, FILEZILLA, GIMP[1], JABREF, HTTPD, KMAIL, NAUTILUS, and UMBRELLO. All open-source systems have a history of several years.

The three industrial systems are closed source and developed by the Debeka-Group. The Debeka-Group offers a variety of insurance and financial services and is one of the top-ten companies in the insurance and home savings business in Germany. The systems we have studied are written in COBOL and each has a history of more than ten years. Systems ZY-ZG and ZY-ZP provide functionality common to different services, whereas the system KV-KL is dedicated to health insurance. All systems are listed in Table 9.1.

For each of the open-source systems, 200 versions with an interval of one week starting from June 2005 to April 2009 have been analyzed. The only exception is ANT, for which there was no activity related to source code reported by the version control

---

[1] The plug-in directory containing roughly half of GIMP's source code has been excluded from the study, because the respective source code contains mostly inevitable clones due to the plug-in mechanism.

system during the first months. ANT's versions have been analyzed from the month where the first source code changes happened (November 2005) resulting in only 175 versions. For the three industrial systems, we analyzed clone evolution over 125 versions with an interval of one week. The first version is from November 2007, the last from March 2010. Earlier versions were not available due to a change in version control mechanisms. Details about the systems and versions analyzed are provided in Table 9.1 on the previous page.

9.1.2 Data Collection

To extract relevant data from the histories of the subject systems, we have used our incremental algorithm. The study has been restricted to type-1 clones, because non-identical clone detection does not yet have the desired precision to base further assumptions on the clones. Thus, fragments of a clone class were required to be identical disregarding whitespace and comments. Each system was analyzed twice to observe the impact of the minimum length clones need to have. The minimum clone length was set to 50 tokens and 100 tokens, roughly corresponding to 5 and 10 source code lines according to our experience. Both values fall in the range of values used by previous studies and ensure that clones are not too short to be relevant. The incremental algorithm has been applied to each system using the different minimum lengths providing Clone Evolution Graphs (CEG) for each system. The CEGs have subsequently been analyzed to investigate the different aspects of clone evolution.

Clone Ratio

For this study, the clone ratio CR for a particular system version v is defined as the number of cloned fragments that exist in that version compared to the version's size measured in SLOC.

$$CR(v) = \frac{\#\text{ Cloned Fragments}(v)}{\#\text{ SLOC}(v)}$$

To analyze how the clone ratio evolves over time, we measure CR for the very first and for the very last version of each system. Comparing both values allows us to tell how the clone ratio has changed during our study period. A more detailed analysis of the clone ratio for each version follows later in this section.

$$\Delta CR = \frac{CR(last) - CR(first)}{CR(first)}$$

Lifetime

For clone management it is important to know whether clones are long-lived or exist only for a short time in a system. Therefore, we have analyzed the lifetime of cloned fragments in each system. First, we have to determine the set of fragments that exist in the CEG. The CEGs, however, contain multiple occurrences of a fragment—one for each version in which the fragment exists. To determine the set of relevant fragments that

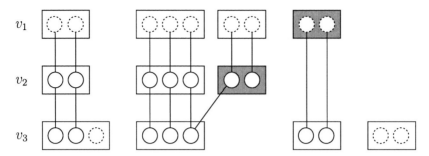

Figure 9.1 – Lifetime of fragments in the Clone Evolution Graph. Dotted fragments denote the begin of the lifetime of distinct fragments.

contains exactly a single occurrence of each fragment, we collect all fragment occurrences that do not have an ancestor. We included subsumed and overlapping fragments since these always belong to different clone classes and although they share a certain number of tokens, they represent different similarity relations.

Fortunately, occurrences of fragments without an ancestor already define the beginning of their lifetime. To determine the age of each fragment, we have to find the occurrence that represents the end of its lifetime. We find this occurrence by traversing the fragment's closest descendants until we have found an occurrence that has no descendant. There is no ambiguity involved because every fragment can have at most one closest descendant. In the case of late propagation, we use ghost fragments to continue tracking them—that is, inconsistent changes that are subsequently propagated do not lead to an end of the lifetime. Please refer to Section 7.1 for a detailed description of fragment ancestry. The lifetime of the fragment is measured in versions and can be computed by counting versions from the beginning to the end of the fragment's lifetime.

Example 9.1 – This example illustrates the calculation of lifetimes using the CEG shown in Figure 9.1. The relevant occurrences of fragments (the beginnings of their lifetimes) are indicated as dotted circles. Their age can be determined by following the ancestry edges until an occurrence with no descendant is found. In this example, there are 12 distinct fragments of which 3 live for 1 version, 1 lives for 2 versions, and 8 live for 3 versions. Consequently, the average lifetime is 2.4 versions. □

Change Consistency

Inconsistent changes to fragments of a clone class are regarded as a major threat related to code clones. To investigate the nature of changes, we have measured to which degree changes to code clones are inconsistent. Information about which clone classes have been changed consistently and inconsistently is included in the CEG. Based on this information, the occurrences of fragments contained in changed classes have been partitioned into two groups: Fragments belonging to an inconsistently changed clone class (*IF*) and fragments belonging to a consistently changed clone class (*CF*). Note, that the occurrence of a fragment is unique to a single version. If a fragment exists for n versions, the n occurrences of the fragment are assigned to different groups depending on

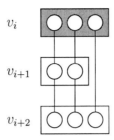

v_i

v_{i+1}

v_{i+2}

Figure 9.2 – Late propagation of an inconsistent change.

the clone class to which the respective occurrence belongs. This is required to recognize repeated changes to fragments.

When a clone class is inconsistently changed, it may happen that the change is made consistent at a later point in time. This situation is referred to as *late propagation*. A schematic example is shown in Figure 9.2, a concrete example taken from *Umbrello* is given in Figure 9.3 on the next page.

Example 9.2 – Figure 9.3 on the next page illustrates late propagation of an inconsistent change that we have found in UMBRELLO. The original source code of both fragments is given in (a). From this version to the next, the explicit iteration has been changed to a `foreach`-loop in both fragments (Figure (b) and (c)). The declaration of the variable `conc`, which is not required any longer, was, however, removed only from one of the fragments. This inconsistent change has been propagated to the other fragment about a month later, making the source code of both fragments be as shown in (c). □

Late propagation is important for analyzing the ratio of inconsistent changes, because an inconsistent change that is resolved by late propagation is, in fact, a consistent change. We measure how many inconsistent changes are made consistent by late propagation, also telling how many inconsistent changes remain unresolved. The set of fragments being part of late propagation is denoted as LP. Based on the sets of fragments CF, IF, and LP, we are now able to define the ratio of inconsistent changes. Let this be the *icratio*:

$$icratio = \frac{|IF| - |LP|}{|IF| - |LP| + |CF| + |LP|} = \frac{|IF| - |LP|}{|IF| + |CF|}$$

To compute the ratio between inconsistent and consistent changes, the size of the set IF is compared to the sum of all changes for each system ($|IF| + |CF|$). Fragments related to late propagation (LP) are, however, subtracted from IF and added to CF, because these are in fact consistent changes and choosing a larger interval between versions would make late propagation appear as consistent change in the first place.

Irregularities

So far, we have described how to investigate different characteristics of clone evolution abstracting from the individual versions of each system. However, we do not assume

```
1  findObjectsRelated(c,includes);
2  UMLPackage *conc;
3  for(UMLPackageListIt includesIt(includes);includesIt.hasNext();) {
4      UMLPackage* conc = includesIt.next();
5      QString headerName =
6          findFileName(conc, ".php");
```

(a) Original source code of both cloned fragments

```
1  findObjectsRelated(c,includes);
2  UMLPackage *conc;
3  foreach(UMLPackage* conc, includes) {
4
5      QString headerName =
6          findFileName(conc, ".php");
```

(b) Modified version of first fragment

```
1  findObjectsRelated(c,includes);
2
3  foreach(UMLPackage* conc, includes) {
4
5      QString headerName =
6          findFileName(conc, ".php");
```

(c) Modified version of second fragment

Figure 9.3 – Inconsistent change in UMBRELLO.

that clone evolution is a constant phenomenon having the same characteristics for every version of a system. Instead, we suppose that particular project phases—major refactorings for example—have a large impact on the characteristics of clone evolution. To test our assumption, we exemplary investigate change consistency of individual versions for some of our subject systems.

To investigate irregularities in clone evolution of individual systems, we have analyzed the number of consistent and inconsistent changes for each individual version. The number of consistently and inconsistently changed fragments can easily be extracted from the CEG. Analyzing these numbers, we are able to identify versions where particularly many cloned fragments are affected by changes. In addition to the number of consistent and inconsistent changes, the total number of fragments is calculated for each version to observe sudden increases or drops in the total number of cloned fragments. The results are combined in a single diagram to relate changes to increases or decreases in the number of fragments.

System	50 Tokens	100 Tokens
GIMP	-4.3	-31.4
HTTPD	-28.3	-47.6
NAUTILUS	9.9	-49.7
FILEZILLA	-2.8	-10.2
KMAIL	29.5	-0.5
UMBRELLO	-4.6	8.4
ANT	-9.7	-33.8
ARGOUML	-26.9	-42.6
JABREF	12.4	46.5
KV-KL	-83.2	5.2
ZY-ZG	-8.7	-12.3
ZY-ZP	0.2	-11.3

Table 9.2 – Evolution of the clone ratio ΔCR [%] between the very first and the very last version of each subject system.

9.2 Results

This section describes the results that were obtained from analyzing the CEGs extracted from the subject systems.

9.2.1 Clone Ratio

To analyze how the ratio of clones evolved over time, we compared the clone ratio of the very first version to the clone ratio of the very last version for each subject system. The difference ΔCR is expressed as percentage. For each system, ΔCR has been computed for both 50 and 100 tokens minimum length of clones. The values for ΔCR are given in Table 9.2.

Looking at the values for 50 tokens minimum length, we can see that the clone ratio increased for only four systems—NAUTILUS, KMAIL, JABREF, and ZY-ZP. The largest increase of 29.5% was observed for KMAIL. Contrary to our expectation, the clone ratio decreased for 8 out of 12 systems. The strongest decrease in an open-source system was observed for HTTPD where the clone ratio decreased by 28.3%. For the industrial systems, KV-KL experienced a significant decrease of 83.2% of the clone ratio due to a major restructuring. For the systems GIMP, FILEZILLA, UMBRELLO, and ZY-ZP, the clone ratio remained relatively stable as the decrease or increase was below 5% for each of these systems.

Using 100 tokens as minimum length changes the values notably. For NAUTILUS, KMAIL, and ZY-ZP, the increase of the clone ratio turns into a decrease when 100 tokens are used as minimum length. In contrast, the decrease turns into an increase for UMBRELLO, and KV-KL. In summary, the clone ratio increased for only three systems and decreased for 9 out of 12 systems.

System	# Versions	Mean Lifetime [#V.]		Median Lifetime [#V.]	
		50 Tokens	100 Tokens	50 Tokens	100 Tokens
GIMP	200	83.9	82.0	52	52
HTTPD	200	121.5	112.2	141	113
NAUTILUS	200	74.8	57.6	58	36
FILEZILLA	200	62.4	51.5	40	29
KMAIL	200	75.4	61.9	61	37
UMBRELLO	200	63.5	60.0	49	47
ANT	175	98.9	77.5	118	43
ARGOUML	200	39.1	39.6	27	25
JABREF	200	90.7	79.8	77	75
KV-KL	125	44.5	77.2	32	87
ZY-ZG	125	102.3	101.2	125	125
ZY-ZP	125	62.5	60.9	52	47

Table 9.3 – Average lifetime of clones.

We believe the significant difference between the results of both minimum lengths is due to the notable difference in the total number of clones. When 50 tokens are used, the number of cloned fragments is roughly six times as large as the number of fragments when using 100 tokens. When the total number of fragments is small, a change to a clone has a stronger impact compared to when the number of fragments is large.

9.2.2   Lifetime

To investigate how long clones exist in a system, we measured the lifetime for each individual fragment. We calculated the average lifetime of fragments for each system and minimum clone length separately. The average has been calculated using the arithmetic mean as well as the median. Table 9.3 provides the results of our analysis.

For clones that are at least 50 tokens long, fragments in HTTPD have the highest life expectancy of 121.5 versions on average. The shortest lifetime has been observed for ARGOUML where fragments exist for only 39.1 versions on average. As we have chosen an interval of one week between versions, fragments in HTTPD live for more than two years on average. Even in ARGOUML, fragments exist for roughly nine months on average. The values of the other systems fall in-between those of HTTPD and ARGOUML. The mean lifetime of cloned fragments across all systems is 76.6 versions corresponding to almost one and a half year.

These values have to be regarded as minimum values, because only a section of each system's history has been analyzed. For clones that already existed in the very first version and those that continue to exist beyond the last version, the actual lifetime is clipped, reducing its actual lifetime to the period of our analysis. Furthermore, we concentrated on type-1 clones in this study. A type-1 clone that disappears might still continue to exist as a non-identical clone, because changes are limited and retain the similarity. Considering all types of clones, the lifetime of many fragments is probably higher compared to considering only type-1 clones. In summary, the average lifetimes reported here are only a minimum bound.

Switching from 50 to 100 tokens minimum clone length, the average lifetime of cloned fragments decreases for all systems, except for ARGOUML and KV-KL where it increases. The difference between these two and the other systems is that they have a much higher clone ratio. The higher coverage of clones causes more changes to affect clones and, consequently, leads to more clone creation and clone removal. Thus, there is more fluctuation of clones in these systems resulting in a shorter life expectancy. When the minimum clone length is increased to 100 tokens, the drop in the clone ratio is larger compared to the other systems, making the remaining clones survive longer. For the other systems, longer clones have a shorter life expectancy. We assume this is caused by longer clones being more susceptible to change due to their size. In addition, the drop in the clone ratio between 50 and 100 tokens minimum length is much smaller in comparison to ARGOUML and KV-KL making the average lifetime decrease.

Looking at the median lifetimes, the values are smaller than the mean lifetimes for most systems. For HTTPD, ANT, KV-KL, and ZY-ZG, the median lifetime is higher than the mean lifetime for at least one of the two minimum lengths. The difference between the mean and the median lifetimes indicates that the distribution is not even. Consequently, we have analyzed the distribution of all lifetimes. The histograms for 50 and 100 tokens respectively are shown in Figure 9.4 on the next page. The histograms show for each possible lifetime, the percentage of fragments that exist for this number of versions. The data have been normalized to give every system an equal weight and prevent systems with many fragments from dominating.

A couple of values stand out in the histogram for 50 tokens minimum length, which is shown in Figure (a). First, it can be seen that most fragments (more than 8%) have a lifetime of 125 versions corresponding to the complete period of analysis for the three industrial systems. Similarly, 5.5% of the fragments survived 200 versions, which equals the analysis period for the majority of the other systems. Most of these fragments probably have an even higher lifetime because they might have existed before the start of analysis and continue to exist beyond the end of the analysis. Likewise, another 2.6% of all fragments exist for 175 versions. Most of these are contributed by ANT for which only 175 versions could be analyzed. Thus, these fragments might have been clipped similarly to those existing 125 and 200 versions.

The 6.6% of the fragments that existed for 33 versions are contributed by the industrial system KV-KL where a larger refactoring terminated the lifetime of many cloned fragments. Another thing to be noticed is that 4% of all fragments are volatile and exist for only one version. Observing the complete histogram, there is a general tendency towards shorter lifetimes. The biggest agglomeration of fragments is found for fragments existing for less than a year.

When 100 tokens are used as minimum length (shown in Figure (b)), the distribution changes only slightly. The most notable difference is that the percentage of fragments existing for 33 versions drops from 6.6% to 0.6%. This indicates, that the refactoring in KV-KL affected primarily fragments shorter than 100 tokens. The percentage of fragments living for 125 versions increases from 8.4% to 11.5%. This is primarily caused by KV-KL, where the average lifetime of fragments significantly higher for longer

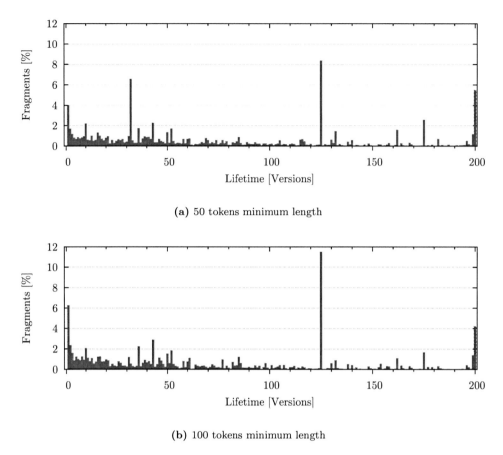

(a) 50 tokens minimum length

(b) 100 tokens minimum length

Figure 9.4 – Distribution of fragment lifetimes.

fragments as can be seen in Table 9.3 on page 146. For all other systems, the average lifetime is lower for longer fragments. Consequently, the percentage of fragments existing for 200 versions is reduced from 5.5% to 4.2% whereas the percentage of fragments existing for only one version increases from 4% to more than 6%. Accordingly, there is a general tendency towards shorter lifetimes for longer clones. This confirms that longer fragments have a shorter lifetime on average with KV-KL being an exception.

An interesting extension of this study would be analyzing the lifetime for cloned fragments of type 1, 2, and 3. Type-1 clones that disappear may, in fact, have changed their type and continue to exist as a type-2 or type-3 clone.

9.2.3 Change Consistency

Change consistency has been measured in terms of the *icratio*, which we defined to be the ratio between the number of fragments contained in clone classes marked as

System	50 Tokens	100 Tokens
GIMP	45.5	35.5
HTTPD	70.0	72.7
NAUTILUS	77.2	68.6
FILEZILLA	62.9	64.9
KMAIL	34.5	27.5
UMBRELLO	37.0	26.4
ANT	78.3	74.2
ARGOUML	69.4	69.6
JABREF	57.7	62.9
KV-KL	89.6	75.4
ZY-ZG	91.3	92.1
ZY-ZP	95.7	80.7

Table 9.4 – Ratio of inconsistent changes to clones (*icratio* [%]).

inconsistently changed and the number of all fragments. The results for 50 and 100 tokens minimum length are summarized in Table 9.4. Considering 50 tokens minimum length, the lowest *icratio* of 34.5% was recorded for KMAIL. Consequently, two thirds of all changes to clones in KMAIL are performed consistently. The highest ratios have been observed for the industrial systems, with 95.7% in ZY-ZP being the maximum ratio. For 9 out of 12 systems, inconsistent changes dominate as the *icratio* is above 50%.

When 100 tokens are used as minimum clone length, the values change slightly. For most systems, it can be observed that low *icratio*s decrease even more, whereas high *icratio*s increase further. For 100 tokens minimum length, UMBRELLO has the lowest *icratio* of 26.4% and ZY-ZG has the highest *icratio* of 92.1%.

Example 9.3 – Figure 9.5 on the next page shows an example of an inconsistent change that we have found in JABREF. The original source code of two identical fragments is shown in (a). Nevertheless, only one of the fragments is modified to remove a defect. The missing length check is added to one fragment (shown in (b)) but not propagated to the other fragment. □

9.2.4 Irregularities

This section presents our results obtained by analyzing the number of fragment affected by consistent and inconsistent changes to clones for individual versions. We present results only for a minimum clone length of 50 tokens, because using 100 tokens did not reveal any additional findings. Furthermore, we concentrate on subject systems with representative characteristics.

The clone evolution of ANT is shown in Figure 9.6 on page 151. Inconsistent changes happened regularly and dominate the consistent changes. This is also reflected by ANT's *icratio* of 78.3%, which is the highest among the open-source systems. In general, the distribution of changes to clones in ANT is equable. While many versions have none or only few changes to cloned fragments, versions where many cloned fragments are

```
1   String [] nameParts = author [1].split (" ");
2   int i = 0;
3
4   for(i=0;i<nameParts.length;i++) {
5       c = nameParts[i].charAt(0);
6   //    System.out.println [...]
7       sb.append(c + ".");
8
9   }
```

(a) Original source code of both cloned fragments

```
1   String [] nameParts = author [1].split (" ");
2   int i = 0;
3
4   for(i=0;i<nameParts.length;i++)
5       if (nameParts[i].length() > 0) {
6           c = nameParts[i].charAt(0);
7   //        System.out.println [...]
8           sb.append(c + ".");
9       }
10  }
```

(b) Inconsistently changed version of one fragment

Figure 9.5 – Inconsistent change in JABREF.

affected by changes occur regularly. The total number of cloned fragments decreased slightly. There is one outstanding drop in the number of fragments in version 44. Manual investigation revealed that this was caused by a reorganization of test cases.

For FILEZILLA (Figure 9.7 on the next page), there was a significant increase in the number of cloned fragments. Interestingly, the clone ratio still decreased, because FILEZILLA is the fastest-growing system among the subject systems and the increase in size was even larger than the increase in the number of cloned fragments. The steep increase in cloned fragments in version 4 was due to new files being added, making the system twice as large. The second largest increase in version 185 was also due to the addition of new files significantly increasing the source code size.

In comparison to ANT, changes to clones occur more frequent and in almost every version. We assume this is caused by an overall increased development activity in FILEZILLA. Analogously to ANT, inconsistent changes dominate as they occur more frequently than consistent changes to clones. The outstanding numbers of inconsistent changes in versions 86 and 192 were due to files with similar functionality being changed. This can be regarded as a potential threat and the inconsistencies should be investigated in detail to identify defects that might have been introduced.

Contrary to the previous systems, clones in HTTPD appear to be much more stable, because they are changed less frequently. This can be seen in Figure 9.8 on page 152. The number of cloned fragments remained almost at the same level until version 182. The

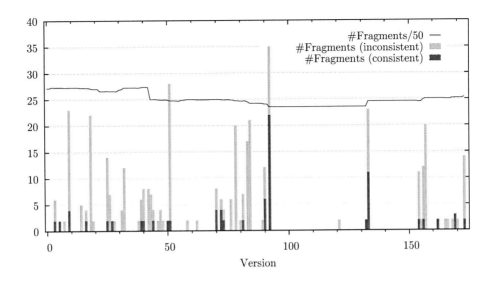

Figure 9.6 – Clone evolution in ANT.

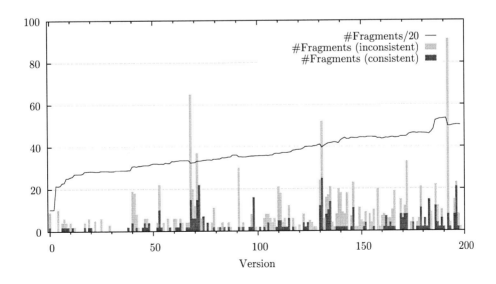

Figure 9.7 – Clone evolution in FILEZILLA.

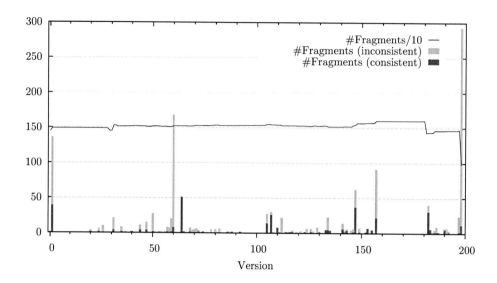

Figure 9.8 – Clone evolution in HTTPD.

significant decrease in fragments from version 182 to the end was caused by files being deleted containing functionality very similar to existing files. As the same functionality had been developed more or less in parallel, this caused a lot of clones being removed by the deletion of one branch. Different changes within those branches also caused the inconsistent changes in version 60.

Figure 9.9 on the next page shows clone evolution in GIMP. A steady increase in the number of cloned fragments can be observed. Nevertheless, the increase in size was even larger and, therefore, the clone ratio decreased—similarly to FILEZILLA. There is an outstanding cluster of consistent as well as inconsistent changes between versions 40 and 50. Inspecting the changes and commit messages from the source repository revealed that a major refactoring happened during this time. Again, the inconsistent changes may be indicators for potential defects and should be observed in detail.

9.3 Discussion

9.3.1 Clone Ratio

The results show that the clone ratio decreased for the majority of our subject systems. Using 50 tokens minimum length, the clone ratio decreased for 6 out of 9 systems. When 100 tokens are used as minimum length, the ratio decreased for 9 out of 12 subject systems. Unfortunately, our results do neither support those of Lagüe and colleagues [123] as well as Livieri and colleagues [134], who found that the clone ratio is stable, nor those of Li and colleagues [130] who found that the clone ratio is steadily increasing. Instead, our results show that a decreasing clone ratio can be observed for

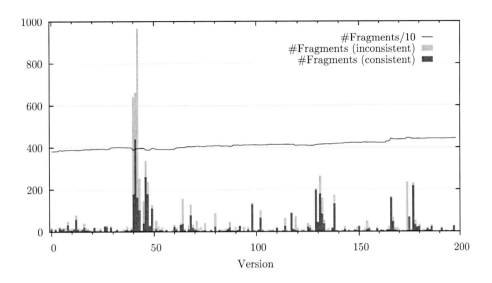

Figure 9.9 – Clone evolution in GIMP.

many systems. However, our results do not falsify those of previous works as these have analyzed different systems and the clone ratio evolution has shown to be very different for individual systems.

We have found that the choice of clone detection parameters has a strong impact on the results. The difference between using 50 tokens and using 100 tokens as minimum clone length is notable and may even turn an increase into a decrease and vice versa. Although the clone ratio decreased in the majority of systems indicating that cloning does not always have to get worse by default, it is hard to make general conclusions due to the diverse results. Furthermore, the results do not indicate a systematic relationship between the programming language used and an increasing or decreasing clone ratio. Likewise, there seems to be no notable difference between open-source and industrial projects. In summary, we conclude that cloning does not naturally have to get worse and may even be reduced as a side effect of other maintenance activities. The evolution of the clone ratio is, however, quite different for individual systems.

9.3.2 Lifetime

The duration that clones exist in a system is important for software maintenance, because volatile clones may require a different form of management compared to long-lived clones. We have analyzed the lifetime of individual cloned fragments. For all systems, the average lifetime of clones is more than half a year. There is, however, a notable difference between systems. While fragments in HTTPD live for more than two years on average, fragments in ARGOUML live for roughly half a year on average.

Future work could be directed at investigating how this relates to the frequency and extent of changes within these systems.

Increasing the minimum length that clones need to have, we can observe that the lifetime of fragments decreases. Consequently, longer fragments live shorter than short fragments. We assume this is due to their increased susceptibility to being changed. We were not able to identify a relation between the programming language used and the average lifetime of fragments. Furthermore, there is no obvious difference between open-source and industrial projects.

The lifetime of cloned fragments has been measured in previous studies [109, 20]. Kim and her colleagues [109] concluded that many cloned fragments are volatile—that is, they disappear shortly after their introduction. Although we found the average lifetime of fragments to be more than half a year for all systems, our analysis of the distribution of lifetimes has shown that there is a clear tendency towards shorter lifetimes. It is, however, debatable where volatility of fragments starts. Hence, our results do not contradict those of Kim and her colleagues. Nevertheless, our findings emphasize that there is a large number of fragments that exist for a long time. Bettenburg and his colleagues [20] have found that clones live for more than half a year on average and, thus, confirm our findings.

We conclude that there is a large number of fragments that exist for only a short time, but also a notable number of fragments that are long-lived. The average lifetime of fragments is above six months. The values are likely to depend on the individual system, its maturity and the maintenance process employed.

9.3.3 Change Consistency

Inconsistent changes are a major threat emerging from the presence of clones. We have analyzed the consistency of changes in the subject systems to investigate how frequently these potentially dangerous situations arise. Our results show that the question whether consistent or inconsistent changes are more frequent can be answered only for individual systems as no general tendency could be observed. Choosing a larger minimum length for clones accentuates the *icratio*—that is, low *icratios* decrease while high *icratios* increase.

For the open-source systems, we were not able to observe a tendency towards certain programming languages facilitating inconsistent changes. Nevertheless, the notably higher *icratios* for the industrial projects written in COBOL suggest, that either COBOL or the data processing domain exacerbate inconsistent changes. For example, COBOL requires more unavoidable and structurally similar parts which, however, are unrelated on a conceptual level. A change to one of these fragments does less often require a change to the other fragments compared to systems written in other programming languages. This results in a much higher number of inconsistent changes— many of which may, however, not be harmful.

Previous studies [8, 121, 178] have analyzed the consistency of changes to clones as well. Aversano, Thummalapenta and their colleagues [8, 178] have found that many clone classes are changed consistently. For ARGOUML they found that more than 50% of changes to clones are consistent changes including late propagation. In contrast, we have found an *icratio* of almost 70% for ARGOUML. The discrepancy may be caused by different techniques and procedures employed. For example, Aversano and colleagues ignored all changes to clone classes where all fragments have been modified in course of the same commit. Furthermore, they excluded all clone classes whose fragments are contained in the same source file.

Krinke [121] has analyzed the consistency of changes to clones as well. Analyzing five subject systems, he found that consistent and inconsistent changes to clones occur with roughly the same frequency. Unfortunately, we cannot confirm these findings based on our results. Again, different techniques and methods used for data collection may explain the discrepancy. According to the significantly different *icratio*s of our subject systems, we conclude that the occurrence of inconsistent changes strongly depends on the individual project and its organization. In general, we cannot conclude that consistent or inconsistent changes are more frequent.

9.3.4   Irregularities

To identify and analyze irregularities in clone evolution, we have investigated the number of cloned fragments that are affected by consistent and by inconsistent changes for each version of our subject systems. In addition, we investigated the total number of cloned fragments for each version. Although we have identified clusters of many changes to clones, there are phases where clones are hardly ever affected by change. In summary, changes to clones do not occur with a constant frequency, but follow an irregular pattern defined by various characteristics of the respective projects.

For all systems, a general observation is that inconsistent changes also happen in closely related files being part of the same subsystem or providing similar functionality. Furthermore, sudden increases or decreases in the number of cloned fragments do not always appear together with a noticeable number of changes. Instead, addition and deletion of complete files can significantly alter the number of clones without individual clones being changed.

On the one hand, irregularities in clone evolution are suited to identify special phases of a project—for example, major restructurings. On the other hand, the irregularities show that even inside a single project, clone evolution is far from having constant characteristics. This applies to all clones as we have found peculiarities independent from the minimum clone length we used. We can conclude that clone evolution can hardly be generalized and has to be investigated for individual systems taking into account special characteristics and constraints of these systems.

9.4   Threats to Validity

This section presents potential threats to the general validity of our results.

Subject systems. Only a section of each system's history has been analyzed. Choosing another section or a different version interval might affect the results. To mitigate this threat and weaken the impact of major restructurings, we have analyzed almost four years of each project's history. We furthermore assumed that all systems were in a comparable state of development. Nevertheless, there may be differences in clone evolution between long-lived systems like HTTPD and newer ones like FILEZILLA.

Clone detection. Token-based clone detection is known to lack precision compared to other approaches. The clone detection parameters were set very restrictive to detect only type-1 clones with identical token sequences to increase precision. Including type-2 and type-3 clones and different filter criteria to discard irrelevant clones might influence the results.

Counting fragments. In contrast to previous studies, the number of cloned fragments instead of cloned source lines has been used to measure the clone ratio. Overlapping fragments and fragments being of different size influences the comparability of the results. To asses the potential threat, we have analyzed the impact of using fragments instead of cloned source lines when calculating the clone ratio for the industrial systems and found that results are comparable.

Diff algorithm. Changes to clones are calculated based on information from the DIFF tool and its underlying algorithm. Therefore, the creation of the CEG depends on DIFF's capabilities and way to handle ambiguity. Nevertheless, DIFF could be replaced by any other method that provides change information, because our approach itself is independent from the source of this information.

9.5 Summary

This chapter presented an extensive study on the diversity of clone evolution. We have analyzed the history of nine open-source systems and three industrial systems which are, however, developed by the same company. The relevant data have been extracted in form of a CEG using our incremental algorithm and analyzed subsequently.

We have found that the ratio of clones decreased over time in many systems and, thus, cloning does not naturally have to get worse. Consequently, the answer to Question 6 on page 42 is that the evolution of the clone ratio depends on the respective systems and there is no general increase or decrease across all systems. Although the lifetime of fragments differed between the systems, cloned fragments existed on average more than a year. Whether consistent or inconsistent changes are more frequent strongly depends on the system and its characteristics. Investigating the increase or decrease in the number of cloned fragments together with the distribution of changes to clones revealed irregularities in clone evolution. These irregularities were related to system-dependent activities and might indicate potential sources of defects. Our observations are summarized in Table 9.5 on the next page.

The observations suggest that the minimum clone length and programming language have only a minor impact on the results. On the one hand, the results indicate that Java and COBOL systems seem to be more susceptible to inconsistent changes. On the other hand, this might be due to the kinds of applications that we have studied. A larger number of subject systems would be required to verify this using statistical tests. In general, the peculiarity of clone evolution was significantly different for each system. Consequently, the answer to Question 10 on page 52 is that clone evolution is very diverse. We conclude that clone evolution has to be investigated separately for each

Observations	50 Tokens				100 Tokens			
	Java	C	C++	COBOL	Java	C	C++	COBOL
Increased clone ratio	1	1	1	1	1	0	1	1
Decreased clone ratio	**2**	**2**	**2**	**2**	**2**	**3**	**2**	**2**
Lifetime >= 1 year	**2**	**3**	1	**2**	1	**2**	0	**2**
Lifetime < 1 year	1	0	**2**	1	**2**	1	**3**	1
More inconsistent changes	**3**	**2**	1	**3**	**3**	**2**	1	**3**
More consistent changes	0	1	**2**	0	0	1	**2**	0

Table 9.5 – Observations by programming language and minimum clone length.

system according to the system's characteristics. Furthermore, the consequence of not being able to generalize clone evolution is that there is no general solution or technique to counter the negative effects and manage clones. Instead, a sophisticated technique to track clones and changes to them is needed which provides relevant information to decide how individual clones are managed. Our Clone Evolution Graph and its extraction algorithm are such a technique.

Chapter 10

Changes to Clones

To counter the negative effects of cloning, a variety of clone detection techniques and tools have evolved to identify duplicated source code in a system. In addition, various tools have been created to assist developers in managing clones. These include refactoring support [16, 78], automated change propagation [41, 182], and change monitoring to prevent unintentional inconsistencies [151].

While there certainly exist clones that are true threats to software maintenance, recent research [103, 109] casts some doubt on the harmfulness of clones in general and lists numerous situations in which clones are a reasonable design decision. From the clone management perspective, it is desirable to detect and manage only the harmful clones, because managing clones that have no negative effects only creates additional effort.

Unfortunately, state-of-the-art clone tools detect and classify clones based only on similar structures in the source code or one of its various representations. When it comes to clone-related problems, however, the most important characteristic of a clone is its change behavior and not its structure. A clone causes additional change effort[1] only if it changes, and unintentional inconsistencies can arise. If, on the other hand, a clone never changes, there is no additional change effort and there is no risk of overlooking propagation of a change. *Our hypothesis is that many clones detected by state-of-the-art tools are "structurally interesting" but irrelevant to software maintenance because they never change during their lifetime.*

Up-to-date clone detectors can efficiently process and detect clones in huge amounts of source code, consequently delivering huge numbers of clones. The real problem, however, is clone assessment. Deciding how to proceed can be very costly even for individual clones as we have experienced with clones in our own code [74]. Hence, having many irrelevant clones in the detection results creates a significant overhead for assessing and managing clones that do not affect maintenance because they never change.

---

[1]With *change effort* we refer to the act of changing itself. This excludes, for example, effort required for reading source code.

To gain a better understanding of clones actual potential for affecting maintenance, we conducted an extensive study on clone evolution in different systems and performed a detailed tracking to detect when and how clones had changed. For this study, we concentrated on two prominent clone-related problems—the additional change effort caused by clones and the risk of unintentional inconsistent changes. Therefore, the case study presented in this chapter provides an answer to Question 11 on page 52 and Question 12 on page 52.

10.1   Setup

This section describes the setup of our case study that we used to collect the data we need to study these research questions. The setup includes the subject systems, parameters for our clone detection tool, and an overview of our procedure to collect relevant data.

10.1.1   Subject Systems

We used the following three subject systems for our case study:

- CLONES. Our first subject system is our token-based clone detection tool— CLONES—itself. CLONES is written in Ada and part of the Bauhaus project.[2] We included this system, because our knowledge of the code allows us to much better assess clones and changes to clones in the code.

- HTTPD. The second system is the webserver HTTPD.[3] HTTPD is part of the Apache project and written in C.

- JABREF. Our final subject system is JABREF.[4] JABREF is a bibliography manager written in Java.

We chose these systems, because they have been used in some previous studies including our study on the diversity of clone evolution presented in Chapter 9. All systems are mature and have a reasonably long history. Each system has had a multitude of developers contributing and is of reasonable size. This mitigates the threat that a system is more or less maintained by a single developer who is an expert regarding every part of the system. For CLONES and JABREF, 15 distinct developers contributed changes relevant to our study. For HTTPD, 45 developers were involved in maintenance.

When analyzing clone evolution based on multiple versions of a system's source code, the interval between each pair of consecutive versions is of great importance. Increasing the interval between versions leads to multiple changes being merged into a single change and consequently results in loss of detail. To capture data with the highest degree of detail that is available, we consider each individual commit to the system's repository as a version. We excluded commits that did not change any source files.

---

[2]http://www.bauhaus-stuttgart.de
[3]http://httpd.apache.org
[4]http://jabref.sourceforge.net

			Revision		∼KLOC	
System	Lang.	#Versions	First	Last	First	Last
CLONES	Ada	820	15271	28900	5	35
HTTPD	C	2186	208366	894526	187	218
JABREF	Java	906	664	3150	52	127

Table 10.1 – Subject systems used in our study.

In addition to the interval between consecutive versions, we require a first and a last version to frame the period of the system's lifetime that we are analyzing. The number of versions that we can analyze is limited by our hardware. We chose to analyze all projects over the period of five years, starting from the very first version in 2005 to the very last version in 2009. Although more versions could have been analyzed for smaller projects, we chose the same scope for all subject systems to make the results comparable. Table 10.1 summarizes our subject systems and gives details of the versions we have analyzed.

10.1.2 Clone Detection Parameters

This section describes the parameters that we used to extract the relevant clone evolution data.

Exclusion of header files. For this study, we were interested only in clones and changes that affect the systems' logic. We excluded all header files (*.h) from HTTPD and all Ada specification files (*.ads) from CLONES.

Exclusion of generated code. Generated code is not maintained by hand and thus, most problems caused by clones do not apply to generated code. Thus, consistent and inconsistent changes to automatically generated files are not relevant to our study. We therefore exclude all generated files from our analysis. For CLONES, all generated files are a kept in a single directory which we excluded. We identified generated files within the other systems by searching directory names, file names, and comments inside a file for indications.

Method Separation. Due to a token-based clone detector's missing knowledge about syntactic structures, clones may embrace more than a single method or function in the source code, that is, clones may start in one method and continue into the next method. To eliminate these artifacts, we preprocess the token sequence of each file before clone detection. We use regular expressions to identify the boundaries of methods and functions and insert unique sentinel tokens that can never be part of a clone. This procedure ensures that clones do not cross method boundaries. For HTTPD, we used a heuristic to identify the boundaries in the presence of preprocessor directives.

Token Exclusion. Another source of less relevant clones are reoccurring patterns imposed by the programming language. Like method separation, this step preprocesses each file's token sequence before clones are detected. This step excludes all `include`-directives in the C code, `import`-statements in the Java code, and `with`-statements in

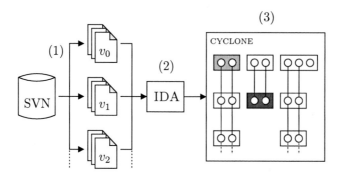

Figure 10.1 – Our study procedure.

the Ada code. It also removes all array initializations (repetitive sequences of identifiers and commas).

Clone types. This parameter determines which types of clones are detected and included in the clone evolution model. In this study, we consider two possible settings for this parameter. The first setting detects only type-1 clones. The second setting detects clones of type 1, 2, and 3. We deliberately analyzed the systems using both settings to evaluate their impact on the results.

Minimum clone length. This value determines how many tokens a clone needs to have to be considered as relevant. This value is of major importance since it influences the results significantly. Choosing a smaller value increases the recall because more clones are found that would not be found otherwise. Choosing a larger value increases the precision because fewer shorter clones are detected that just happen to be similar due to common programming patterns. We decided to use three distinct values. This allows us to compare the impact of the minimum length on the results. The values we chose are 30, 50, and 100 tokens.

10.1.3 Study Procedure

This section describes the overall procedure we used during our analysis. The process is illustrated in Figure 10.1.

(1) We extracted the relevant versions of each subject system from its SUBVERSION repository and stored them locally. This step is necessary since fast access to the source code—for detection and analysis—is important. It allows us to repeatedly access the source code without the overhead of accessing a distant repository. Note that we store only changed source code for each version, keeping the space requirements low. This step had to be done only once for each system, whereas every following step had to be done for each combination of parameters.

(2) We used our incremental detection algorithm (*IDA*) to extract the clone evolution data.

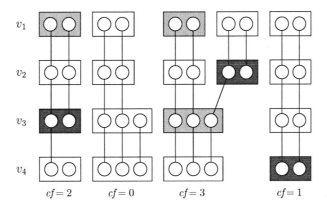

Figure 10.2 – Example of a Clone Evolution Graph.

(3) We used our tool CYCLONE to analyze and visualize the evolution data. This includes creation of genealogies, calculation of change frequencies, and support for manual inspection of clones and changes to clones.

10.2 Results

This section describes how we collected relevant data and presents the results. Before being able to estimate the additional change effort and the threat of new defects introduced by inconsistent changes, the clone information had to be extracted from the history of the subject systems.

Our first objective was a quantification of the clones and changes found in the system. For each subject system and each possible combination of clone type and minimum length, we calculated the total number of clone classes aggregated over all versions, the number of genealogies that were obtained from linking the clone classes, and the number of situations in which a clone class was changed. Consider our example of an evolution graph in Figure 10.2. That graph contains 18 clone classes which are grouped into four distinct genealogies based on the ancestry of their fragments. There are six situations in which clone classes have been changed, indicated by the colored clone classes.

We have analyzed the evolution of real clones in our subject systems. The quantities are given in Table 10.2 on the next page. Not surprisingly, increasing the minimum clone length reduces the number of detected clones for each system. When searching for all types of clones, more clones are detected compared to only looking for type-1 clones. For every system, the number of genealogies is proportional to the number of detected clones. Nevertheless, the number of clone classes for each genealogy differs between the systems. In CLONES, each genealogy contains roughly 100 clone classes, in HTTPD 1000 clone classes, and in JABREF 200 clone classes. Although we have analyzed only twice as many versions of HTTPD than the other systems, the number of clone classes per genealogy is up to ten times higher in HTTPD. This may be due to clones in HTTPD changing less frequently compared to the other two systems. If clones change

System	Type	Min.	#Clone Classes	#Genealogies	Changes
CLONES	1	30	101,807	876	736
	1	50	32,131	317	304
	1	100	9,315	86	90
	1–3	30	109,714	1,027	923
	1–3	50	49,888	523	544
	1–3	100	19,708	189	238
HTTPD	1	30	1,723,091	1,532	678
	1	50	743,762	742	388
	1	100	198,295	245	168
	1–3	30	2,163,465	1,902	990
	1–3	50	1,211,477	1,145	717
	1–3	100	433,733	461	369
JABREF	1	30	281,957	927	548
	1	50	98,493	416	244
	1	100	26,299	132	72
	1–3	30	376,383	1,220	754
	1–3	50	196,489	731	466
	1–3	100	60,692	269	177

Table 10.2 – Detected clones and changes. Clones classes and changes are accumulated for all versions.

less frequently, genealogies are more stable, that is, new genealogies appear only rarely and existing genealogies disappear only rarely. Consequently, genealogies contain more clone classes due to their longer life expectancy. This is supported by the number of changes displayed in the last column of Table 10.2. The number of situations in which clones were changed is not much higher than for the other systems—although we have analyzed more than twice as many versions for HTTPD and the number of detected clone classes is significantly higher.

10.2.1 Change Effort

We now use the information about clone genealogies and changes to clones to answer Question 11 on page 52 and estimate the additional change effort caused by clones in each system. We assume that clones may cause additional change effort only when they are modified. Clones that are never changed can never be responsible for increased change effort. Note that—in this study—we refer to the act of changing the source code and exclude the effort to understand or test the code. As code understanding causes most of the maintenance effort, future work should investigate how code clones affect the effort for program understanding.

To analyze how often clones are changed during their lifetime, we counted the number of changes for each genealogy. Let the *change frequency (cf)* of a genealogy be the number of the genealogy's clone classes marked as changed. Change frequencies are

System	Type	Min.	#Geneal.	Change frequency														
				0	[%]	1	[%]	2	[%]	3	[%]	4	[%]	5	[%]	>5	[%]
CLONES	1	30	876	385	43.9	356	40.6	84	9.6	30	3.4	7	0.8	8	0.9	6	0.7
	1	50	317	109	34.4	154	48.6	34	10.7	15	4.7	1	0.3	1	0.3	3	0.9
	1	100	86	24	27.9	46	53.5	10	11.6	4	4.7	–	–	1	1.2	1	1.2
	1–3	30	1,027	434	42.3	429	41.8	89	8.69	40	3.9	12	1.2	12	1.2	11	1.1
	1–3	50	523	179	34.2	247	47.2	51	9.8	26	5.0	7	1.3	5	1.0	8	1.5
	1–3	100	189	53	28.0	90	47.6	22	11.6	12	6.3	4	2.1	3	1.6	5	2.6
HTTPD	1	30	1,532	961	62.7	497	32.4	54	3.5	14	0.9	4	0.3	1	0.1	1	0.1
	1	50	742	421	56.7	275	37.1	33	4.4	8	1.1	3	0.4	1	0.1	1	0.1
	1	100	245	109	44.5	116	47.3	12	4.9	5	2.0	2	0.8	1	0.4	–	–
	1–3	30	1,902	1,134	59.6	634	33.3	82	4.3	35	1.8	8	0.4	4	0.2	5	0.3
	1–3	50	1,145	609	53.2	430	37.6	59	5.2	33	2.9	6	0.5	3	0.3	5	0.4
	1–3	100	461	196	42.5	205	44.5	34	7.4	17	3.7	4	0.9	2	0.4	3	0.7
JABREF	1	30	927	515	55.6	321	34.6	63	6.8	16	1.7	10	1.1	1	0.1	1	0.1
	1	50	416	221	53.1	160	38.5	25	6.0	6	1.4	4	1.0	–	–	–	–
	1	100	132	72	54.5	51	38.6	7	5.3	1	0.8	1	0.8	–	–	–	–
	1–3	30	1,220	675	55.3	410	33.6	90	7.4	27	2.2	13	1.1	4	0.3	1	0.1
	1–3	50	731	386	52.8	264	36.1	56	7.7	13	1.8	9	1.2	3	0.4	–	–
	1–3	100	269	147	54.6	87	32.3	25	9.3	3	1.1	4	1.5	3	1.1	–	–
CLONES	*	*	–	–	35.1	–	46.6	–	10.3	–	4.7	–	1.0	–	1.0	–	1.3
HTTPD	*	*	–	–	53.2	–	38.7	–	5.0	–	2.1	–	0.6	–	0.3	–	0.3
JABREF	*	*	–	–	54.3	–	35.6	–	7.1	–	1.5	–	1.1	–	0.3	–	0.0
*	1	*	–	–	48.1	–	41.2	–	7.0	–	2.3	–	0.6	–	0.3	–	0.3
*	1–3	*	–	–	46.9	–	39.3	–	7.9	–	3.2	–	1.1	–	0.7	–	0.7
*	*	30	–	–	53.2	–	36.1	–	6.7	–	2.3	–	0.8	–	0.5	–	0.4
*	*	50	–	–	47.4	–	40.9	–	7.3	–	2.8	–	0.8	–	0.4	–	0.5
*	*	100	–	–	42.0	–	44.0	–	8.4	–	3.1	–	1.0	–	0.8	–	0.8
*	*	*	–	–	47.5	–	40.3	–	7.5	–	2.7	–	0.9	–	0.5	–	0.5

Table 10.3 – Change frequency of clone genealogies.

given for the genealogies shown in Figure 10.2 on page 163. The number of genealogies and its percentage compared to all genealogies is shown in Table 10.3 for each change frequency. The numbers of genealogies with a change frequency higher than 5 have been combined due to space limitations. We provide averages at the bottom of the table. The * represents the combination of all values.

Never changed. We first look at the clones that never changed. The column labeled "0" shows how many genealogies were never affected by change during their lifetime. The next column to the right gives the percentage when compared to the number of all genealogies. The surprising result is that for HTTPD and JABREF, more than half of the clone genealogies are never changed. These numbers tell us that roughly half of the clones can—under no circumstances—be made responsible for increased change effort. For CLONES, 35.1% of the genealogies are never changed. This may be due to the high number of changes—considering CLONES' size and the number of versions analyzed— compared to the other systems. Taking the arithmetic mean for all three systems with each having equal weight, 47.5% of all genealogies are never changed.

The numbers are almost the same, independent of whether we consider only type-1 clones or clones of all types. Increasing the minimum length of clones reduces the percentage of genealogies that are never changed. We think this is due to longer clones being more susceptible to change. When the smaller clones are not considered, the remaining longer ones are more likely to be affected by changes.

Changed once. Apart from the genealogies that never changed, the genealogies that changed only once are also of interest to us. During the lifetime of these genealogies, there has been a single change applied to one clone class of the genealogy. Assuming that removing a clone requires changing it at least once, genealogies that were changed only once did not increase the change effort compared to when the clone would have been removed. It is, however, debatable, whether removing a clone or performing an arbitrary change to it requires more effort. The answer may also depend on the type of clone detection used. For example, clones detected by a syntax-aware technique like NICAD [160] may be easier to remove.

In CLONES 46.6%, in HTTPD 38.7%, and in JABREF 35.6% of the genealogies were changed exactly once. For CLONES the number of genealogies changed once is higher than the number of genealogies that never changed. For the other two systems, more genealogies were never changed than changed once. The overall average of genealogies that changed exactly once is 40.3%, being almost as high as the percentage of clones that never changed.

The type of clones has only a minor impact on the results. When considering only type-1 clones, 41.2% of the genealogies were changed exactly once. Considering all types of clones, 39.3% of genealogies were changed once. Increasing the minimum length of clones also increases the percentage of genealogies changed once. Interestingly, this is the inverse compared to the genealogies that never change, where the percentage of genealogies decreases as the minimum length is increased.

Changed more than once. The remaining category are clone genealogies that were changed more than once. Table 10.3 on the previous page lists the number of genealogies for change frequencies from 2 to 5 and the aggregated number of genealogies that changed more than five times. In general, the number of genealogies decreases as the change frequency increases. While there are still some genealogies that changed twice (7.5%) or three times (2.7%), higher change frequencies are only scattered. Clone genealogies that change multiple times are likely to increase the change effort and could thus be regarded as harmful clones. These clones should be inspected and removed where possible.

When considering clones of all types, the percentage of genealogies that are changed more than once increases compared to considering only clones of type 1. Increasing the minimum length of clones also increases the number of genealogies that are changed more than once.

In general, switching from type-1 clones to clones of all types decreases the percentage of genealogies that were never changed or changed only once and increases the percentage of genealogies that were changed more than once. Increasing the minimum length of clones decreases the percentage of genealogies that are never changed while increasing the percentage of all genealogies that changed at least once. We believe that this is caused by the increased likelihood of larger clones being affected by change. Excluding clones of shorter length—most of which are not changed—leaves only the longer clones that are more susceptible to change due to their increased length.

10.2.2 Unintentional Inconsistencies

Apart from increasing the change effort, clones are also said to facilitate problems caused by unintentional inconsistent changes. To explore this assumption and to answer Question 12 on page 52, we analyzed the changes to clones in detail. Unfortunately, manual assessment requires significant effort and always involves the threat of bias. Experience shows that assessing the impact of changes to code we are not familiar with can be difficult or impossible for the majority of changes. To ensure familiarity with the code and its history, we restricted this part of our study to the system CLONES. Consequently, we are in a much better position to judge the changes and to explain our findings than if we were analyzing an unfamiliar system. The disadvantage of studying CLONES is that some of its developers were aware of clone-related problems (see our threats to validity in Section 10.3).

In this part of the study, we used only a single parameter setting to keep the assessment effort manageable. We chose to look at changes to type-1 clones only, because having identical fragments before the change makes the evaluation of the change itself much easier. For the minimum clone length, we chose 50 tokens. This setting provided us with a total number of 304 changes to clone classes. To answer Question 12 on page 52, every change was analyzed to decide whether it contains an unintentional inconsistency—that is, a missing propagation of the change. We further assign each unwanted inconsistency one of two severity levels:

- **Low**: The change *should be consistent*. It does not cause the program to crash or produce wrong results, but may complicate future maintenance and facilitate further inconsistencies.

- **High**: The change *must be consistent*. The inconsistency may cause the program to crash or produce wrong results.

The following paragraphs summarize the kinds of changes that we have encountered.

Consistent changes. Our objective is to identify unintentional inconsistent changes within the set of all changes. Consequently, we first removed all consistent changes— that is, changes where exactly the same modifications have been done to each fragment of the clone class. In total, 173 (56.9%) of the changes were consistent. The remaining 131 inconsistent changes were inspected manually.

Semantics-preserving. Inconsistent changes are detected based on the changes to the token sequences of the respective fragments. However, not every change to the token sequence changes the semantics of the program. For example, the rewriting of the parameter list as shown in Figure 10.3 on the next page does not change the semantics (in is the default mode for parameters in Ada), but may still be responsible for an inconsistent change. If semantics-preserving changes are unwanted inconsistencies, their severity can only be low.

We manually checked each inconsistent change whether it altered the semantics of the program or not. We found that almost half (51 out of 131) of the inconsistent changes did not change the semantics of the program. Many of the inconsistencies resulted from unused variable declarations or unnecessary uses of fully qualified names being removed.

```
1  function Is_Right_Extensible          1  function Is_Right_Extensible
2    (A, B  :  Token_Table_Index;        2    (A   : in Token_Table_Index;
3    Len    :  Natural)                   3    B   : in Token_Table_Index;
4    return Boolean                       4    Len : in Natural)
5  is                                     5    return Boolean
6    ...                                  6  is
7                                         7    ...
```

         (a) Version i (b) Version $i+1$

Figure 10.3 – Semantics-preserving change. The more elaborate notation of parameters in (b) has the same semantics as the more compact notation in (a) (**in** is the default mode for parameters in Ada).

Total	304	100.0%
Consistent	173	56.9%
Inconsistent	131	43.1%
Semantics-preserving	51	16.8%
Unintentionally Inconsistent	45	14.8%
Low severity	36	11.8%
High severity	9	3.0%

Table 10.4 – Classification of changes in CLONES.

Unwanted Inconsistencies. The final and most important assessment for each change is whether it features a missing change propagation and if it does, whether the severity is low or high.

Example 10.1 – An example of an inconsistency with high severity is shown in Figure 10.4 on the next page. The missing check to prevent `Ceiling_Prime` being called with 0 (the type `Positive` expects numbers greater than 0) is inserted in only one of the fragments making this an incomplete bug removal. The change has high severity, because the change *must be* propagated to all fragments. Unless the missing check is inserted in all fragments, the program may crash when encountering empty token sequences. □

Analyzing the 131 inconsistent changes, we found that 45 of them were unintentionally inconsistent. This amounts to 14.8% of the total number of changes to clones. Four out of five problematic changes had low severity—for example changes to debugging code. Of all 36 changes classified as low, 20 are also semantics-preserving. In total, only 9 inconsistencies with high severity were found. This amounts to 3% of all changes. Table 10.4 summarizes our results regarding the classification of changes. Note that some changes belong to multiple categories.

```
 1    function Ceiling_Prime
 2      (Number : in Positive)
 3        return Positive
 4    is
 5      ...
 6
 7
 8    procedure Initialize
 9    is
10        Table_Size : Natural := Natural
11          (Float (Number_Of_Tokens) * 2.4);
12    begin
13        if Table_Size > 0 then
14            Table_Size :=
15                Ceiling_Prime (Table_Size);
16            ...
17    end Initialize;
```

Figure 10.4 – Unintentional inconsistency with high severity. The figure shows the original source code of both cloned fragments. However, line 13 is added to only one of the fragments.

10.3 Threats to Validity

There are certain threats to the general validity of our case study's results. This section presents the threats we have identified.

Clone detection parameters. As with most studies on clones, the parameters used for detecting clones have a major impact on the results. We deliberately used different combinations of parameters to analyze their impact. This included the type of clones that were detected and the minimum length that clones were required to have. We presented detailed results in Table 10.3 on page 165 and described the impact of the parameters.

Precision. The precision of a clone detection tool influences the validity of the results. Although token-based clone detection has—in general—lower precision than approaches using abstract syntax trees or graphs, we carefully selected our parameters to exclude irrelevant clones from the results. Furthermore, we used a novel approach that requires clones to have identical parts of sufficient length to detect type-2 and type-3 clones—a frequent source of irrelevant clones using traditional approaches. We manually inspected a sample of clones to ensure that detected clones are relevant. The only clones we found to be less relevant are those in handling of command line parameters.

Study period. The part of a system's history that we used for our study also has an impact on the result. For each of the subject systems, we have analyzed five years of maintenance history to reduce the impact of special phases (e.g., major refactorings). Using only a part of a system's history also crops genealogies, that is, genealogies that might have existed before the beginning of the study period and might exist beyond the end of the study period. When considering only genealogies that appear after the first version and disappear before the last version of the study period, the majority of genealogies have a change frequency of 1 (instead of 0). Nevertheless, the percentage of genealogies changed more than once remains almost the same. Consequently, the ratio between genealogies changed never or once and genealogies changed more than once remains also roughly the same.

Mapping. The mapping between fragments of consecutive versions is another potential threat to validity. As genealogies are created based on the mapping of fragments, a missing connection will break genealogies apart, leaving two genealogies each of which has a change frequency equal or less to the combined genealogy. The reason for an incomplete mapping can be the algorithm to calculate differences between token sequences—which has to deal with ambiguous situations—and clone classes becoming left-extensible or right-extensible due to changes or removal of fragments. However, according to our experience from previous studies and careful analysis of the clone evolution data, we have found that these situations are rare.

Analyzing CLONES. Another threat may arise from the analysis of our own program CLONES. Although 15 different developers have contributed to CLONES, most of them knew about clone-related problems—and they may have been aware of them during development. This might have an impact on the number of unintentional inconsistencies. Thus, the percentage of unwanted inconsistencies might be higher for projects where developers are completely unaware of clones.

Manual assessment. Manual assessment of changes to clones depends on the judges and their expertise. We have deliberately chosen a system we are familiar with to reliably judge the impact of changes.

10.4   Summary

Clones are said to increase the change effort when software is maintained, because changes may have to be propagated to all clones. However, a prerequisite for change propagation is that clones are actually changed. Looking at the results we have presented in Section 10.2.1, we see that almost half of the clones have never been changed during their lifetime. Thus, these clones have never caused any additional change effort. Apart from the clones that never changed, another 40.3% changed only once during their lifetime.

We assume that removal is the only option to prevent additional change effort since semi-automated change propagation (e.g., [182]) still requires effort for manual verification of the suggested propagation. We also assume that the additional effort caused by a single change to a clone class is less than the effort to remove the respective clones by refactoring. That means, for 87.8% of the clones (the ones that never changed or changed once), removal would not have been beneficial because the effort to remove the clones would have been larger than the additional change effort that would have been prevented. This answers Question 11 on page 52.

Only for the remaining 12.2% of clones that changed more than once, removal might have been beneficial. It is, however, debatable how many arbitrary changes to a clone class require the same effort as its removal. Furthermore, we counted all changes including those that are meant to be independent—that is, they do not need to be propagated to the other clones of the class. Hence, the 87.8% is an under-estimation of the true percentage.

Our results show that the major percentage of clones in our example systems has not caused additional effort, independent of whether the clone is "structurally interesting" or not. Based on our findings, we suggest that it may be appropriate to consult change information when deciding which clones are relevant and which clones are not relevant. Although the data describes only the past evolution of clones, we believe it provides important information to predict their future evolution.

When a cloned fragment is changed, the change might need to be propagated to the other copies. If this is not done—or not done correctly—new problems may arise or existing problems might not be completely mitigated. We analyzed changes to clones in our own code and found that 14.8% of all changes were unintentionally inconsistent— answering Question 12 on page 52. 11.8% of the changes had only low severity, that is, the inconsistency does not cause the program to crash or produce wrong results. Only 9 (3.0%) of all changes were found to have high severity—less than two changes a year. We have analyzed consecutive changes to clones [67] to identify characteristics that indicate unwanted inconsistencies. However, our initial study did not yield any suitable characteristic.

On the one hand, we can confirm the results of previous studies [13, 90, 96, 130] that identified faults based on inconsistencies between clones or their contexts. There are clones that can exacerbate problems when they are changed. On the other hand, our results show that 85.2% of the changes in our example systems were consistent or intentionally inconsistent, confirming findings of previous studies [8, 178]. This is important for developing clone-management tools (for example, CLEVER [151] or CLONEBOARD [41]), because too many false alarms about potential problems caused by inconsistent changes may be counterproductive for the adoption of clone management in practice.

Please note that our study focused on two prominent clone-related threats. Apart from these, there are other problems caused by the presences of code clones. These include, for example, increased system size and additional effort to read and understand the code. Hence, our results are not to be regarded as a general acquittal of clones.

The implication of our results is, that the history of clones is helpful in determining their relevance and threat potential. This is important in light of the increasing number of clone management tools. To successfully establish these tools in daily maintenance practice, it is important to reliably identify clones with high threat potential and not besiege maintainers with false alarms.

Chapter 11

Clone Removal

The purpose of clone management is to exploit the positive effects of cloning and reduce the threats that emerge from clones. To be successful, clone management requires a substantial understanding of a clone's evolution from creation to removal. While reasons for the creation of code clones and their effects have been elaborately investigated [103, 105, 126], their removal has not. Although there are a variety of methods that provide support to eliminate duplication [15, 16, 18, 54, 78, 97, 111, 112, 166, 174], there is no systematic study of situations where developers remove clones from a system. We do, however, believe that a comprehensive understanding of how developers see and deal with duplication is crucial to efficiently support software maintainers. Without this knowledge it is impossible to construct efficient tools that truly add value to tool-supported software maintenance. We identified two major benefits of better understanding a software maintainer's point of view regarding clones.

(1) Clone detection results are usually used for subsequent maintenance activities. For example, they may be given to a system developer whose task it is to understand and eliminate the duplication as much as possible. Hence, the conformance between detected clones and the schema of duplication the maintainer has in mind is essential to successfully make use of the clone detection results. Analyzing how developers have removed clones in the past helps to get an impression of how maintainers see duplication. Comparing these insights to the detected code clones allows us to estimate the conformance between the clone detector's and the developer's point of view. A possible discrepancy could be reduced by improving clone detectors and training the developer's understanding of code duplication.

(2) One of the major purposes of clone detection is to subsequently remove the clones via refactoring [159]. A number of different approaches have been presented that suggest and apply refactorings to remove clones [15, 16, 18, 54, 78, 97, 111, 112, 166, 174]. However, the application of an arbitrary refactoring may not always be beneficial. Although the duplication is removed, the refactoring might negatively affect program comprehensibility or introduce bugs. Investigating which clones

maintainers select and which refactorings they chose to remove these clones provides the foundation to improve existing tool support.

This chapter presents our study of intentional clone removals—an aspect of code clones that has not been analyzed before. The removal of a clone defines the end of its lifetime and is an evolutionary aspect that can be analyzed using our Clone Evolution Graph. The study presented in this chapter analyzes the characteristics of deliberate clones removal and answers Question 13 on page 53. The intention of our study is to campaign for more observance of a maintainer's point of view and deliver insight into how developers approach code duplication. We first search for deliberate removals of code clones in different systems, to show that these in fact exist and are not fictitious. Based on the results, we analyze various aspects of clone removals to get an impression of the developers' perspective. Our findings can be used to improve existing clone detection as well as clone refactoring tools.

11.1   Setup

This section describes the subject systems that have been used in this case study and the procedure that has been used to collect relevant data.

11.1.1   Subject Systems

The subject systems we use need to match different criteria to be suitable for our case study. Their source code has to be freely available and accessible via SUBVERSION, because our analysis infrastructure currently supports only SUBVERSION repositories. The source code should have a reasonable size to obtain meaningful results but, on the other hand, should make manual inspection of all clone removals possible. Most important, there should be indications of deliberate clone removals that we can investigate. We test this criteria by looking for commit messages that include suspicious keywords. Among others, we search for variations of the terms "duplication", "redundancy", "refactoring", "clone", and "removal". In addition, we build our Clone Evolution Graph for the respective system and take a sample of disappearing clones to judge whether any of these have been intentionally removed. Systems where we cannot find relevant commit messages or any deliberate clone removals in the sample are not considered for our case study.

While finding SUBVERSION-accessible systems of appropriate size is straightforward, the detection of deliberate clone removals is much harder. During our search for suitable subject systems we found that only very few systems show traces of deliberate clone removal upon preliminary investigation. For many systems, we did neither find relevant commit messages, nor deliberately removed clones. This matches our assumption that intentional removal of clones is a rare phenomenon. Among others, the APACHE WEBSERVER, the GNU COMPILER COLLECTION, and MOZILLA are examples where we could not identify traces of intentional clone removal at first sight. Nevertheless, we found intentional clone removals in the following systems, which we use in our case study accordingly.

System	Language	KSLOC	Source Directories
ADEMPIERE-CLIENT	Java	62–69	15–20
ARGOUML	Java	151–157	88–92
KDE-UTILS	C++	92–107	106–130
TORTOISESVN	C++	157–167	25–28

Table 11.1 – Subject systems used in our case study

ADempiere is an open-source application that supports business processes by providing ERP, CRM, and SCM functionality. We restrict our study to the client part of ADempiere to keep the source code size at a manageable level.

ArgoUML is a UML modeling tool supporting all standard diagram types. We exclude all source files containing test code from our analysis because these contain mostly inevitable redundancy.

KDE is a desktop environment for UNIX-based systems. Due to the large number of different applications and consequently large amount of source code, we pick the utility package of KDE as subject system for our study.

TortoiseSVN is a graphical interface to the subversion version control system.

For each subject system, we analyze the time period from January 7 to October 29, 2009. The time span is chosen to base results on recent development activity and keep manual inspection at a reasonable level. We chose an interval of one week between versions, resulting in 43 versions per system. A summary of the systems we use is given in Table 11.1.

All systems are mature, continuously maintained, and have a history of at least five years each. We deliberately excluded younger systems from our study, because we assume their code and the clones contained are more volatile due to frequent major refactorings. However, volatile clones have only minor opportunity to show their negative effects. Thus, their removal is more likely to be a consequence of a larger refactoring that an intentional elimination of duplication.

11.1.2 Data Collection

The first step of our analysis is to find situations where developers deliberately removed code duplication. We refer to each of these situations as *ROD* (Removal of Duplication). A naïve way to identify RODs is searching for commit messages that include suspicious keywords in the history of the version control system. However, from our experience we know that these messages are all too often fairly short or inaccurate. Although we might be able to identify some RODs, we would most likely miss the majority of them. Instead of starting with commit messages, we start our search with the cloned fragments detected by our clone detection tool. We assume that removal of duplication is always accompanied by a deletion of tokens from the respective fragments. Based on this assumption, we can identify RODs by inspecting all cloned fragments from which tokens are deleted during the evolution of the system. We consider changed tokens as a

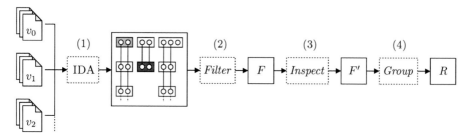

Figure 11.1 – Detecting removals of duplication.

deletion followed by an addition, therefore changed fragments can also indicate RODs. The process for identifying RODs is summarized in Figure 11.1.

(1) **Incremental clone detection.** Our first objective is to determine the set of fragments from which tokens are deleted. We use our incremental clone detection algorithm to create the Clone Evolution Graph for the versions of each system under study. To increase recall, we use tolerant clone detection parameters. We configured our algorithm to detect identical (type-1) as well as non-identical (type-2 and type-3) clones. We applied a minimum clone length of 50 tokens.

(2) **Filtering.** Among other information, the Clone Evolution Graph provides us with the set of cloned fragments for each version. Due to the nature of clone classes, many fragments are subsumed by other fragments. Therefore, we exclude all fragments that are completely contained within another fragment within the same version. Using this approach, we avoid analyzing the same situation multiple times which would bias our results. Within the set of remaining fragments, we identify fragments from which tokens are deleted by consulting the change information that is also provided by the Clone Evolution Graph. We further reduce the set of fragments by considering only those that have more than a given number of tokens deleted. In our pre-study we manually investigated all fragments detected in TORTOISESVN with at least a single token deleted. We found that there are no RODs where fewer than 15 tokens have been deleted. We therefore require cloned fragments to have at least 15 tokens deleted. This excludes all fragments that are only marginally changed. Let F be the resulting set of fragments.

(3) **Identifying intentional removals.** Unfortunately, F still contains many fragments from which tokens just happen to be deleted without the intention to remove duplication. We therefore have to manually analyze each fragment in set F. The purpose of manual inspection is to determine the subset F' of F, such that F' contains only intentional removals whereas $F \setminus F'$ contains only unintentional removals. The decision whether a removal is deliberate or not is critical to our study and exposed to subjective judgment. Therefore, we describe the criteria we apply as well as possible to make our decisions comprehensible.

Basically, we look for variants of refactorings that are used to eliminate duplication, for example, the replacement of a statement sequence with a single method call. When analyzing a particular removal $f \in F$, we do not require the scope of f to match the scope of a potential refactoring. We search for an arbitrarily sized refactoring inside the bounds of f as our preliminary investigations showed that the scope of f and the scope of the refactoring hardly ever match. We consult the identifiers in f before and after the change to help picturing the modification. In some cases it does not suffice to investigate the source code only within the scope of f. Especially if new methods are created, these have to be analyzed to understand their functionality and judge whether they are a proper replacement. In other cases, tokens are removed only from f and no new tokens are introduced. In these situations, the class hierarchy has to be analyzed to find out whether the functionality has been moved to an ancestor class. Finally, we consult the change message relevant to f from the subversion repository. If we find explicit indications that cloned code has been refactored and our observations from the source code match the description, then f is an element of F'. Note, that if the commit message does not explicitly mention clone removal, f can still be classified as intentional if the other observations speak for it. Using our experience in code clone research, as well as experience in the programming languages of the subject systems, helps us to make a substantiated decision whether f relates to a deliberate clone removal or not.

A situation that frequently occurs is the sole deletion of tokens from a fragment because the code is not needed anymore. Without a proper replacement for the deleted part or a clarifying commit message, we do not regard pure deletion as a deliberate removal of duplication. This includes deletion of complete files that contain cloned fragments.

Example 11.1 – To demonsrate our decisions, we provide an example taken from TortoiseSVN. Figure 11.2 on the next page shows a deliberate removal of a loop that deletes an array of font objects (shown in (a)). The loop is intentionally refactored and replaced by a call to a new function that provides the same functionality (shown in (b)). $\square$

(4) **Grouping.** In the end, the fragments related to elimination of duplication have to be grouped, because most situations where clones are removed affect more than a single fragment. We group the fragments related to clone removal according to the RODs (*Removals of Duplication*: situations where clones have been deliberately removed) they belong to, because our case study aims to investigate RODs rather than individual fragments. For this manual grouping, we also consult the information that was used to classify the fragments in the previous step. Fragments are combined to a ROD if the respective refactorings originate from a common intention. As an example, let there be three fragments within which code to show a particular message box is replaced by a call to the same new method. These three fragments are combined in a single ROD. However, if the common code is replaced by calls to different methods, the fragments do not belong to the same ROD.

```
1   ...                                            1   ...
2   for (int i=0; i<MAXFONTS; i++) {                2
3     if (m_apFonts[i] != NULL) {                   3
4       m_apFonts[i]->DeleteObject();               4
5       delete m_apFonts[i];                        5   deleteFonts();
6     }                                             6
7     m_apFonts[i] = NULL;                          7
8   }                                               8
9   ...                                             9   ...
```

(a) Prior to change (2009-08-20)   (b) After change (2009-08-27)

Figure 11.2 – Deliberate removal of a cloned fragment in TORTOISESVN (BaseView.cpp).

Under special circumstances, RODs can have only one fragment assigned. This occurs, for example, when a statement sequence somewhere in the code is identical to the statement sequence resembling a method body. A developer realizes that the method already provides the functionality and replaces the statement sequence in the code with a call to the method. In such a case, the ROD contains only one fragment, because the fragment inside the method body is not changed at all. Let R be the final set of RODs.

Committers and Commit Messages

Given the set R we are now able to analyze the RODs themselves. We start by investigating the involvement of different committers and distribution of removals over time. Identifying the commits that relate to a given ROD is straight-forward. We count the number of distinct committers based on these commits for each system to estimate the number of developers involved in removing clones. However, our preliminary investigations showed that some commits are performed on behalf of others. To identify these situations, we inspect the relevant commit messages and search for hints. Wherever we find an indication that someone else than the committer is responsible for the change, we count the other person instead. Nonetheless, committing on behalf of others might not always be documented and therefore the number of developers that remove clones has to be regarded as a lower bound. We proceed in the same way to count the total number of people that commit changes by considering all commits during the period of study. Apart from developer involvement, we analyze the distribution of RODs with respect to the time they occurred. Therefore, we count the number of RODs that happen within each week of our study period. The time of each ROD can be determined from its respective commit.

Removal Techniques

Apart from quantitative analysis, details about how duplication is removed are helpful to analyze how developers approach clone removal. This insight might help to improve tool support for semi-automated clone removal and adjust clone detectors to produce more useful results. We first aim to analyze which refactorings developers apply to remove duplication. Knowing which techniques developers prefer allows us to improve semi-automated refactorings. We further investigate how well the scope of detected clones matches those of RODs. A good matching is desirable, because clone detection results are the basis for developers to manage clones and should therefore be easily comprehensible. A bad matching indicates that either clone detection is not accurate enough, developers are not aware of the duplication's extent, or our clone detection method has merged two separate clones that happen to be adjacent. We are also interested in knowing whether developers only refactor cloned code that is identical or also take the effort to create a unification for similar but not identical duplication.

To investigate which removal techniques have been used, we categorize RODs according to the refactoring that has been performed. The taxonomy used for classification is a result of this process, because there are no previous studies on how developers remove clones. We guide our classification by refactorings commonly quoted as suitable to remove duplication—for example, the *Extract Method* refactoring.

For each ROD, we compare the scope of its fragments to that of the respective refactoring. This is done manually by deciding whether the removal affects only a part of the fragments, matches the fragments, or exceeds the fragments' bounds. Doing this manually allows us to abstract from various artifacts of token-based clone detection at the beginning and end of fragments—for example, brackets and semicolons. Each cloned fragment is classified to either *Superior* if it contains statements that are not part of the refactoring, *Inferior* if the refactoring includes statements not part of the fragment, or *Match* if all statements of the fragment are part of the refactoring and vice versa. We have not encountered any refactorings that only partially overlap with cloned fragments. We perform the classification on individual fragments, because the fragments of a single ROD may not belong to the same clone class and therefore fall into different categories.

We determine for each ROD whether the token sequences that are removed by the refactoring are identical or only similar. Note that this token sequences might extend beyond the bounds of the detected clone fragments. RODs that embrace only a single fragment are not considered.

Clone Characteristics

There is an ongoing uncertainty as to which clones are to be regarded as relevant and which are to be regarded as irrelevant to software maintenance. We believe, that an important contribution to this answer may lie in the analysis of which clones developers select to be removed. We might be able to identify certain characteristics of clones that make them attractive for removal. There is a wide range of attributes that might be taken into account to answer this question. In this respect, we regard our study as a prototype and limit our study to the simple attributes length, similarity, and distance in the source tree. Further research is needed to investigate a larger variety and more complex attributes—for example, their relation to defects or their change frequency.

We first analyze whether particularly long or short clones attract the attention of maintainers and invoke clone removal. The length of each ROD is calculated by taking the average length of its fragments measured in tokens. Our previous results have shown that the scope of cloned fragments detected by our token-based method and the scope of the respective refactoring hardly ever match. Nevertheless, we believe the length of the fragments as detected is a reasonable measure to approximate the length of the duplication that attracts attention.

Apart from the length, we also analyze the similarity among the fragments of each ROD. The results indicate whether only identical or also similar clones attract attention. We distinguish between RODs whose fragments are completely identical and those where fragments are only similar. Due to the use of clone classes, there might be two classes with fragments a, b, c and a', b' such that a is contained in a' and b is contained in b'. A ROD affecting the common part of all fragments will have the fragments a', b', c related, because we excluded subsumed fragments in the first place. In such cases, we determine the similarity based on fragments a, b, c, because otherwise the ROD's fragments could never be classified as identical. We also exclude RODs with only a single fragment.

We investigate whether developers prefer to remove clones contained within the same or closely related source code files. We therefore measure the distance of the files containing the fragments of a ROD in the source tree. We assign the value *Same File* to a ROD if all fragments are contained within the same source file. If all fragments' files are contained within the same directory but not in the same file, we categorize the ROD as *Same Directory*. If the respective files are not contained within the same directory, we classify the ROD as *Different Directories*. A similar categorization of the distance between cloned fragments has previously been used by Kapser and Godfrey [102]. Apart from the distance, we calculate the *Magnitude* of each ROD. We define the magnitude to be the number of source code files that contain the fragments of the ROD.

11.2   Results

This section describes the results that were obtained from analyzing the deliberate removal of duplication that we have identified using the Clone Evolution Graphs extracted from the subject systems.

Applying our clone detection algorithm to the versions of the four subject systems resulted in more than 1.1 million cloned fragments in total. Excluding subsumed fragments and removing those that have fewer than 15 tokens deleted, reduced this number to a reasonable level. For all systems, 977 fragments in total were left to manual inspection. From these fragments, 167 were found to be directly related to a deliberate removal of duplication. Grouping those fragments resulted in 43 distinct RODs. The numbers for the individual systems are given in Table 11.2 on the next page.

TORTOISESVN contributed the majority of the RODs whereas the other systems contributed only five or fewer. The most voluminous ROD was found in ARGOUML

System	Clone Classes	Fragments	$|F|$	$|F'|$	$|R|$
ADEMPIERE	58,791	150,728	406	10	5
ARGOUM	95,040	278,519	204	60	4
KDE-UTILS	136,003	494,892	138	5	2
TORTOISESVN	74,778	180,143	229	92	32
Total	**364,612**	**1,104,282**	**977**	**167**	**43**

Table 11.2 – Number of clones and removals.

where 49 cloned fragments were part of the removal. In particular, all occurrences of the expression

```
((org.omg.uml.UmlPackage) ((ModelElement) handle).refOutermostPackage())
```

have been replaced by

```
getRefOutermostPackage(handle)
```

The corresponding method `getRefOutermostPackage` has been newly created. There were several RODs that just included a single fragment. This occurs, for example, when a sequence of statements is replaced by a single method call, and the method already existed elsewhere.

11.2.1 Committers and Commit Messages

The number of commits, distinct committers, and removers is given in Table 11.3 on the next page for each system. KDE-UTILS clearly had the most contributors, whereas in TORTOISESVN, only seven developers contributed changes during the period of study. Interestingly, there seems to be no relation between the size of the subject system and the number of people contributing changes. Compared to the total number of committers, the fraction of developers involved in clone removal is relatively small. In KDE-UTILS, both RODs were performed by the same developer and in ADEMPIERE two developers removed duplication. The four RODs in ARGOUML were performed by an individual developer each. Four developers in TORTOISESVN were involved in clone removal. Comparing these numbers to the total number of committers shows that in TORTOISESVN more than half of the people involved were actually aware of duplication and took measures to reduce duplication. For ARGOUML, almost every second developer performed a clone removal. For KDE-UTILS, only a single developer out of 56 committers was involved in clone removal.

The distribution of RODs is shown in Figure 11.3 on the next page. Unfortunately, the number of RODs is too small to observe a general tendency. For ADEMPIERE, ARGOUML, and KDE-UTILS, RODs were spread across the study period and no two RODs were performed within the same week for each of these systems. Looking at the RODs in TORTOISESVN shows that there is a clear cluster around August, caused by two distinct developers. All in all, clones seem to be removed every now and then with the bigger refactoring in TORTOISESVN being an exception.

System	Commits	Committers	Removers
ADEMPIERE	183	14	2
ARGoUML	676	10	4
KDE-UTILS	1271	56	1
TORTOISESVN	987	7	4

Table 11.3 – Developers involved in clone removal.

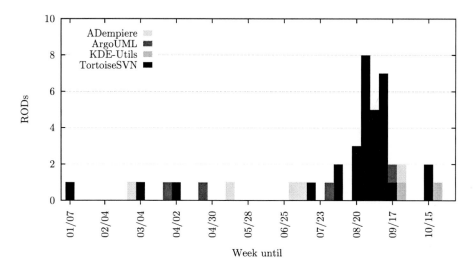

Figure 11.3 – Distribution of RODs.

11.2.2 Removal Techniques

We first decided for each ROD which refactoring has been applied to remove the duplication. We identified three major categories: *Replacement, Unification,* and *Movement.* Our classification is summarized in Figure 11.4 on the next page. This classification is not exhaustive as it is based only on the results from our subject systems. Further analysis might very well reveal more and refined categories.

Replacement A sequence of statements is replaced by a single method call. We further distinguish whether the called method existed before, existed but is modified, or is newly created.

Unification Two cloned fragments with similar functionality are unified in a single place. The unification preserves the functionality of both fragments. In contrast to replacement, this affects complete methods and, hence, there is no method call inserted as replacement. However, the calls to the previously similar methods are adjusted to now call the unified method.

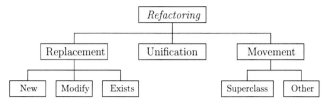

Figure 11.4 – Classification of removals.

		Fragments		
Refactoring	RODs	Superior	Inferior	Match
Replacement	**37**	**106**	**25**	**24**
New Method	24	90	15	21
Modify Existing Method	4	9	3	2
Method Exists	9	7	7	1
Unification	**1**	-	**2**	-
Movement	**5**	**4**	**4**	**2**
Move to Superclass	2	4	-	-
Move to Other Class	3	-	4	2
Total	43	110	31	26

Table 11.4 – Removal strategies used by developers.

Movement Field declarations or methods are moved and gathered in a single place. We differentiate between moving functionality from a specialized class to its parent and moving functionality to another class.

After manually classifying the RODs, we determined the frequency for each particular type of refactoring. The number of RODs for each category is given in the first column of Table 11.4. The dominating type of refactoring used by developers was *Replacement.* In 37 out of 43 RODs, developers replaced cloned code by a single method call. This was mostly related to introducing a new method. Nonetheless, we found situations where existing methods were called with and without modifications to that method. There are some instances where functionality had been moved to the parent class or a common utility class. There is only a single situation where duplication was removed due to cloned code being unified.

A result from our preliminary investigations is, that refactorings performed by developers hardly ever match the scope of clones detected by our token-based method. To analyze this relation, we manually judged for each refactoring whether it matches the scope of the respective cloned fragments as detected by the clone detector. The result of the classification is given in the last three columns of Table 11.4. Of the RODs' fragments, 66% were classified as *Superior*, 19% as *Inferior*, and only 16% as *Match*. To illustrate the classification, we provide an example of *Superior* in Figure 11.5 on the next page. Only the loop that replaces characters in a given buffer was extracted to a new method, whereas the other part of the clone remained unchanged.

```
 1   ...                                 1   ...
 2    filelist += _T("/");               2    filelist += _T("/");
 3   }                                   3   }
 4   filelist += _T("/");                4   filelist += _T("/");
 5   int len = filelist.GetLength();     5   int len = filelist.GetLength();
 6   TCHAR * buf = new TCHAR[len+2];      6   TCHAR * buf = new TCHAR[len+2];
 7   _tcscpy_s(buf, len+2, filelist)     7   _tcscpy_s(buf, len+2, filelist);
 8   for (int i=0; i<len; ++i)           8
 9     if (buf[i] == '/')                9   CStringUtils::PipesToNulls(buf, len);
10       buf[i] = 0;                    10
11   SHFILEOPSTRUCT fileop;             11   SHFILEOPSTRUCT fileop;
12   ...                                12   ...
```

(a) Prior to change (2009-08-27)   (b) After change (2009-09-03)

Figure 11.5 – Refactoring affecting only a fraction of the code detected as clone in TORTOISESVN (DelUnversionedCommand.cpp).

In most cases, developers refactored only a small part of a larger clone. For the unification, the two fragments classified as *Inferior* are the beginning and end of method that was unified with its similar sibling. Due to differences in the middle section of the cloned methods, the two fragments were detected separately. Still, the refactoring affected the complete method. This special situation suggests a more tolerant merging of neighboring clones.

Analyzing whether developers take the effort to remove clones that are only similar, we found that in only 46% of the cases, fragments of the respective ROD were identical. That means, maintainers also removed clones that were only similar, which naturally requires a more sophisticated refactoring.

11.2.3   Clone Characteristics

The RODs that we analyzed had an average length of 127.2 tokens (median 99). The fragments of the longest ROD had an average length of 549.5 tokens. The fragments of the shortest ROD had a length of 50 tokens which equals the minimum length we used to configure our clone detector. All but three RODs had a length between 50 and 181 tokens. This distribution is similar to the overall distribution of fragment lengths. Therefore, we cannot observe a tendency towards removing particularly short or particularly long clones. Analogous to the length, we could not observe a tendency towards identical or only similar fragments. In 51% of the cases, the fragments of the ROD were identical; in 49% of the cases they were only similar, with some being type-2 and most being type-3 clones.

We analyzed the distance of the source code files that contain the fragments of a ROD. For each system, the total number of directories containing source code files (not recursively) is given in the last column of Table 11.1 on page 175. Of all RODs, 28 were classified as *Same File*. Hence, 65% of all RODs affected only a single source code file. From the remaining RODs, 7 were classified as *Same Directory*. Thus, the removal was not limited to a single file, but affected more than one file contained within the same source directory. The remaining 8 RODs affected source code files that were spread across the source tree as the respective fragments were not contained in files within the same directory. These 8 RODs all happened in TORTOISESVN. For ADEMPIERE, ARGOUML, and KDE-UTILS, all RODs were classified as *Same File* or *Same Directory*. The results indicate that developers prefer to remove clones contained within the same or closely related files. Nevertheless, it may also indicate that developers were unable to locate the other fragments. We also found situations where duplication was removed that was not contained within the same source directory. The average magnitude of RODs is 1.6 files (median 1). Coherent with our previous observation, most removals affected only a single source code file. The maximum magnitude found was 8 for the ROD from which the example in Figure 11.5 on the previous page is taken, whereas the next smaller RODs had a magnitude of 4.

11.3   Threats to Validity

There are certain threats to the general validity of our case study's results.

   Subject systems. The subject systems we studied were not chosen randomly and may not be regarded as a representative sample. Our selection was guided by technical constraints and the objective to find deliberate elimination of duplication. Although we could not find intentional removals in the majority of systems we have investigated, other systems may contain more frequent removals that have different characteristics.

   Clone detection. Another threat emerges from the use of our token-based clone detector. Although token-based clone detection is known to have a reasonable recall, we might still miss certain clones that are not detected or filtered, for example, by imposing a length restriction. We tried to reduce this threat by using tolerant settings to maximize recall. Furthermore, token-based clone detection is known to disregard the syntactic structure of the program. Syntax-tree or graph-based approaches might produce results closer to the developer's point of view, because they report clones based on syntactic units. Since these syntactic units are the starting point for refactoring, clones detected by these methods are likely to be more appropriate for clone removal.

   ROD identification. Our case study is based on the RODs that we initially detect in the subject systems. Chances are that we missed individual RODs, because there is no reliable record of these. We mitigated this threat by doing an extensive pre-study on one of the subject systems, manually investigating all cloned fragments that have at least a single token deleted. After all, substantial changes to the source code with no clarifying commit message can still hide individual RODs.

   Human judgment. Finally, human judgment is involved in analyzing various aspects of the RODs and therefore the results are threatened by subjectivity. We tried to limit subjectivity and overcome this threat by making decisions according to well-defined criteria.

11.4   Summary

This chapter presented a case study of deliberate clone removal by software developers. Our intention was to approach duplication from a maintainer's point of view to gain insights that help to improve clone detection as well as clone refactoring tools. The answer to Question 13 on page 53 is that intentional clone removal happens and is not fictitious, since we have found many situations where duplication has been eliminated. Still, clone removal does not appear to be part of daily maintenance activity as it occurs only selectively. Interestingly, the fewer people are involved in a project, the more intentional removal of duplication seems to take place.

Analyzing the removals in our example systems showed that method extraction was the most frequent refactoring used to eliminate duplication. However, the scope of the refactorings hardly ever matched the scope of detected clones. Recently, Tairas and Gray [176, 177] also found that clone-related refactorings often affect only part of a clone. On the one hand, this might indicate that developers are not aware of the whole extent of the duplication. On the other hand, clone detection results might be too imprecise from a developer's perspective as they are only parts of a larger abstraction, or combinations of two or more smaller abstractions.

Our preliminary investigations to find attributes of clones that developers prefer to remove did not yield clear results. Length and similarity do not seem to make clones attractive for removal. On the other hand, when clones are removed, these are mostly located in the same source code file. Developers do not refrain from removing clones that are only similar but not identical. We suspect that more complex attributes are needed to identify which clones are attractive for removal—for example, change frequency or relation to bugs. In summary, our case study highlights a discrepancy between clones detected by token-based clone detection and the way maintainers approach duplication.

Part IV

Finale

Chapter 12

Conclusion

This chapter summarizes the conclusions of this thesis with respect to the research problems stated in Section 1.1. In summary, this thesis has presented a comprehensive model of clone evolution and an efficient incremental algorithm to extract the relevant data from evolving systems. The techniques have been applied in several case studies on real-world systems and the results are an important contribution towards a better understanding on how clones evolve and their impact on maintainability.

12.1   Modeling Clone Evolution

Although several previous studies analyzed clone evolution, no common model was used to represent the relevant data. These studies differ in whether individual fragments or clone classes are tracked and used similar but yet different patterns for their analysis. In Chapter 4 we have introduced Clone Evolution Graphs—a more comprehensive model of clone evolution. The graphs are a fine-grained representation of clones and changes to them, but also allow us to derive higher-level patterns. Clone Evolution Graphs are capable of representing all patterns that have been previously used to analyze clone evolution.

To analyze how clones evolve, they have to be detected in all relevant versions of a system. So far, studies on clone evolution applied traditional clone detection approaches to each version of a system individually. We have presented an incremental clone detection approach in Chapter 6, which efficiently detects clones in a sequence of versions. The algorithm reuses data from the previous version's analysis as much as possible to mitigate redundant calculations and significantly decrease processing time.

For analyzing clone evolution, it is not sufficient to only detect clones in every version. Clones of subsequent versions have to be mapped to track them as the system evolves. Clone tracking has previously been done by finding best matches between clones of two versions. This approach is quite costly due to its quadratic nature and suffers from imprecision. Chapter 7 introduced our clone tracking approach that makes use of fine-grained change information to precisely track clones as the system evolves. The change information is also used to determine the consistency of changes to clones and to track clones that temporarily disappear.

A major requirement of our incremental approach is its applicability to research as well as practice. It must have a reasonable performance to allow for a retroactive analysis of clone evolution as well as live analysis while a system is maintained. We have presented the results of our extensive performance analysis in Chapter 8 and shown that the overall performance makes our algorithm applicable to both scenarios.

In summary, this thesis has solved the problem of extracting relevant clone evolution data by providing a comprehensive model of clone evolution and an efficient incremental technique to detect and track clones in evolving systems.

12.2   How Clones Evolve

Despite ongoing research, the phenomenon of cloning and the impact of software clones on maintainability is not yet sufficiently understood. Clone evolution is a rich source of information because the majority of positive as well as negative effects of clones is related to change. To gain a better understanding of how clones evolve we have conducted three comprehensive case studies that analyzed various aspects of clone evolution. All case studies made use of Clone Evolution Graphs and the incremental extraction as described in this thesis.

Chapter 9 presented the first study in which we have analyzed different aspects of how clones evolve in nine open-source and three industrial systems. Investigating the number of clones and system size we have found that the clone rate does not increase in all of our subject systems. Our results show that many clones are long-lived and exist for more than a year on average. That is, once duplication has been created, it is likely to stay for a long time. Regarding change consistency, inconsistent changes to clones dominate in some systems whereas in other systems consistent changes are more frequent. In summary, we have found clone evolution to be very versatile prohibiting general conclusions. Instead, our results highlight the need for sophisticated techniques to analyze clone evolution in individual systems.

Chapter 10 described our case study on the frequency and risks of changes to clones. We have tracked individual clones in different systems over the period of five years and investigated how they were changed. We have found that the majority of clones changes at most once during their lifetime. Almost half of all clones are never changed throughout their existence. The results show that many clones do not cause additional change effort. We have further analyzed changes to clones in detail to evaluate the danger of incomplete propagation of changes. In total, 15% of all changes to clones are related to a missing propagation of the change to all identical fragments. Nevertheless, the majority of these incomplete changes were related to debugging code and coding style.

In our third case study we specifically focused on the deliberate removal of duplication from a system. Deliberate removals provide indication of which clones developers consider as relevant and worth to be refactored. The results of our case study presented in Chapter 11 indicate that the intentional removal of clones is a rare phenomenon. Nevertheless, we have found some deliberate removals in four systems. Our results suggest that the fewer developers are involved, the more likely is clone removal. Furthermore, developers tend to remove clones in the same or closely related files. Our study has, however, also shown that the scope of a clone removal hardly ever matches the scope of detected clones.

In summary, our studies have solved the problem of gaining deeper insight into the nature of code clones. Although the phenomenon of cloning is still not completely understood, the studies presented in this thesis are an important step towards a better understanding of clone evolution.

12.3 Future Work

This section presents opportunities for improvements of our incremental algorithm and future work on clone evolution.

12.3.1 Extend the Clone Evolution Graph

The Clone Evolution Graph is intended to be a comprehensive model of clone evolution. As such it might need to be extended when new patterns are discovered that are relevant to the analysis of clone evolution and cannot be represented with the Clone Evolution Graph in its current form. Another possible extension is the inclusion of more detailed change information in the graph. Currently, the model distinguishes between clones classes whose fragments were not changed, were consistently changed, and were inconsistently changed. Nevertheless, not all inconsistent changes are harmful as code may be syntactically similar but otherwise unrelated. More detailed change information would allow further differentiation between changes.

12.3.2 Improved Differencing Algorithm

Although our incremental algorithm itself is independent from the source of the difference information, the information about how source code was changed between versions has a major impact on the mapping—and consequently the tracking—of clones. Retroactive analysis of how source code has changed always faces ambiguity which may result in an unintuitive mapping and tracking. The quality of the mapping can, however, be improved by using a more sophisticated differencing algorithm. For example, Canfora and colleagues [30, 31] introduced LDIFF that is aware not only of addition, deletion, and modification, but also movement of entities. Future research should investigate the effect of the differencing algorithm on the mapping.

12.3.3 Parallel Processing

Currently, our incremental extraction algorithm is implemented using a single processor only. Its performance can be further improved by using parallel processing, especially because computers are more and more equipped with multiple processors. Reading relevant source code files and creating the token tables is one of the activities that is suitable for parallel processing. In addition, large parts of the clone detection and merging of non-identical clones clones could be carried out in parallel. Still, not all parts of the algorithm are suited for parallel processing. For example, modifications of the generalized suffix tree have to be done in sequence.

12.3.4   Reduce Memory Consumption

Our analysis has shown that the incremental algorithm has a reasonable memory consumption that allows running it on common hardware. Nevertheless, further reduction of the memory consumption is desirable, especially with respect to larger systems. Our detailed investigation has shown that the major part of the memory is required for storing the generalized suffix tree. To reduce the memory consumption, one could try to replace the suffix tree with a more compact data structure.

A possible replacement is the suffix array, which has been introduced by Manber and Myers [139] as an alternative to suffix trees. Although both require linear space, a suffix array is a much more compact representation of the suffixes of a given sequence while providing the same functionality. Abouelhoda and colleagues [1] showed that every algorithm using suffix trees can be transformed to using suffix arrays. However, our incremental algorithm uses a generalized suffix tree that is built for a set of sequences and allows subsequent modification—addition and removal of individual sequences— after the tree's initial construction. Despite first work on modifying a suffix array after its initial construction [165] the concept of a *generalized suffix array* as our algorithm would require it has not been established. Nevertheless, the concept of a generalized suffix array could significantly improve the performance of the incremental algorithm.

12.3.5   IDE Integration

The usage scenarios of the incremental algorithm do not include only a retroactive analysis, but also a live analysis of clone evolution during development. To provide a seamless integration into the daily maintenance activities, the algorithm could be integrated into an IDE. The algorithm could benefit from detailed and precise change information recorded by the IDE and provide up-to-date information that helps to spot clone-related problems as soon as they appear. In Chapter 8 we have shown that such an integration is feasible as our algorithm has the required performance.

12.3.6   Harmful Inconsistent Changes

Inconsistent changes are an indication of clone-related problems as the incomplete propagation of changes may result in incomplete removal of bugs or facilitate new problems. Nevertheless, many inconsistent changes are not harmful because the respective source code fragments are sufficiently independent despite being structurally similar. Further analysis of which inconsistent changes may not pose threats and which are truly harmful could reduce false alarms and increase efficiency when rating clones.

12.3.7   Evaluate Detection of Type-3 Clones

Although non-identical clones are of great importance for software maintenance, current methods are not able to reliably and precisely detect such non-identical clones. Previous studies showed that many non-identical clones that are detected are irrelevant. We have tried to overcome this problem by using a less tolerant approach that requires non-identical clones to have identical subsequences of a certain length. The output of a traditional clone detection approach has been compared to the output of our new technique for detecting non-identical clones (Section 6.4.2). Different categories of clones that are no longer detected have been presented. So far, we have limited our comparison to type-2 clones. Future research should include a similar comparison for type-3 clones.

12.3.8   Postprocessing Clone Information

Among the benefits of token-based clone detection are its performance and its independence from particular programming languages (except for a scanner). One of the major drawbacks, however, is missing knowledge about the syntactic structure of the program. This results in clones whose bounds do often not align with the boundaries of syntactic structures within a program.

Developers, however, make heavy use of the syntactic structures to decompose and understand the program. For example, we have found a general discrepancy between detected clones and what developers recognize as duplication worth to be removed. In addition, refactorings are defined based on syntactic structure of the program and, therefore, cannot always be applied to cloned fragments detected by a token-based technique.

To make clone detection results more comprehensible and to ease further processing of clone information (for example, refactoring), one could postprocess the cloned fragments and extract the syntactic structure of the code regions that contain the clones. This would allow to adjust the clones' bounds and improve the alignment with the syntactic units in the source code.

12.4   Closing Words

The phenomenon of cloning has attracted much research in the past and will continue to be an inspiring field of research in the future. The concept of software clones that looks simple at first sight soon turns into a complex and challenging problem. Most likely, there will never be a universal solution to all clone-related problems. Nevertheless, the awareness of code clones and a tool set to manage duplication in a software system are important in practice. A major building block of effective clone management is analyzing the evolution of clones as the impact of clones becomes recognizable only when the system and the clones within it evolve. After all, this thesis provides techniques and knowledge that help to gain a much better understanding of clone evolution.

I enjoyed creating it.

List of Figures

List of Tables

List of Examples

Glossary

AST

An AST (Abstract Syntax Tree) represents the syntactic structure of a program.

Bad Smell

Indication for quality deficiencies.

CEG

→ *Clone Evolution Graph*

Clone Class

Similarity relation between two or more *fragments*.

Clone Evolution Graph

Comprehensive model for clone evolution. Nodes are the occurrences of cloned *fragments*. Different types of edges tell which fragments occur in the same version, are similar to each other, and are ancestors of each other.

Clone Pair

Similarity relation between exactly two *fragments*.

Consistent Change

Change where the fragments of a *clone class* or *clone pair* are changed in exactly the same way.

cyclone

Tool for multi-perspective analysis of clone evolution data.

Extensible

A *clone class* or *clone pair* is extensible, if it is *left-extensible*, *right-extensible*, or both.

Fragment

Contiguous section of source code (*token* sequence) with a well-defined location characterized by the file that contains the fragment, as well as a start and end position within that file.

Gapped Clone

→ *Type-3 Clone*

Generalized Suffix Tree

Data structure for efficient extraction of identical subsequences within a set of sequences of elements.

Ghost Fragment

Source code fragment that has previously been part of a clone class but is now without similar counterpart due to an inconsistent change.

iClones

Implementation of *IDA*.

IDA

Our Incremental Detection Algorithm which detects clones in multiple versions of a system and extracts information about their ancestry and change characteristics.

Inconsistent Change

Change where the fragments of a *clone class* or *clone pair* are changed differently or the change is not propagated to all fragments.

Late Propagation

Resolves an earlier *inconsistent change* by propagating the change to all fragments of a *clone class* or *clone pair*.

Left-Extensible

A set of *fragments* is left-extensible, if the tokens directly before the starting position of each fragment are equal.

LOC

LOC (Lines of Code) measures the size of a system or component by counting all lines in the corresponding source files.

Maximal

A *clone class* or *clone pair* is maximal, if it is not *extensible*.

Near-Miss Clone

→ *Non-Identical Clone*

Non-Identical Clone

Collective term for clones with certain differences, namely *type-2 clones* and *type-3 clones*.

PDG

A PDG (Program Dependency Graph) represents control or data dependencies between different entities of a program.

Refactoring

Code restructuring to improve non-functional characteristics of a system—for example, maintainability.

Right-Extensible

A set of *fragments* is right-extensible, if the tokens directly after the end position of each fragment are equal.

ROD (Removal of Duplication)

A situation where one or more cloned source code fragments have been deliberately removed.

SLOC

SLOC (Source Lines of Code) measures the size of a system or component by counting all source lines in the corresponding source files that contain at least one non-comment token.

Suffix Tree

Data structure for efficient extraction of identical subsequences within a sequence of elements.

System

Arbitrary collection of source code files within which clones should be detected.

Token

Atomic syntactic element of a programming language—for example, a keyword, an operator, or an identifier.

Token Table

Stores a sequence of tokens along with their properties.

Type-1 Clone

Clone class or *clone pair* whose *fragments* have identical *token* sequences disregarding comments and whitespace.

Type-2 Clone

Clone class or *clone pair* whose *fragments* have identical *token* sequences disregarding comments, whitespace, and the textual representation of identifiers and literals.

Type-3 Clone

Clone class or *clone pair* whose *fragments* have similar token sequences but some tokens do not occur in all fragments (gaps).

Version

State of a *system*'s source code at a specific point in time.

Bibliography

[1] M. I. Abouelhoda, S. Kurtz, and E. Ohlebusch. Replacing suffix trees with enhanced suffix arrays. *Journal of Discrete Algorithms*, 2(1):53–86, 2004.

[2] A. V. Aho, R. Sethi, and J. D. Ullman. *Compilers: Principles, Techniques, and Tools*. Addison-Wesley, Boston, MA, USA, 1986.

[3] A. Amir, M. Farach, Z. Galil, R. Giancarlo, and K. Park. Dynamic dictionary matching. *Journal of Computer and System Sciences*, 49(2):208–222, 1994.

[4] G. Antoniol, G. Casazza, M. Di Penta, and E. Merlo. Modeling clones evolution through time series. In *Proceedings of the International Conference on Software Maintenance*, pages 273–280. IEEE Computer Society, 2001.

[5] G. Antoniol, U. Villano, E. Merlo, and M. Di Penta. Analyzing cloning evolution in the linux kernel. *Information and Software Technology*, 44(13):755–765, 2002.

[6] T. Apiwattanapong, A. Orso, and M. J. Harrold. A differencing algorithm for object-oriented programs. In *Proceedings of the 19th International Conference on Automated Software Engineering*, pages 2–13. IEEE Computer Society, 2004.

[7] A. Apostolico and Z.Galil, editors. *Pattern Matching Algorithms*. Oxford University Press, Cary, NC, USA, 1997.

[8] L. Aversano, L. Cerulo, and M. Di Penta. How clones are maintained: An empirical study. In *Proceedings of the 11th European Conference on Software Maintenance and Reengineering*, pages 81–90. IEEE Computer Society, 2007.

[9] B. S. Baker. A program for identifying duplicated code. In *Computing Science and Statistics: Proceedings of the 24th Symposium on the Interface*, volume 24, pages 49–57, 1992.

[10] B. S. Baker. On finding duplication and near-duplication in large software systems. In *Proceedings of the 2nd Working Conference on Reverse Engineering*, pages 86–95. IEEE Computer Society, 1995.

[11] B. S. Baker. Parameterized pattern matching: Algorithms and applications. *Journal of Computer and System Sciences*, 52(1):28–42, 1996.

[12] B. S. Baker. Parameterized duplication in strings: Algorithms and an application to software maintenance. *SIAM Journal on Computing*, 26(5):1343–1362, 1997.

[13] T. Bakota, R. Ferenc, and T. Gyimóthy. Clone smells in software evolution. In *Proceedings of the 23rd International Conference on Software Maintenance*, pages 24–33. IEEE Computer Society, 2007.

[14] M. Balazinska, E. Merlo, M. Dagenais, B. Lagüe, and K. Kontogiannis. Measuring clone based reengineering opportunities. In *Proceedings of the 6th International Symposium on Software Metrics*, pages 292–304. IEEE Computer Society, 1999.

[15] M. Balazinska, E. Merlo, M. Dagenais, B. Lagüe, and K. Kontogiannis. Partial redesign of java software systems based on clone analysis. In *Proceedings of the 6th Working Conference on Reverse Engineering*, pages 326–336. IEEE Computer Society, 1999.

[16] M. Balazinska, E. Merlo, M. Dagenais, B. Lagüe, and K. Kontogiannis. Advanced clone-analysis to support object-oriented system refactoring. In *Proceedings of the 7th Working Conference on Reverse Engineering*, pages 98–107. IEEE Computer Society, 2000.

[17] H. A. Basit, S. J. Puglisi, W. F. Smyth, A. Turpin, and S. Jarzabek. Efficient token based clone detection with flexible tokenization. In *Proceedings of the 6th Joint Meeting on European Software Engineering Conference and the ACM SIGSOFT Symposium on the Foundations of Software Engineering*, pages 513–516. ACM, 2007.

[18] I. D. Baxter, A. Yahin, L. Moura, M. Sant'Anna, and L. Bier. Clone detection using abstract syntax trees. In *Proceedings of the International Conference on Software Maintenance*, pages 368–377. IEEE Computer Society, 1998.

[19] S. Bellon, R. Koschke, G. Antoniol, J. Krinke, and E. Merlo. Comparison and evaluation of clone detection tools. *IEEE Transactions on Software Engineering*, 33(9):577–591, 2007.

[20] N. Bettenburg, W. Shang, W. Ibrahim, B. Adams, Y. Zou, and A. E. Hassan. An empirical study on inconsistent changes to code clones at release level. In *Proceedings of the 25th Working Conference on Reverse Engineering*, pages 85–94. IEEE Computer Society, 2009.

[21] B. Biegel and S. Diehl. Highly configurable and extensible code clone detection. In *Proceedings of the 17th Working Conference on Reverse Engineering*, pages 237–241. IEEE Computer Society, 2010.

[22] B. Biegel and S. Diehl. JCCD: A flexible and extensible api for implementing custom code clone detectors. In *Proceedings of the 25th International Conference on Automated Software Engineering*, pages 167–168. IEEE Computer Society, 2010.

[23] R. Brixtel, M. Fontaine, B. Lesner, C. Bazin, and R. Robbes. Language-independent clone detection applied to plagiarism detection. In *Proceedings of the 10th International Working Conference on Source Code Analysis and Manipulation*, pages 77–86. IEEE Computer Society, 2010.

[24] M. Bruntink. Aspect mining using clone class metrics. In *Proceedings of the 1st Workshop on Aspect Reverse Engineering*, 2004.

[25] M. Bruntink, A. van Deursen, T. Tourwé, and R. van Engelen. An evaluation of clone detection techniques for identifying crosscutting concerns. In *Proceedings of the 20th IEEE International Conference on Software Maintenance*, pages 200–209. IEEE Computer Society, 2004.

[26] M. Bruntink, A. van Deursen, R. van Engelen, and T. Tourwé. On the use of clone detection for identifying crosscutting concern code. *IEEE Transactions on Software Engineering*, 31(10):804–818, 2005.

[27] P. Bulychev and M. Minea. Duplicate code detection using anti-unification. In *Proceedings of the 2nd Spring Young Researchers' Colloquium on Software Engineering*, pages 51–54, 2008.

[28] E. Burd and M. Munro. Investigating the maintenance implications of the replication of code. In *Proceedings of the International Conference on Software Maintenance*, pages 322–329. IEEE Computer Society, 1997.

[29] F. Calefato, F. Lanubile, and T. Mallardo. Function clone detection in web applications: A semiautomated approach. *Journal of Web Engineering*, 3(1):3–21, 2004.

[30] G. Canfora, L. Cerulo, and M. Di Penta. Identifying changed source code lines from version repositories. In *Proceedings of the 4th International Workshop on Mining Software Repositories*, pages 14–21. IEEE Computer Society, 2007.

[31] G. Canfora, L. Cerulo, and M. Di Penta. Ldiff: an enhanced line differencing tool. In *Proceedings of the 31st International Conference on Software Engineering*, pages 595–598. IEEE Computer Society, 2009.

[32] W. Chen, B. Li, and R. Gupta. Code compaction of matching single-entry multiple-exit regions. In *Proceedings of the 10th International Conference on Static Analysis*, pages 401–417. Springer-Verlag, 2003.

[33] A. Ciu and D. Hirtle. Beyond clone detection. Technical report, University at Waterloo, Ontario, Canada, 2007.

[34] J. R. Cordy. Comprehending reality – practical barriers to industrial adoption of software maintenance automation. In *Proceedings of the 11th IEEE International Workshop on Program Comprehension*, pages 196–205. IEEE Computer Society, 2003.

[35] J. R. Cordy. The TXL source transformation language. *Science of Computer Programming*, 61(3):190–210, 2006.

[36] J. R. Cordy, T. R. Dean, and N. Synytskyy. Practical language-independent detection of near-miss clones. In *Proceedings of the Conference of the Centre for Advanced Studies on Collaborative Research*, pages 1–12. IBM Press, 2004.

[37] M. Dagenais, E. Merlo, B. Laguë, and D. Proulx. Clones occurrence in large object oriented software packages. In *Proceedings of the Conference of the Centre for Advanced Studies on Collaborative Research*. IBM Press, 1998.

[38] N. Davey, P. Barson, S. Field, R. Frank, and S. Tansley. The development of a software clone detector. *International Journal of Applied Software Technology*, 1995.

[39] I. J. Davis and M. W. Godfrey. Clone detection by exploiting assembler. In *Proceedings of the 4th International Workshop on Software Clones*, pages 77–78. ACM, 2010.

[40] I. J. Davis and M. W. Godfrey. From whence it came: Detecting source code clones by analyzing assembler. In *Proceedings of the 17th Working Conference on Reverse Engineering*, pages 242–246. IEEE Computer Society, 2010.

[41] M. de Wit, A. Zaidman, and A. van Deursen. Managing code clones using dynamic change tracking and resolution. In *Proceedings of the International Conference on Software Maintenance*, pages 169–178. IEEE Computer Society, 2009.

[42] Saumya K. Debray, W. Evans, R. Muth, and B. de Sutter. Compiler techniques for code compaction. *ACM Transactions on Programming Languages and Systems*, 22(2):378–415, 2000.

[43] F. Deissenboeck, B. Hummel, E. Juergens, M. Pfaehler, and B. Schaetz. Model clone detection in practice. In *Proceedings of the 4th International Workshop on Software Clones*, pages 57–64. ACM, 2010.

[44] F. Deissenboeck, B. Hummel, E. Juergens, B. Schätz, S. Wagner, Jean-François Girard, and Stefan Teuchert. Clone detection in automotive model-based development. In *Proceedings of the 30th International Conference on Software Engineering*, pages 603–612. ACM, 2008.

[45] S. Demeyer, S. Ducasse, and O. Nierstrasz. Finding refactorings via change metrics. In *Proceedings of the 15th Conference on Object-oriented Programming, Systems, Languages, and Applications*, pages 166–177. ACM, 2000.

[46] G. A. Di Lucca, M. Di Penta, and A. R. Fasolino. An approach to identify duplicated web pages. In *Proceedings of the 26th International Computer Software and Applications Conference on Prolonging Software Life: Development and Redevelopment*, pages 481–486. IEEE Computer Society, 2002.

[47] C. Domann, E. Juergens, and J. Streit. The curse of copy&paste—cloning in requirements specifications. In *Proceedings of the 3rd International Symposium on Empirical Software Engineering and Measurement*, pages 443–446. IEEE Computer Society, 2009.

[48] E. Duala-Ekoko and M. P. Robillard. Tracking code clones in evolving software. In *Proceedings of the 29th International Conference on Software Engineering*, pages 158–167. IEEE Computer Society, 2007.

[49] E. Duala-Ekoko and M. P. Robillard. Clonetracker: Tool support for code clone management. In *Proceedings of the 30th International Conference on Software Engineering*, pages 843–846. ACM, 2008.

[50] E. Duala-Ekoko and M. P. Robillard. Clone region descriptors: Representing and tracking duplication in source code. *ACM Transactions on Software Engineering and Methodology*, 20(1):1–31, 2010.

[51] S. Ducasse, O. Nierstrasz, and M. Rieger. On the effectiveness of clone detection by string matching. *Journal of Software Maintenance and Evolution: Research and Practice*, 18(1):37–58, 2006.

[52] S. Ducasse, M. Rieger, and S. Demeyer. A language independent approach for detecting duplicated code. In *Proceedings of the International Conference on Software Maintenance*, pages 109–118. IEEE Computer Society, 1999.

[53] W. S. Evans, C. W. Fraser, and F. Ma. Clone detection via structural abstraction. In *Proceedings of the 14th Working Conference on Reverse Engineering*, pages 150–159. IEEE Computer Society, 2007.

[54] R. Fanta and V. Rajlich. Removing clones from the code. *Journal of Software Maintenance*, 11(4):223–243, 1999.

[55] P. Ferragina, R. Grossi, and M. Montagero. A note on updating suffix tree labels. In *Proceedings of the 3rd Italian Conference on Algorithms and Complexity*, pages 181–192. Springer-Verlag, 1997.

[56] M. Fowler. *Refactoring: Improving the Design of Existing Code*. Addison-Wesley, Boston, MA, USA, 1999.

[57] M. Gabel, L. Jiang, and Z. Su. Scalable detection of semantic clones. In *Proceedings of the 30th International Conference on Software Engineering*, pages 321–330. ACM, 2008.

[58] M. Gallé, P. Peterlongo, and F. Coste. In-place update of suffix array while recoding words. In *Proceedings of the Prague Stringology Conference*, pages 54–67. Department of Computer Science and Engineering, Faculty of Electrical Engineering, Czech Technical University in Prague, 2008.

[59] R. Geiger, B. Fluri, H. Gall, and M. Pinzger. Relation of code clones and change couplings. *Lecture Notes in Computer Science*, 3922:411–425, 2006.

[60] N. Göde. Incremental clone detection. Diploma thesis, University of Bremen, 2008.

[61] N. Göde. Evolution of type-1 clones. In *Proceedings of the 9th International Working Conference on Source Code Analysis and Manipulation*, pages 77–86. IEEE Computer Society, 2009.

[62] N. Göde. Mapping code clones using incremental clone detection. *Softwaretechnik-Trends*, 29(2):28–29, 2009.

[63] N. Göde. Clone evolution revisited. *Softwaretechnik-Trends*, 30(2):60–61, 2010.

[64] N. Göde. Clone removal: Fact or fiction? In *Proceedings of the 4th International Workshop on Software Clones*, pages 33–40. ACM, 2010.

[65] N. Göde. Not all that glitters is gold. *Softwaretechnik-Trends*, 2011. Accepted for publication.

[66] N. Göde and J. Harder. Clone stability. In *Proceedings of the 15th European Conference on Software Maintenance and Reengineering*, pages 65–74. IEEE Computer Society, 2011.

[67] N. Göde and J. Harder. Oops!... I changed it again. In *Proceedings of the 5th International Workshop on Software Clones*, 2011. Accepted for publication.

[68] N. Göde and R. Koschke. Incremental clone detection. In *Proceedings of the 13th European Conference on Software Maintenance and Reengineering*, pages 219–228. IEEE Computer Society, 2009.

[69] N. Göde and R. Koschke. Studying clone evolution using incremental clone detection. *Journal of Software Maintenance and Evolution: Research and Practice*, 2010. Published online.

[70] N. Göde and R. Koschke. Frequency and risks of changes to clones. In *Proceedings of the 33rd International Conference on Software Engineering*, 2011. Accepted for puplication.

[71] M. W. Godfrey and Q. Tu. Tracking structural evolution using origin analysis. In *Proceedings of the International Workshop on Principles of Software Evolution*, pages 117–119. ACM, 2002.

[72] D. Gusfield, G. M. Landau, and B. Schieber. An efficient algorithm for the all pairs suffix-prefix problem. *Information Processing Letters*, 41(4):181–185, 1992.

[73] J. Harder and N. Göde. Modeling clone evolution. In *Workshop Proceedings of the 13th European Conference on Software Maintenance and Reengineering*, pages 17–21, 2009.

[74] J. Harder and N. Göde. Quo vadis, clone management? In *Proceedings of the 4th International Workshop on Software Clones*, pages 85–86. ACM, 2010.

[75] J. Harder and N. Göde. Efficiently handling clone data: RCF and cyclone. In *Proceedings of the 5th International Workshop on Software Clones*, 2011. Accepted for publication.

[76] J. Harder, N. Göde, and M. Rausch. Stability of cobol clones. *Softwaretechnik-Trends*, 2011. Accepted for publication.

[77] Y. Higo, T. Kamiya, S. Kusumoto, and K. Inoue. Aries: Refactoring support environment based on code clone analysis. In *Proceedings of the 8th International Conference on Software Engineering and Applications*, pages 222–229, 2004.

[78] Y. Higo, T. Kamiya, S. Kusumoto, and K. Inoue. Refactoring support based on code clone analysis. *Lecture Notes in Computer Science*, 3009:220–233, 2004.

[79] D. Hofmann. Entwurf und implementierung der klonerkennung mittels suffix-arrays. Diploma thesis, University of Stuttgart and University of Bremen, 2010.

[80] W. Hordijk, M. L. Ponisio, and R. Wieringa. Harmfulness of code duplication – a structured review of the evidence. In *Proceedings of the 13th International Conference on Evaluation and Assessment in Software Engineering*. IEEE Computer Society, 2009.

[81] S. Horwitz. Identifying the semantic and textual differences between two versions of a program. In *Proceedings of the Conference on Programming Language Design and Implementation*, pages 234–245. ACM, 1990.

[82] K. Hotta, Y. Sano, Y. Higo, and S. Kusumoto. Is duplicate code more frequently modified than non-duplicate code in software evolution?: An empirical study on open source software. In *Proceedings of the Joint Workshop on Software Evolution and International Workshop on Principles of Software Evolution*, pages 73–82. ACM, 2010.

[83] B. Hummel, E. Juergens, L. Heinemann, and M. Conradt. Index-based code clone detection: Incremental, distributed, scalable. In *Proceedings of the 26th International Conference on Software Maintenance*. IEEE Computer Society, 2010.

[84] J. J. Hunt and W. F. Tichy. Extensible language-aware merging. In *Proceedings of the International Conference on Software Maintenance*, pages 511–520. IEEE Computer Society, 2002.

[85] J. W. Hunt and T. G. Szymanski. A fast algorithm for computing longest common subsequences. *Communications of the ACM*, 20(5):350–353, 1977.

[86] P. Jablonski and D. Hou. CReN: A tool for tracking copy-and-paste code clones and renaming identifiers consistently in the ide. In *Proceedings of the OOPSLA Workshop on Eclipse Technology Exchange*, pages 16–20. ACM, 2007.

[87] D. Jackson and D. A. Ladd. Semantic diff: A tool for summarizing the effects of modifications. In *Proceedings of the International Conference on Software Maintenance*, pages 243–252. IEEE Computer Society, 1994.

[88] F. Jacob, D. Hou, and P. Jablonski. Actively comparing clones inside the code editor. In *Proceedings of the 4th International Workshop on Software Clones*, pages 9–16. ACM, 2010.

[89] L. Jiang, G. Misherghi, Z. Su, and S. Glondu. DECKARD: Scalable and accurate tree-based detection of code clones. In *Proceedings of the 29th International Conference on Software Engineering*, pages 96–105. IEEE Computer Society, 2007.

[90] L. Jiang, Z. Su, and E. Chiu. Context-based detection of clone-related bugs. In *Proceedings of the 6th Joint Meeting on European Software Engineering Conference and the ACM SIGSOFT Symposium on the Foundations of Software Engineering*, pages 55–64. ACM, 2007.

[91] J. H. Johnson. Identifying redundancy in source code using fingerprints. In *Proceedings of the Conference of the Centre for Advanced Studies on Collaborative Research*, pages 171–183. IBM Press, 1993.

[92] J. H. Johnson. Substring matching for clone detection and change tracking. In *Proceedings of the International Conference on Software Maintenance*, pages 120–126. IEEE Computer Society, 1994.

[93] E. Juergens and F. Deissenboeck. How much is a clone? In *Proceedings of the 4th International Workshop on Software Quality and Maintainability*, 2010.

[94] E. Juergens, F. Deissenboeck, M. Feilkas, B. Hummel, B. Schaetz, S. Wagner, Christoph Domann, and Jonathan Streit. Can clone detection support quality assessments of requirements specifications? In *Proceedings of the 32nd International Conference on Software Engineering*, pages 79–88. ACM, 2010.

[95] E. Juergens, F. Deissenboeck, and B. Hummel. Clonedetective – a workbench for clone detection research. In *Proceedings of the 31st International Conference on Software Engineering*, pages 603–606. IEEE Computer Society, 2009.

[96] E. Juergens, F. Deissenboeck, B. Hummel, and S. Wagner. Do code clones matter? In *Proceedings of the 31st International Conference on Software Engineering*, pages 485–495. IEEE Computer Society, 2009.

[97] N. Juillerat and B. Hirsbrunner. An algorithm for detecting and removing clones in java code. In *Proceedings of the 3rd International Workshop on Software Evolution through Transformations*, pages 63–74, 2006.

[98] T. Kamiya, S. Kusumoto, and K. Inoue. CCFinder: A multilinguistic token-based code clone detection system for large scale source code. *IEEE Transactions on Software Engineering*, 28(7):654–670, 2002.

[99] C. J. Kapser and M. W. Godfrey. Toward a taxonomy of clones in source code: A case study. In *Proceedings of the Workshop on Evolution of Large-scale Industrial Software Applications*, pages 67–78, 2003.

[100] C. J. Kapser and M. W. Godfrey. Aiding comprehension of cloning through categorization. In *Proceedings of the 7th International Workshop on Principles of Software Evolution*, pages 85–94. IEEE Computer Society, 2004.

[101] C. J. Kapser and M. W. Godfrey. "Cloning considered harmful" considered harmful. In *Proceedings of the 13th Working Conference on Reverse Engineering*, pages 19–28. IEEE Computer Society, 2006.

[102] C. J. Kapser and M. W. Godfrey. Supporting the analysis of clones in software systems: a case study. *Journal of Software Maintenance and Evolution: Research and Practice*, 18(2):61–82, 2006.

[103] C. J. Kapser and M. W. Godfrey. "Cloning considered harmful" considered harmful: patterns of cloning in software. *Empirical Software Engineering*, 13(6):645–692, 2008.

[104] S. Kawaguchi, T. Yamashina, H. Uwano, K. Fushida, Y. Kamei, M. Nagura, and Hajimu Iida. SHINOBI: A tool for automatic code clone detection in the ide. In *Proceedings of the 16th Working Conference on Reverse Engineering*, pages 313–314. IEEE Computer Society, 2009.

[105] M. Kim, L. Bergman, T. Lau, and D. Notkin. An ethnographic study of copy and paste programming practices in OOPL. In *Proceedings of the International Symposium on Empirical Software Engineering*, pages 83–92. IEEE Computer Society, 2004.

[106] M. Kim and D. Notkin. Using a clone genealogy extractor for understanding and supporting evolution of code clones. *SIGSOFT Software Engineering Notes*, 30(4):1–5, 2005.

[107] M. Kim and D. Notkin. Program element matching for multi-version program analyses. In *Proceedings of the International Workshop on Mining Software Repositories*, pages 58–64. ACM, 2006.

[108] M. Kim and D. Notkin. Discovering and representing systematic code changes. In *Proceedings of the 31st International Conference on Software Engineering*, pages 309–319. IEEE Computer Society, 2009.

[109] M. Kim, V. Sazawal, D. Notkin, and G. C. Murphy. An empirical study of code clone genealogies. In *Proceedings of the Joint 10th European Software Engineering Conference and the 13th ACM SIGSOFT Symposium on the Foundations of Software Engineering*, pages 187–196. ACM, 2005.

[110] S. Kim, K. Pan, and Jr. E. J. Whitehead. When functions change their names: Automatic detection of origin relationships. In *Proceedings of the 12th Working Conference on Reverse Engineering*, pages 143–152. IEEE Computer Society, 2005.

[111] R. Komondoor and S. Horwitz. Semantics-preserving procedure extraction. In *Proceedings of the 27th ACM SIGPLAN-SIGACT Symposium on Principles of Programming Languages*, pages 155–169. ACM, 2000.

[112] R. Komondoor and S. Horwitz. Effective, automatic procedure extraction. In *Proceedings of the 11th IEEE International Workshop on Program Comprehension*, pages 33–42. IEEE Computer Society, 2003.

[113] R. V. Komondoor and S. Horwitz. Using slicing to identify duplication in source code. In *Proceedings of the 8th International Symposium on Static Analysis*, pages 40–56. Springer-Verlag, 2001.

[114] K. Kontogiannis. Evaluation experiments on the detection of programming patterns using software metrics. In *Proceedings of the 4th Working Conference on Reverse Engineering*, pages 44–54. IEEE Computer Society, 1997.

[115] K. Kontogiannis, R. Demori, E. Merlo, M. Galler, and M. Bernstein. Pattern matching for clone and concept detection. *Automated Software Engineering*, 3(1–2):77–108, 1996.

[116] R. Koschke. Survey of research on software clones. In R. Koschke, E. Merlo, and A. Walenstein, editors, *Duplication, Redundancy, and Similarity in Software*, number 06301 in Dagstuhl Seminar Proceedings, Dagstuhl, Germany, 2007. Internationales Begegnungs- und Forschungszentrum für Informatik (IBFI), Schloss Dagstuhl, Germany.

[117] R. Koschke. Frontiers of software clone management. In *Proceedings of Frontiers of Software Maintenance*, pages 119–128. IEEE Computer Society, 2008.

[118] R. Koschke, R. Falke, and P. Frenzel. Clone detection using abstract syntax suffix trees. In *Proceedings of the 13th Working Conference on Reverse Engineering*, pages 253–262. IEEE Computer Society, 2006.

[119] N. Kraft, B. Bonds, and R. Smith. Cross-language clone detection. In *Proceedings of the 20th International Conference on Software Engineering and Knowledge Engineering*, pages 54–59. Knowledge Systems Institute Graduate School, 2008.

[120] J. Krinke. Identifying similar code with program dependence graphs. In *Proceedings of the 8th Working Conference on Reverse Engineering*, pages 301–309. IEEE Computer Society, 2001.

[121] J. Krinke. A study of consistent and inconsistent changes to code clones. In *Proceedings of the 14th Working Conference on Reverse Engineering*, pages 170–178. IEEE Computer Society, 2007.

[122] J. Krinke. Is cloned code more stable than non-cloned code? In *Proceedings of the 8th International Working Conference on Source Code Analysis and Manipulation*, pages 57–66. IEEE Computer Society, 2008.

[123] B. Laguë, D. Proulx, J. Mayrand, E. Merlo, and J. Hudepohl. Assessing the benefits of incorporating function clone detection in a development process. In *Proceedings of the International Conference on Software Maintenance*, pages 314–321. IEEE Computer Society, 1997.

[124] B. M. Lange and T. G. Moher. Some strategies of reuse in an object-oriented programming environment. In *Proceedings of the SIGCHI Conference on Human Factors in Computing Systems*, pages 69–73. ACM, 1989.

[125] J. Laski and W. Szermer. Identification of program modifications and its applications in software maintenance. In *Proceedings of the International Conference on Software Maintenance*, pages 282–290. IEEE Computer Society, 1992.

[126] T. D. LaToza, G. Venolia, and R. DeLine. Maintaining mental models: a study of developer work habits. In *Proceedings of the 28th International Conference on Software Engineering*, pages 492–501. ACM, 2006.

[127] M. Lee, J. Roh, S. Hwang, and S. Kim. Instant code clone search. In *Proceedings of the 18th International Symposium on Foundations of Software Engineering*, pages 167–176. ACM, 2010.

[128] S. Lee and I. Jeong. Sdd: high performance code clone detection system for large scale source code. In *Companion to the 20th Conference on Object-oriented Programming, Systems, Languages and Applications*, pages 140–141. ACM, 2005.

[129] Z. Li, S. Lu, S. Myagmar, and Y. Zhou. CP-Miner: A tool for finding copy-paste and related bugs in operating system code. In *Proceedings of the 6th Conference on Opearting Systems Design & Implementation*, pages 20–33. USENIX Association, 2004.

[130] Z. Li, S. Lu, S. Myagmar, and Y. Zhou. CP-Miner: Finding copy-paste and related bugs in large-scale software code. *IEEE Transactions on Software Engineering*, 32(3):176–192, 2006.

[131] E. Lippe and N. van Oosterom. Operation-based merging. *SIGSOFT Software Engineering Notes*, 17(5):78–87, 1992.

[132] C. Liu, C. Chen, J. Han, and P. S. Yu. GPLAG: Detection of software plagiarism by program dependence graph analysis. In *Proceedings of the 12th ACM SIGKDD International Conference on Knowledge Discovery and Data Mining*, pages 872–881. ACM, 2006.

[133] H. Liu, Z. Ma, L. Zhang, and W. Shao. Detecting duplications in sequence diagrams based on suffix trees. In *Proceedings of the 13th Asia Pacific Software Engineering Conference*, pages 269–276. IEEE Computer Society, 2006.

[134] S. Livieri, Y. Higo, M. Matsushita, and K. Inoue. Analysis of the linux kernel evolution using code clone coverage. In *Proceedings of the 4th International Workshop on Mining Software Repositories*, pages 22–25. IEEE Computer Society, 2007.

[135] S. Livieri, Y. Higo, M. Matushita, and K. Inoue. Very-large scale code clone analysis and visualization of open source programs using distributed CCFinder: D-CCFinder. In *Proceedings of the 29th International Conference on Software Engineering*, pages 106–115. IEEE Computer Society, 2007.

[136] A. Lozano and M. Wermelinger. Assessing the effect of clones on changeability. In *Proceedings of the 24th International Conference on Software Maintenance*, pages 227–236. IEEE Computer Society, 2008.

[137] A. Lozano, M. Wermelinger, and B. Nuseibeh. Evaluating the harmfulness of cloning: A change based experiment. In *Proceedings of the 4th International Workshop on Mining Software Repositories*, pages 18–21. IEEE Computer Society, 2007.

[138] U. Manber. Finding similar files in a large file system. In *Proceedings of the USENIX Winter 1994 Technical Conference*, pages 1–10, 1994.

[139] U. Manber and G. Myers. Suffix arrays: A new method for on-line string searches. *SIAM Journal on Computing*, 22(5):935–948, 1991.

[140] A. Marcus and J. I. Maletic. Identification of high-level concept clones in source code. In *Proceedings of the 16th IEEE International Conference on Automated Software Engineering*, pages 107–114. IEEE Computer Society, 2001.

[141] J. Mayrand, C. Leblanc, and E. Merlo. Experiment on the automatic detection of function clones in a software system using metrics. In *Proceedings of the International Conference on Software Maintenance*, pages 244–253. IEEE Computer Society, 1996.

[142] E. McCreight. A space-economical suffix tree construction algorithm. *Journal of the ACM*, 32(2):262–272, 1976.

[143] E. Merlo, G. Antoniol, M. Di Penta, and V. F. Rollo. Linear complexity object-oriented similarity for clone detection and software evolution analyses. In *Proceedings of the 20th International Conference on Software Maintenance*, pages 412–416. IEEE Computer Society, 2004.

[144] E. Merlo, M. Dagenais, P. Bachand, J. S. Sormani, S. Gradara, and G. Antoniol. Investigating large software system evolution: The linux kernel. In *Proceedings of the 26th International Computer Software and Applications Conference on Prolonging Software Life: Development and Redevelopment*, pages 421–426. IEEE Computer Society, 2002.

[145] E. Merlo and T. Lavoie. Computing structural types of clone syntactic blocks. In *Proceedings of the 16th Working Conference on Reverse Engineering*, pages 274–278. IEEE Computer Society, 2009.

[146] A. Monden, D. Nakae, T. Kamiya, S. Sato, and K. Matsumoto. Software quality analysis by code clones in industrial legacy software. In *Proceedings of the 8th International Symposium on Software Metrics*, page 87. IEEE Computer Society, 2002.

[147] E. W. Myers. An O(ND) difference algorithm and its variations. *Algorithmica*, 1(2):251–266, 1986.

[148] I. Neamtiu, J. S. Foster, and M. Hicks. Understanding source code evolution using abstract syntax tree matching. In *Proceedings of the International Workshop on Mining Software Repositories*, pages 2–6. ACM, 2005.

[149] H. A. Nguyen, T. T. Nguyen, N. H. Pham, J. M. Al-Kofahi, and T. N. Nguyen. Accurate and efficient structural characteristic feature extraction for clone detection. In *Proceedings of the 12th International Conference on Fundamental Approaches to Software Engineering*, pages 440–455. Springer-Verlag, 2009.

[150] T. T. Nguyen, H. A. Nguyen, J.M. Al-Kofahi, N. H. Pham, and T. N. Nguyen. Scalable and incremental clone detection for evolving software. In *Proceedings of the International Conference on Software Maintenance*, pages 491–494. IEEE Computer Society, 2009.

[151] T. T. Nguyen, H. A. Nguyen, N. H. Pham, J. M. Al-Kofahi, and T. N. Nguyen. Clone-aware configuration management. In *Proceedings of the 24th International Conference on Automated Software Engineering*, pages 123–134. IEEE Computer Society, 2009.

[152] J.-F. Patenaude, E. Merlo, M. Dagenais, and B. Laguë. Extending software quality assessment techniques to java systems. In *Proceedings of the 7th International Workshop on Program Comprehension*, pages 49–56. IEEE Computer Society, 1999.

[153] N. H. Pham, H. A. Nguyen, T. T. Nguyen, J. M. Al-Kofahi, and T. N. Nguyen. Complete and accurate clone detection in graph-based models. In *Proceedings of the 31st International Conference on Software Engineering*, pages 276–286. IEEE Computer Society, 2009.

[154] F. Rahman, C. Bird, and P. Devanbu. Clones: What is that smell? In *Proceedings of the 7th International Working Conference on Mining Software Repositories*, pages 72–81. IEEE Computer Society, 2010.

[155] M. Rieger. *Effective Clone Detection Without Language Barriers*. PhD thesis, University of Bern, 2005.

[156] R. Robbes and M. Lanza. A change-based approach to software evolution. *Electronic Notes in Theoretical Computer Science*, 166:93–109, 2007.

[157] R. Robbes, M. Lanza, and M. Lungu. An approach to software evolution based on semantic change. *Lecture Notes in Computer Science*, 4422:27–41, 2007.

[158] M. B. Rosson and J. M. Carroll. Active programming strategies in reuse. In *Proceedings of the 7th European Conference on Object-Oriented Programming*, pages 4–20. Springer-Verlag, 1993.

[159] C. K. Roy and J. R. Cordy. A survey on software clone detection research. Technical report, Queens University at Kingston, Ontario, Canada, 2007.

[160] C. K. Roy and J. R. Cordy. NICAD: Accurate detection of near-miss intentional clones using flexible pretty-printing and code normalization. In *Proceedings of the 16th International Conference on Program Comprehension*, pages 172–181. IEEE Computer Society, 2008.

[161] C. K. Roy, J. R. Cordy, and R. Koschke. Comparison and evaluation of code clone detection techniques and tools: A qualitative approach. *Science of Computer Programming*, 74(7):470–495, 2009.

[162] A. Sæbjørnsen, J. Willcock, T. Panas, D. Quinlan, and Z. Su. Detecting code clones in binary executables. In *Proceedings of the 18th International Symposium on Software Testing and Analysis*, pages 117–128. ACM, 2009.

[163] T. Sager, A. Bernstein, M. Pinzger, and C. Kiefer. Detecting similar java classes using tree algorithms. In *Proceedings of the International Workshop on Mining Software Repositories*, pages 65–71. ACM, 2006.

[164] R. K. Saha, M. Asaduzzaman, M. F. Zibran, C. K. Roy, and K. A. Schneider. Evaluating code clone genealogies at release level: An empirical study. In *Proceedings of the 10th International Working Conference on Source Code Analysis and Manipulation*, pages 87–96. IEEE Computer Society, 2010.

[165] M. Salson, T. Lecroq, M. Léonard, and L. Mouchard. Dynamic extended suffix arrays. *Journal of Discrete Algorithms*, 8(2):241–257, 2010.

[166] S. Schulze and M. Kuhlemann. Advanced analysis for code clone removal. *Softwaretechnik-Trends*, 29(2):26–27, 2009.

[167] G. M. K. Selim, L. Barbour, W. Shang, B. Adams, A. E. Hassan, and Y. Zou. Studying the impact of clones on software defects. In *Proceedings of the 17th Working Conference on Reverse Engineering*, pages 13–21. IEEE Computer Society, 2010.

[168] G. M. K. Selim, K. C.n Foo, and Y. Zou. Enhancing source-based clone detection using intermediate representation. In *Proceedings of the 17th Working Conference on Reverse Engineering*, pages 227–236. IEEE Computer Society, 2010.

[169] D. M. Shawky and A. F. Ali. An approach for assessing similarity metrics used in metric-based clone detection techniques. In *Proceedings of the 3rd International Conference on Computer Science and Information Technology*, pages 580–584. IEEE Computer Society, 2010.

[170] B. Shneiderman. Tree visualization with tree-maps: 2-d space-filling approach. *ACM Transactions on Graphics*, 11(1):92–99, 1992.

[171] J. Śliwerski, T. Zimmermann, and A. Zeller. When do changes induce fixes? In *Proceedings of the International Workshop on Mining Software Repositories*, pages 24–28. ACM, 2005.

[172] R. Smith and S. Horwitz. Detecting and measuring similarity in code clones. In *Workshop Proceedings of the 13th European Conference on Software Maintenance and Reengineering*, pages 28–34, 2009.

[173] H. Störrle. Towards clone detection in UML domain models. In *Proceedings of the Fourth European Conference on Software Architecture: Companion Volume*, pages 285–293. ACM, 2010.

[174] N. Synytskyy, J. R. Cordy, and T. Dean. Resolution of static clones in dynamic web pages. In *Proceedings of the International Workshop on Web Site Evolution*, pages 49–56. IEEE Computer Society, 2003.

[175] R. Tairas and J. Gray. Phoenix-based clone detection using suffix trees. In *Proceedings of the 44th ACM Annual Southeast Regional Conference*, pages 679–684. ACM, 2006.

[176] R. Tairas and J. Gray. Sub-clone refactoring in open source software artifacts. In *Proceedings of the Symposium on Applied Computing*, pages 2373–2374. ACM, 2010.

[177] R. Tairas and J. Gray. Sub-clones: Considering the part rather than the whole. In *Proceedings of the International Conference on Software Engineering Research & Practice*, pages 284–290. CSREA Press, 2010.

[178] S. Thummalapenta, L. Cerulo, L. Aversano, and M. Di Penta. An empirical study on the maintenance of source code clones. *Empirical Software Engineering*, 15(1):1–34, 2010.

[179] R. Tiarks, R. Koschke, and R. Falke. An assessment of type-3 clones as detected by state-of-the-art tools. In *Proceedings of the 9th International Working Conference on Source Code Analysis and Manipulation*, pages 67–76. IEEE Computer Society, 2009.

[180] R. Tiarks, R. Koschke, and R. Falke. An extended assessment of type-3 clones as detected by state-of-the-art tools. *Software Quality Journal*, 19(2):295–331, 2010.

[181] W. F. Tichy. The string-to-string correction problem with block moves. *ACM Transactions on Computer Systems*, 2(4):309–321, 1984.

[182] M. Toomim, A. Begel, and S. L. Graham. Managing duplicated code with linked editing. In *Symposium on Visual Languages and Human Centric Computing*, pages 173–180. IEEE Computer Society, 2004.

[183] Y. Ueda, T. Kamiya, S. Kusumoto, and K. Inoue. Gemini: Maintenance support environment based on code clone analysis. In *Proceedings of the 8th Symposium on Software Metrics*, pages 67–76, 2002.

[184] Y. Ueda, T. Kamiya, S. Kusumoto, and K. Inoue. On detection of gapped code clones using gap locations. In *Proceedings of the 9th Asia-Pacific Software Engineering Conference*, pages 327–336. IEEE Computer Society, 2002.

[185] E. Ukkonen. On-line construction of suffix trees. *Algorithmica*, 14(3):249–260, 1995.

[186] V. Wahler, D. Seipel, J. W. v. Gudenberg, and G. Fischer. Clone detection in source code by frequent itemset techniques. In *Proceedings of the 4th International Workshop on Source Code Analysis and Manipulation*, pages 128–135. IEEE Computer Society, 2004.

[187] A. Walenstein and A. Lakhotia. The software similarity problem in malware analysis. In R. Koschke, E. Merlo, and A. Walenstein, editors, *Duplication, Redundancy, and Similarity in Software*, number 06301 in Dagstuhl Seminar Proceedings, Dagstuhl, Germany, 2007. Internationales Begegnungs- und Forschungszentrum für Informatik (IBFI), Schloss Dagstuhl, Germany.

[188] Z. Wang, K. Pierce, and S. McFarling. BMAT – a binary matching tool for stale profile propagation. *Journal of Instruction-Level Parallelism*, 2, 2000.

[189] V. Weckerle. CPC an eclipse framework for automated clone life cycle tracking and update anomaly detection. Diploma thesis, Freie Universität Berlin, 2008.

[190] R. Wettel and R. Marinescu. Archeology of code duplication: Recovering duplication chains from small duplication fragments. In *Proceedings of the 7th International Symposium on Symbolic and Numeric Algorithms for Scientific Computing*. IEEE Computer Society, 2005.

[191] T. Yamashina, H. Uwano, K. Fushida, Y. Kamei, M. Nagura, S. Kawaguchi, and H. Iida. SHINOBI: A real-time code clone detection tool for software maintenance. Technical report, Nara Institute of Science and Technology, Takayama, Ikoma Nara, Japan, 2008.

[192] W. Yang. Identifying syntactic differences between two programs. *Software – Practice & Experience*, 21(7):739–755, 1991.

[193] A. T. T. Ying, G. C. Murphy, R. Ng, and M. C. Chu-Carroll. Predicting source code changes by mining change history. *IEEE Transactions on Software Engineering*, 30(9):574–586, 2004.

[194] T. Zimmermann, P. Weißgerber, S. Diehl, and A. Zeller. Mining version histories to guide software changes. *IEEE Transactions on Software Engineering*, 31(6):429–445, 2005.

[195] L. Zou and M. W. Godfrey. Detecting merging and splitting using origin analysis. In *Proceedings of the 10th Working Conference on Reverse Engineering*, pages 146–154. IEEE Computer Society, 2003.

[196] L. Zou and M. W. Godfrey. Using origin analysis to detect merging and splitting of source code entities. *IEEE Transactions on Software Engineering*, 31(2):166–181, 2005.